The Men of No Property

Irish Radicals and Popular Politics in the Late Eighteenth Century

Jim Smyth

Research Fellow
Trinity Hall, Cambridge

Gill and Macmillan

Published in Ireland by
Gill and Macmillan Ltd
Goldenbridge
Dublin 8
with associated companies in
Auckland, Budapest, Gaborone, Harare, Hong Kong,
Kampala, Kuala Lumpur, Lagos, London, Madras,
Manzini, Melbourne, Mexico City, Nairobi,
New York, Singapore, Sydney, Tokyo, Windhoek

© Jim Smyth 1992

Published in Great Britain by
The Macmillan Press Ltd

0 7171 1991 2
Printed in Hong Kong

A catalogue record for this book is available from the
British Library.

Contents

Acknowledgements

I have incurred many debts of gratitude in writing this book and the Ph.D. dissertation on which it is based. Firstly, I must thank Dr Brendan Bradshaw who supervised my dissertation and who kept a practiced eye on the development of the book. I can only marvel at his patience. Professor Louis Cullen kindled my interest in this period of Irish history and his work on this subject continues to inspire. Dr David Dickson introduced me – in the appropriate setting of Trinity College – to the fascinations and specific pleasures of that 'unruly town', eighteenth-century Dublin. I am grateful too, to those historians who read and commented upon all or part of earlier drafts of the manuscript: Dr Tom Bartlett, Dr Sean Connolly, Dr Jacqueline Hill, Dr Gareth Stedman Jones and Dr Jonathan Steinberg. Any errors or infelicities which remain in the text are, as they say, all my own.

The professional staffs of the following libraries and archives were unfailingly helpful and courteous: the Linen Hall library and the Public Record Office of Northern Ireland, Belfast, the National Library of Ireland, the library of Trinity College Dublin, the State Paper Office and the Public Record Office of Ireland, Dublin, the Public Record Office, Kew, and the University Library, Cambridge. I was also given kind permission to consult the records of the Irish Grand Lodge of Free Masons.

In practical, but no less important, terms, Liam Lynch and Hamish Park dug me out of the word-processing morasses into which I wandered more than once, while Jim Burgess saved me more time and trouble than he perhaps realises. I was also assisted at a practical, as well as an intellectual, level by Professor R. H. Buchannan and the fellows of the Institute of Irish Studies, Queen's University, Belfast, where I started to write this book. It was completed in the serene *environs* of Trinity Hall. I cannot imagine more stimulating and congenial conditions in which to pursue scholarship of any kind, than those sustained by the Master and fellows of this ancient college.

Finally, I owe a great deal personally, to Colin Wisdom and, of course, to my mother. But a special word of appreciation must go to my sternest critic, editor and encourager-in-chief, my wife Mary. This book is for her.

JIM SMYTH

List of Abbreviations

B.N.L	*Belfast Newsletter*
D.E.P	*Dublin Evening Post*
Dub.Soc.	*The Dublin Society of United Irishmen* (Dublin, 1794)
F.D.J	*Faulkners Dublin Journal*
H.M.C	*Historical Manuscripts Commission*
Hib. Jrnl.	*Hibernian Journal*
I.H.S	*Irish Historical Studies*
I.S.P.O.	Irish State Paper Office
J.H.C.	*Journal of the House of Commons*
Lecky	W. E. H. Lecky, *A history of Ireland in the eighteenth century* (London, 1892) 5 vols
McDowell, *Age*	R. B. McDowell, *Ireland in the age of imperialism and revolution* (Oxford, 1979)
Musgrave	Sir Richard Musgrave, *Memoirs of the different rebellions in Ireland* (Dublin, 1801)
N.E.S.	*National Evening Star*
N.L.I.	National Library of Ireland
N.S.	*Northern Star*
Parl. reg.	*Parliamentary register*
P.R.O.	Public Record Office
P.R.O.I.	Public Record Office of Ireland
P.R.O.N.I.	Public Record Office of Northern Ireland
Reb. papers	Rebellion papers
S.N.L.	*Saunders Newsletter*
S.O.C.P.	State of the Country papers
S.P.P.	State Prisoners Petitions
T.C.D.	Trinity College, Dublin

A Note on the Title

Irish readers (and others) will recognise the phrase 'the men of no property' as a quotation from the journals of Theobald Wolfe Tone. The passage from which it is taken was written by Tone on 11 March, 1796, when he was in Paris negotiating for a French invasion of Ireland. 'My life is of little consequence . . . ', he wrote,

> Our independence must be had at all hazards, if the men of property will not support us, they must fall: we can support ourselves by the aid of that numerous and respectable class of the community, *the men of no property*.[1]

In the politics of historical quotation this passage is rivalled only by Tone's other celebrated statement about uniting catholic, protestant and dissenter under the common name of Irishman. The Young Irelander, John Mitchel, adopted this phrase as the motto for his paper, *The United Irishman,* in 1848. To Patrick Pearse in 1916 these words revealed his hero as 'the greatest of modern Irish democrats'. Four years later during the civil war, Liam Mellows wrote from his cell in Mountjoy prison, 'We are back to Tone – and it is just as well – relying on that great body "the men of no property". The "stake in the country" people were never with the Republic.'[2] And since Mellows's time a number of left-wing writers, notably T. A. Jackson, Peter Berrisford Ellis and Sean Cronin, have used the phrase to emphasise the social-radical character of Tone and the United Irishmen.[3] Moreover, its use, we have been warned, 'is on the increase'.[4]

It was inevitable, perhaps, that sooner or later the professional historians would get around to 'demythologizing' such a well-known quotation. Thus it has been argued that the passage did not reflect Tone's true sentiments so much as his political desperation by 1796, and that the phrase 'men of no property' has been misunderstood. According to the first argument, Tone, despairing of suppport from the country's 'natural leaders', turned to the poor as a last resort. According to the second argument he didn't turn to the poor at all, that by 'property' he meant, in typical eighteenth-century fashion, 'landed property', and by 'men of no property' the middle class.[5] According to both views the quotation has been wrenched from its historical context and put to work for later polemical purposes.

Is it still permissible, then, to use Tone's phrase in the straightfoward, pre-revisionist, sense in which it was used by Mellows or by C. S. Andrews?[6] Two points should be made here. Firstly, the revisionist interpretations may be more thoughtful than the older 'populist' one, but, as the existence of alternative readings demonstrates, they cannot be considered definitive. Secondly, irrespective of what Tone did or did not intend, his words have subsequently assumed a life and a commonly-understood meaning independent of their author. That commonly-understood meaning *might* be a popular misconception, and as such may irritate austere historians, but, whether they like it or not, that meaning is now contained in tradition. Irish readers will not only recognise 'the men of no property' as a quotation from Tone, they will also almost certainly read it as a reference to the propertyless, the poor, the common people. And these are, indeed, the people to whom the title refers.

IRELAND by courtesy of the University of Wisconsin Press from Clark and Donnelly, *Irish Peasants: Violence and Political Unrest, 1780–1914.*

Introduction

The study of Ireland in the 1790s is still in its heroic phase. To say so is not to deny the quality of the scholarship devoted to this period, but simply to suggest the tremendous range and complexity of the problems thrown up by this crowded decade. These were years which witnessed the emergence of an assertive middle-class catholic leadership, a multi-pronged challenge to the 'Protestant Ascendancy' (a challenge which forced that ascendancy to define itself), rebellion and the extinction of the Irish parliament. Furthermore, the nineties were significant as well as dramatic. In this respect Ireland, so often remarkable for its unique development, is typical of the wider 'Atlantic world'.[1] The importance of this period in French history requires no comment, but it is worth noting that it has also been seen as decisive in the making of the English working class. In Ireland the legacy of the last decade of the eighteenth century is strong. Both the Orange Order and the 'physical force', separatist, republican tradition originated during these years.

Not surprisingly, these phenomena have generated a voluminous historical literature. Beginning with the extremely partisan accounts of contemporaries, notably Sir Richard Musgrave's *Memoirs of the different rebellions in Ireland* (1801) on the loyalist side, and Edward Hay's *History of the insurrection in county Wexford* (1803) written from the catholic standpoint, through the memoirs of various participants in the rebellion and R. R. Madden's hagiographic compendium *The lives of the United Irishmen* (1842–6), to W. E. H. Lecky's *History of Ireland in the eighteenth century* (1892) and R. B. McDowell's *Ireland in the age of imperialism and revolution* (1979), students of the period have not lacked commentaries. The attention which the 1790s have attracted emerges all the more strongly when this rich historiography is contrasted with the dearth of material concerning the earlier eighteenth century. Three of Lecky's five volumes are devoted to the last decade alone. Lecky's influence upon later historians may itself be one reason for what Professor E. M. Johnston has identified as an 'imbalance'.[2] This 'by now notorious' bias is evident, for instance, in the eighteenth-century volume of the *New history of Ireland* where just eighteen pages are taken to summarize the political history of the years 1714–60, whereas the years 1789–1800 merit eighty-two.[3] The work of Lecky and McDowell stands as a major contribution to our knowledge of late eighteenth-century Irish politics. Like all history, however, it is open to

1

revision. At a general level new evidence may come to light, or long familiar evidence may yield unexpected conclusions when interrogated in novel ways. Specifically, in this instance the scale, magisterial tone and seamless narrative of these books are deceptive. Such 'balanced' and authoritative accounts are rarely as value free as they at first appear. Lecky's loyalist and patrician assumptions and McDowell's elitist perspective skewed their interpretation of this critical period. Lecky maintained that 'the peasantry, sunk in poverty and ignorance, had no political interests'. McDowell states that 'the great bulk of the people were restricted by poverty and persecution to political speculations of the simplest kind'. The 'outlook of the masses', in his view, is scarcely worth examining.[4]

It will be argued here that the evidence suggests otherwise; that the lower classes did have 'political interests' and that an appreciation of the popular dimension of politics is in fact central to a proper understanding of the 1790s. None of these propositions is controversial. Indeed most recent studies have shifted the emphasis towards 'history from below'[5] although in the Irish case without any specific Marxist analysis or intent.[6] This approach has produced some important new insights. To cite only one example: McDowell depicts the secret society, the Defenders, as 'rural rioters', whose 'aims were agrarian'. In contrast, Dr Elliott shows that 'Defenderism was never a peasant movement', and that it had a 'distinct revolutionary tone'.[7] Yet stimulating though contributions such as Elliott's have been, Dr Beames's observation remains valid: 'The complex events of the mid-1790s still await satisfactory analysis. The interrelationship between the various strands of agrarian discontent, sectarian nationalism and United Irish republicanism remain to be unravelled.'[8]

If this was the great age of 'bourgeois' revolution, of French Jacobins and United Irishmen, it was also the age of the *sans culottes* and, in Ireland, of the Defenders. Never before did the lower classes play so active or critical a role in politics, although, as we shall see, these interventions were not entirely without precedent. The Dublin crowd exhibited clear signs of politicisation as early at least as the 1750s. The Volunteer movement, which began in 1778, eventually enrolled up to 80,000 citizens in arms and 'created a heady involvement [in politics] for many below the level of gentry'.[9] Nor can the 'archaic' or 'primitive' agrarian rebellions of the Whiteboys and others in the 1760s, 1770s and 1780s, be written off as non-political simply because they do not conform to later conceptions of 'politics'. Nevertheless, during the 1790s a threshold is crossed. Most obviously, levels of violence spiralled out of control. Just as tellingly, the language of popular protest changed. In addition to the by then familiar grievances about rents and tithes the Defenders 'talked of the famous system of liberty and equality in the most extravagant manner. Why should others have land and property and they want it?'[10] The 'Protestant Ascendancy' (or state) became objects of popular animosity alongside the local landlord and tithe-proctor. Cheap editions of Thomas Paine's *Rights of Man* circulated in the backstreet taverns of Dublin. In its scale and intensity the politicisation of the lower classes during the 1790s is of a qualitatively different order.

What did politicisation mean? There are, as Peter Burke points out, two problems here, one conceptual, the other empirical. Burke defines 'politics' in the context of early modern European popular culture as '"affairs of state", not local issues but the concerns of rulers, in other words the succession, war, taxation, and economic and religious problems . . . political consciousness might be defined as awareness of these problems and their possible solutions . . . '[11] Thus the United Irish handbill which urged its readers to 'think of your rulers; think of republics; think of kings; think of the murderous wars they are carrying on . . . ' Certainly by this time many ordinary people were in fact involved in the great public issues of the day, and above all in the struggle for catholic relief.

To Burke's understanding of politicisation may be added the popular assimilation of abstract ideas: 'the famous system of liberty and equality' proclaimed by the Meath Defenders, 'republicanism', 'nationalism' and so on. We should not, however, expect to find these abstractions in their pure form. Popular ideology has been characterised as a compound of pre-existing 'inherent' elements and ideas 'derived' from outside. The first are based on folk-memory, custom and 'common sense' – popular estimates of 'just' rents or the right to land, for example, or in Ireland the sense of dispossession. The second consists of more sophisticated notions – in the 1790s the 'Rights of Man' – imbibed from newspapers, from pulpits, from radical and conservative elites. Typically these ideas are vulgarised or adapted as they fuse, in the process of transmission, with older beliefs.[12] Defenderism, a hybrid of traditional agrarian aspirations and half-digested 'French' principles, is a model of popular ideology conceived in this way.

The possibility of investigating Defender ideology arises from the survival of some of the movement's catechisms. Unfortunately, evidence of politicisation is not usually available in such neat bundles. This brings us to Burke's empirical problem: 'the historian's notorious inability to subject the dead to an opinion poll'. How then can we recover what ordinary people believed? When Samuel McSkimmin remarked that 'every illiterate bumpkin considered himself a consummate politician'[13] this is evidence of politicisation (if not literacy), but it is second hand and tells us nothing about the 'bumpkins'' ideas. Similarly, the content of radical literature offers direct evidence about radical, not popular, ideology. On the other hand, the use of French revolutionary slogans, songs and symbols by the Wexford rebels in 1798 does show radical and popular ideologies meshing. Moreover, it is reasonable to deduce popular political attitudes from popular political behaviour; to correlate actions with collective ideas. It may safely be assumed that the tens of thousands who signed petitions for catholic relief or who joined the United Irishmen, also opposed the doctrine of 'Protestant Ascendancy'. Admittedly such generalised sentiments are not very illuminating, but they do provide a lead.

Politicisation is a dynamic process: popular ideology is shaped by action, by experience, by participation in public affairs. Thus the mobilisation of the common people in the catholic relief and parliamentary reform campaigns of 1792–3 probably had a greater politicising effect than all the 'writings disseminating the poison of disaffection and sedition [which] found their way into all parts of the country' in such enormous quantities in these years.[14] Yet radical and conservative alike took a more naive view of the efficacy of propaganda. In a memorial prepared for the French government in 1794 Wolfe Tone declared that the catholics, 'the great body of the nation . . . have, within these two years received a great degree of information, and manifested a proportional degree of discontent'.[15] 'Our great aim and design' announced the United Irish newspaper, the *Northern Star,* is 'a general diffusion of knowledge among our countrymen'; 'the ignorance of the people is the only security of despotic governments. Enlighten mankind and they will be free'.[16] It was that simple. Public opinion, properly organised and informed, would prove irresistible.

This optimistic strategy overestimated the power of the printed word. Propaganda in itself cannot create consciousness. For example, protestant evangelicals distributed five million or so religious tracts among the catholic population in the 1810s, but the anticipated mass conversions – the so-called second reformation – never materialised.[17] The printed word is only effective when addressed to a receptive audience. Eighteenth-century radicals, like nineteenth-century evangelicals, undoubtedly invested too great faith in the opinion-making capacities of propaganda, although in the Ireland of the 1790s they did strike a popular chord. Any study of politics and 'the men of no property' must therefore take the content and impact of radical literature into account.

A large number of United Irish publications were precisely targeted at a plebeian constituency – at the 'poorer classes of the community' as one of their broadsheets put it.[18] In this respect the *form* of the propaganda is as important as the content, and, as in so much else, Paine set the example. Paine's plain, accessible, language proceeded from the assumption that 'everybody's thought is adequate for political participation'. His achievement was to show that 'common sense, the understanding of the ordinary citizen, enabled all to grasp the true (and simple) nature of politics; and to say that politics was simple was to say something very radical indeed'.[19] That democratic 'Paineite' assumption underpins the argument of a handbill distributed in counties Armagh, Down and Louth in 1794:

> Friends and fellow-countrymen – You have been often told that politics is a subject upon which you should never think; that to the rich and great men of the country you should give up your judgment in the business of government; and that to your own occupations alone you should turn your minds. But you should carefully enquire who gives this advice. Is it disinterested men, or men who wish your welfare? No; it is men in power; it is men who profit by your ignorance and inattention, who keep you in darkness that they may the more easily fleece you of your property and deprive you of your rights; men who hesitate not to say, that you do not deserve the light that shines because you are poor. But is there any sensible, honest man will say that the poor man is not as useful in society as the rich? Will he not assert that the poor are the support of society . . . why not think of politics? Think seriously; think of your rulers; think of republics; think of kings; think of the murderous wars they are carrying on; think of the money they are robbing you of to keep you in slavery and ignorance . . . [20]

In the 1790s radical and catholic activists systematically solicited the active support of 'the people'. Thomas Russell rejected the 'infamous intolerable proposition . . . that the mass of the people have no right to meddle in politics'. In his view it was 'not only the right, but the *essential duty* of every man to interest himself in the conduct of government'.[21] Thomas Addis Emmet, though more moderate than Russell, explained that the United Irish movement sought to 'make every man a politican'.[22] How far did they succeed? In the summer of 1794 an alarmed loyalist reported from south Armagh that 'the change in the natives here is truly astonishing. Formerly a newspaper would have been a phenomenon amongst them. At present, they may vie with the northerns in their thirst after politics. He who can read has generally a large audience about the door of his cabin . . . '[23] Evidence of this kind is plentiful, and there is little doubt that the United

Irishmen did, to some extent, politicise the lower classes. The question is
to what extent.

Politicisation necessarily entailed a break-down of deference. Lower-
class political initiatives, or the mobilisation of lower-class support by
others, when it is inimicial to, or even simply independent of, the interests
of the landed elite, represents a challenge to traditional authority. A
decisive breach in gentry hegemony has been identified in the mid-1820s
when tenants, organised in Daniel O'Connell's Catholic Association, voted
en masse in defiance of their landlords' wishes.[24] However, it is equally
plausible to pinpoint the break over thirty years earlier: 'In an aggressive
campaign [in 1792], which adopted the Volunteering tactic of organising
through extra-parliamentary representative institutions, the new Catholic
Committee helped break the mould of deference which had kept many
catholic tenants in the hold of their gentry.'[25] The startling escalation of
collective violence likewise indicates a collapse of deference-based social
control. This can be seen in the Defender practice of raiding gentry homes
for arms, or in the unprecedented scale of the anti-militia riots in 1793.

The erosion of the structures of authority created a space where an
autonomous popular awareness could develop. 'Every man who can read'
the government informer, Leonard McNally, warned his employers, 'or
who can hear and understand what is read to him, begins in religion as
in politics, to think for himself.'[26] Indeed the definition of politicisation
might be elaborated as working men thinking for themselves, thinking
about kings, rulers, wars and republics; and refusing to *defer*, to 'give up
[their] judgement', to the 'rich and great men of the country'.

McNally mentions religion as well as politics. This may allude to
free-thinking, popular deism, the supposed impact of Paine's *Age of
Reason,* or, what seems more likely, to the declining influence of the
catholic clergy over its flock. Priest and bishop exercised an alternative, and
arguably stronger, authority to that of the largely protestant gentry. But this
authority, invariably exercised in support of the status quo, was never absolute. The priest-ridden Irish peasantry beloved of protestant pamphleteers is
a gross caricature. The Whiteboys defied excommunication as early as the
1760s, while the 1780s and 1790s have been described as 'the high-point
of popular anticlericalism'.[27] Of course McNally, like so many informers,
was prone to exaggeration. The hierarchical, deferential social order may
have appeared to appalled conservatives to be disintegrating – 'the lower
order of papists' declared a loyalist newspaper, 'want *equality*, they will
allow of no *lords* or *gentlemen*'[28] – but in reality the political innovations
of the 1790s fell far short of a complete social revolution. Looked at
in a longer perspective the (intermittant) anticlericalism of this period

is atypical. Again, the role of deference in nineteenth-century electoral politics underlines the limited (or reversible) nature of the weakening of landlord authority which was one aspect of the end of century crisis.

Politicisation is an historians' term. The words 'politics' and 'politician' were common enough at the time, but contemporaries, magistrates or newspapers for instance, referred not to the 'politicised' but to the 'disaffected'. This was a term of abuse, and it is not synonymous with politicisation insofar as its excludes popular loyalism. The Orange Order was a political but not a disaffected movement.[29] In the context of the 1790s, however, the concept of disaffection is still useful: it helps explain conservative attitudes and reminds us that, almost by definition, popular politics happened beyond the narrow pale of legitimacy circumscribed by the Anglo-Irish governing elite.

'Popular' in the sense in which it is used here is an historians' term as well. It has been chosen to describe a category elastic enough to comprehend the subtly graded, open-ended nature of the late eighteenth-century class structure. Any simple three-tier model of upper, middle and lower classes would be inaccurate, just as constructs like 'peasantry' and 'proletariat' are usually inappropriate. Ireland was a transitional, proto-industrial society, based increasingly on a cash economy. Journeymen weavers rubbed shoulders with tenant farmers and landless labourers in the countryside; 'independent' artisan craftsmen with wage-earning employees in the city. Arguably the imprecision of the range of contemporary descriptions, 'the people', 'common people', 'lower orders', 'lower ranks', 'artificers', 'mechanics', 'manufacturers', 'operatives' or 'men of no property' more accurately conveys the multifarious contemporary social reality than would modern sociological terminology. Because of that lack of clear definition or demarcation it would be impossible to fix the point at which a shopkeeper, say, left *le menu peuple* and joined the 'middling sort'. The popular character of the catholic agitation of 1791–3, and of the United Irish movement, thus extends to the middle as well as to the lower classes,[30] and in practice there was often a perceived identity of political interest between these two social groupings. This is not to say that it was ever an equal partnership. The middle classes – specifically, the Belfast (presbyterian) and Dublin (catholic) mercantile elites – led. Perhaps the most meaningful line of demarcation was the one which divided this broad popular category from the landed gentry and aristocracy. In Ireland, of course, land ownership was concentrated almost exclusively in the hands of the ruling anglican caste. Class antagonisms were confused, if not always submerged, by political and religious differences. It was no accident that the two areas with a numerous middling and lower-class anglican population, Armagh and north Wexford/south Wicklow, were the areas in which the Orange Order was strongest.

Politics could transcend class, but class still shaped politics. E. P. Thompson traces the beginnings of an English working-class consciousness to this period. In Ireland no such consciousness – or class – developed. There lower-class solidarity and collective awareness found expression through opposition to the ascendancy, religion and an as yet inchoate nationalism. The populist strategy and rhetoric of the United Irishmen did, however, raise the possibility of social revolution. For its part the ascendancy – nobility and gentry – exhibited pride and consciousness of class. The language of class which it used suggested as much and could often, 'upon the fatal warning of France', slide into a language of invective and fear. In the vocabulary of the 'great', wrote Russell, the labouring poor were 'the mob, the rabble, the beggars on the bridge, the grey-coated men whose views are anarchy and plunder, and whose means are bloodshed and murder'.[31] When the lord lieutenant observed that Catholic Committee propaganda appealed to the 'popular mind',[32] his own mind must have been haunted by the spectre of the French revolution, French 'levelling principles' and the threat of social upheaval. Class tensions informed, conditioned and sharpened the political conflicts of the 1790s.

In conclusion it may be helpful to clarify what this book is not about. It is not about the background, causes and course of the 1798 rebellion. Although all of the events, ideas and politics which are examined did lead, in some sense, to the rebellion, and while obviously that cannot be ignored, it is possible to analyse these things without reference to a rigid teleological framework. The criteria for the selection (and exclusion) of material is therefore more generous than it would be for a study of the genesis of the rebellion. The field of inquiry opens out and corresponds more closely to the untidy diversity of historical experience. For example, that key element in popular politics, Defenderism, was particularly strong in south Ulster, a region which stayed comparatively quiet during the insurrection. There was no direct correlation between the geography of politicisation and the incidence of rebellion, and an analysis of the background to the rebellion would have to pay more attention to Wexford than to Monaghan or Cavan.

Nor would there be much point, at this stage, in a straight narrative account of the 1790s. What follows is concerned more with popular perceptions of the catholic agitation than with the details of catholic relief legislation; more with the impact of the Fitzwilliam episode on public opinion than with the high political intrigue which led to that lord lieutenant's recall. This was a two-way process, of course. The question is not simply how far and in what ways did events politicise the common man; but to what extent were the course of events shaped by the 'men of no property'. These are some of the themes which this study attempts to address.

1 Eighteenth-Century Ireland: Politics, Economy, Society

The social and political stability of eighteenth-century Ireland was something of a facade. By the late 1770s the facade began to crack; in the 1790s it collapsed. The image of stability is based on the long domestic peace which followed the Treaty of Limerick in 1691, and indeed the contrast between the eighteenth century and the turbulence of the seventeenth is striking. This is the era of (long unchallenged) protestant dominance and self-confidence. A confidence expressed – and an image of stability reinforced – by the great public buildings and elegant Georgian squares which grace Dublin to this day. Above all, the monumental Palladian colonnades of the new parliament, erected in College Green between 1729 and 1739, symbolised the burgeoning sense of security now enjoyed by the governing protestant elite. The eighteenth century witnessed the finest flowering, in literature as in architecture, of J. C. Beckett's 'Anglo-Irish tradition'.[1]

The obverse of this powerful image is that of a submerged catholic and Gaelic culture, of Daniel Corkery's 'hidden Ireland'. As a result, 'among the confraternity of Irish historians, there used to be an unspoken assumption that . . . only scholars with a protestant background would find [the eighteenth century] an intellectually stimulating age to investigate'.[2] Moreover, later perceptions of peace and stability contributed to the view of the period before the late 1770s as one largely bereft of 'politics' or 'history'. However implausible this 'tension-free' model of eighteenth-century Irish society now seems,[3] the paucity of detailed studies has ensured that it is not yet possible to replace it with a new synthesis, even if the outlines of that synthesis can now be discerned. Recent scholarship, probing behind the facade of stability, protestant self-confidence and catholic passivity, has emphasised the persistence of protestant anxieties and sectarian tensions.

Viewed in this way the crisis of the 1790s is more explicable – and the depth and extent of that crisis does require explanation. The French Revolution encouraged formidable radical movements in Scotland and England, yet, put to the test, Britain's celebrated social and political stability held.[4] In Ireland, on the other hand, the long eighteenth-century peace culminated in a rebellion little short of civil war. Why? Ultimately, the explanation for the dramatic turn of events in Ireland – for the explosive impact of the French Revolution – must lie in the country's distinctive power structures and specific historical experience.

I POLITICAL STRUCTURES AND IDEOLOGY

The formal political structures of eighteenth-century Ireland were strictly confessional. Full membership of the political nation depended upon conformity to the anglican communion; catholics, and to a lesser degree, dissenters, were excluded. Of course in terms of official ideology and legal monopoly confessionalism defined the *ancien regime* in England as elsewhere. What made Ireland different was the minority position of members of the established church. The confessional state rested on a body of legislation known as the penal code.[5] After the trauma of James II's reign, the 'patriot parliament' and the Williamite wars, the victorious protestants determined never to allow a catholic revival. What is more, in the context of war with France the containment of catholic Ireland was crucial to England's security as well.

The penal laws, most of which were enacted by the Irish parliament between 1695 and 1709, tackled the problem on three fronts. Firstly, they attempted to throttle the Catholic Church. Bishops and regular clergy were banished and parish priests compelled to register and to take oaths of abjuration renouncing loyalty to the Stuart line. As priests may not be ordained except by bishops the logic of these laws, if vigorously enforced, would have resulted in the extinction of organised catholic religion within a generation. Secondly, catholics were excluded from parliament, public office, the university, the bar, the bench, the army, trade guilds and corporations. No catholic, as every Irish schoolboy knows, could own a horse worth more than £5, or more pointedly, fire-arms. The right to bear arms was a badge of citizenship, a good horse the mark of a gentleman, so both these restrictions diminished the catholic's social status. Finally, the penal code cut to the source of political power in an early modern pre-industrial society: land. Catholics could only obtain thirty-one year leases and could not purchase or inherit land from protestants. When a catholic landowner died his holding had to be sub-divided between his sons, unless the eldest converted to the established church, which entitled him to the whole estate. If a son converted during the father's lifetime, the father's legal status became 'tenant for life'. Again, if vigorously enforced these laws would have led to the eventual disappearance of the catholic landed class – the catholic majority's 'natural' political leadership.

The fearsome spirit of these laws offers a chilling insight into protestant attitudes in post-Jacobite Ireland. But how much do the statute books tell us about eighteenth-century society as it actually evolved? Almost 400 regular clergy left Ireland in 1698. Some bishops were arrested; others went into exile.[6] Yet, although in the early years of the century the Church suffered sustained legal harassment its hierarchy and organisation survived largely intact. By the 1790s catholic bishops received *de facto* recognition from the authorities and were welcomed in certain governing circles as conservative allies against the radical movement. In contrast to the popular legends about persecution and mass rocks, the secondary literature used to minimise the religious impulse behind the penal code. Consequently eighteenth-century society witnessed the advance of 'religious indifferentism' and practical toleration.[7] This thesis echoes the sentiments of a number of protestant reformers later in the period. Joseph Pollock (1779), Peter Burrowes (1784) and Wolfe Tone (1791), all argued that as catholicism – in 'enlightened' opinion a backward superstitious creed – had entered irreversible decline, religious bigotry was now out of joint with the times.[8] The 'liberal protestant' thesis obviously fits the 'tension-free' model quite neatly. The problem with this thesis, however, is the need to account for the sudden sharp reversal of that supposed liberalism in the sectarian-wracked 1790s. As the events of that decade demonstrated the (wholly typical) optimism of the reformers was misplaced. Perhaps previous generations of historians were predisposed to underestimate the dogged continuity of sectarianism in Irish life because they, not unnaturally, found it 'unattractive [and] depressing'.[9] In their desire to 'exorcise passion' from the *writing* of Irish history,[10] these scholars sometimes filtered unpleasant passions out of history itself.

The rather anodyne versions of eighteenth-century politics and society which inescapably proceeded from these genteel perspectives are no longer convincing. It has recently been argued that the original religious impulse behind the framing of the penal laws was strong and authentic, that that impulse frequently reasserted itself throughout our period, and that the reversal of protestant liberalism in the 1790s does not need to be explained because liberalism was never, in fact, an important ideological force.[11] If the penal laws directed at the Catholic Church failed in their avowed purpose, this in the end was due to lax application. But it would be wrong to infer that this resulted from protestant tolerance or indifference. Rather the coercive machinery available to the government – a thinly-spread unpaid magistry – was inadequate to the task. As the periodic closures of mass-houses – in 1744, for example[12] – the annual commemoration's of the 1641 massacres on 23 October and the establishment of the conversionist charter schools in 1733 all show, the men of no popery were alive and kicking. Eighteenth-century man, Jonathan Clark reminds us in another context, lived in an intellectual and political world where religion mattered.[13]

Those penal laws which did not require active coercion proved more effective. It was a comparatively simple matter excluding catholics from Trinity College, the corporations, or the franchise. The apparent success of the laws relating to land ownership is more problematic. Catholics possessed an estimated twenty-two per cent of the land in Ireland in 1688, fourteen per cent in 1703 and only five per cent by 1778. Yet the story which these statistics tell, in one respect plain enough, needs to be qualified. Firstly, a distinction should be made between ownership and leasehold. Secondly and more subtly, L. M. Cullen has identified a 'convert interest' – a network of landowning families with catholic relatives and catholic sympathies.[14] Even among barristers many converts were suspected of only nominal protestantism.[15] In other words, the impact of the penal code upon catholic property was not as clear-cut or as devastating as the bare statistics suggest.

Its effects across the country were also uneven: prosperous catholic communities survived in counties Galway, Kilkenny and Meath, for instance. Nor was land the only source of wealth. Catholics were excluded from the trade guilds but not from trade. The penal laws in no way hindered the steady growth of a middle-class catholic mercantile elite. Edward Byrne, a prominent member of the Catholic Committee in the 1790s, was reputedly the richest man in Ireland. This complex catholic presence had important political implications: protestant anxieties, though exaggerated, were not baseless. Sectarian tensions reflected social realities. Thus the bitterly contested Tipperary bye-election of 1760 involved accusations of crypto-catholicism against one of the candidates, a convert.

The impact of the penal code reached far beyond its practical effects (or, from the legislators standpoint, failures). It institutionalised sectarianism in Irish life. The majority were not only excluded but alienated from the political nation. Conversely, as Lecky observed, even 'the most worthless protestant had the satisfaction of being a member of a dominant race'.[16] A sense of historic grievance entrenched catholic resentments. Travellers such as Arthur Young in the 1770s and DeLatocayne in the 1790s noted a strong popular consciousness of dispossession. Just as the memory of 1641 continued to haunt the protestant imagination, catholics, as the memoirs of Charles Teeling, James Coigly, Miles Byrne and Thomas Cloney all testify, never forgot the confiscations of the seventeenth century. Again it is clear that protestant fears of catholic revanchism were not baseless.

Again too, before the 1790s, these fears were exaggerated. Nevertheless, nagging anxiety kept alive a profound distrust of catholic loyalty.

Rural disturbances, like the Whiteboy unrest in Munster in the 1760s, were, despite their social character and identifiable economic causes, quickly labelled popish insurrections by edgy local protestants. Characteristically, the Anglo-Irish elite were also quick to detect the hand of France, catholic Ireland's traditional ally, stirring up unrest. French agents were even rumoured to be involved in fomenting riots in Dublin in 1784. Indeed, the stubborn persistence of Francophobia in Anglo-Irish governing circles compared with the more relaxed attitudes of their English counterparts serves as an illuminating commentary on the differing levels of confidence. The Anglo-Irish were the more francophobe because, conditioned by recent historical experience, they believed they had more to fear from a potentially hostile, francophile, catholic population.[17]

'Race memories', francophobia and protestant anxieties reveal a fissured sociey. Ireland's facade of social and political stability was structurally flawed. Unlike the sturdier English construction it could not absorb the reverberations set off by the French revolution. Yet the collapse of stability in the 1790s does not *prove* that the protestant nation founded in the 1690s was inevitably doomed. That conclusion would be as lopsided and inaccurate as the old 'tension-free' model of eighteenth-century politics and society. The Anglo-Irish governing elite may not have been as successful or secure as its English counterpart, but as the recent debate about the genesis of the term 'Protestant Ascendancy' indicates, it was not without ideological resources. Even as the facade began to crack, 'there was possibly more life in the Anglo-Irish ascendancy . . . ' argues Anthony Malcomson, 'than eighteenth-century historians or, more important, the late eighteenth-century British government, allowed'.[18] Perhaps hindsight, our knowledge that in the long run the ascendancy 'lost' the political battle, combined in some quarters with distaste for the 'colonial past', accounts for the slim historiography of ascendancy political culture. Yet it is essential for historians of radical or popular politics to explore that culture and appreciate its vitality. Consideration of the strengths and character of the old order can only enhance our understanding of the strengths, weaknesses and priorities of those who challenged it.

The debate about what has been called 'the meaning and significance of "Protestant Ascendancy"' has already been alluded to. Other terms, such as 'Anglo-Irish', 'protestant nation' 'political nation' and *ancien regime* have also been employed. Yet others, like 'protestant interest', or simply, 'Irish nation', were used at the time. If, up to a point, these terms can be used, as they sometimes are, interchangeably, their meanings nonetheless differ.

Ulster's presbyterian community might belong to the 'protestant interest' (as understood by Eamon O'Flaherty, for example),[19] but it was excluded from, and often hostile to, the 'Anglo-Irish ascendancy' (as defined by Malcomson). The term 'political nation' can reasonably be read in a way which encompasses the enfranchised, anglican or dissenter, rich or poor; 'ascendancy', on the other hand, whether protestant or Anglo-Irish, has a definite social-elitist resonance.

Since the divisions between presbyterians and the established church were almost as important, in a political sense, as those between 'protestant' and catholic, concepts like 'political nation' or 'protestant interest' may conceal as much as they reveal. With 'Protestant Ascendancy' this problem of descriptive imprecision is reversed. That concept was articulated in the particular contexts of public debate between 1786 and 1792. It is chronologically too specific. In the light of new scholarship on the subject, 'Protestant Ascendancy' now seems an inappropriate term when applied earlier in the century. Malcomson's 'Anglo-Irish ascendancy' – and he acknowledges that it is an historian's definition – comes closest to describing eighteenth-century political structures as they were actually experienced and functioned. This he depicts as 'a narrow social and political elite, to be defined along social and political rather than ethnic lines'. Membership of the elite depended upon conformity to the anglican communion, and was composed of 'those who themselves sat in the Irish parliament or who exercised significant influence over the return of the 300 members of the House of Commons'.[20]

As we shall see, eighteenth-century radicals likewise located parliament at the centre of their analysis of society. Virtually all the political energies of radicalism focused on parliamentary reform. If this analysis now strikes us as inadequate and the energies misdirected, those MPs who sat in the unreformed commons and the great landed magnates – the borough-owners – who controlled so many of their seats, shared their radical critics estimation of parliament's importance. Evidence of this self-perception stands in imposing, graceful, stone in College Green today. It is visible too in the street plan of Dublin city centre. The first broad thoroughfares laid out by the Wide Streets Commissioners – significantly, a statutory body – after 1757, were intended to improve the approaches to parliament. Assertive architecture and the new urban streetscape reflected the enhanced prestige of the eighteenth-century legislature.

Like its mother institution, Westminster, the Irish parliament first became a regular and indispensible feature of the constitution after the Glorious Revolution of 1688 and its settlement. The commons sat every second year from 1692 to 1785 and annually thereafter. Unlike Westminster, and before the octennial act of 1768, the life of each parliament was coterminus with the reign of the monarch. Thus there were no general elections between 1715 and 1727, or between 1727 and 1760. Other dissimilarities had greater practical effect. In spite of the flamboyant symbolism of the College Green building, or the high claims made for the parliaments' autonomous status under the crown, most cogently advanced by William Molyneux's *Case of Ireland . . . stated* (1698), the Irish legislature never achieved complete independence. Under Poynings' law (1494–1782) parliament could not initiate legislation, only 'heads of bills'. Heads of bills were transmitted via the Irish privy council to the English privy council, which could suppress them, or return them with amendments. At that stage the Irish parliament had either to accept or reject the amended legislation in full. Westminster, moreover, could pass laws binding in Ireland. It was an example of this practice, the 1697 Woollen act, which provoked Molyneux's celebrated pamphlet. Nor did the Irish parliament control its own executive. The principal officers of the crown, the lord lieutenant and his chief secretary, were always Englishmen appointed by the British government. With certain exceptions – notably the Woods ha'pence episode in the 1720s, the money bill dispute in the 1750s, the crisis of 1779–82 or the regency affair in 1789 – power resided in Dublin Castle, not College Green.

These well-known limitations on the prerogatives of the Irish parliament never reduced it to the British ministry's rubber stamp. It always required careful management, the judicious distribution of places, pensions, honours and sinecures to purchase votes for the administration. At first this management devolved on parliamentary 'undertakers' who secured government majorities in return for control of government patronage.[21] But as the money bill dispute in the 1750s demonstrated, the undertakers were not entirely reliable, and during the Townsend lord lieutenancy (1767–72) the Castle took direct control of patronage. Successful though management generally was, parliament could and did revolt. Popular measures, unwelcome to government, could be carried by galvanising the 'floating' votes of the independent country gentlemen. At a certain critical level placemen could be expected to desert their political pay-masters. Voting patterns of this sort often coalesced in response to 'public opinion'. 'Free Trade' in 1779, and the repeal of Poynings' law and the declaratory act in 1782, were carried against a background of sustained out-of-doors campaigns.

In certain circumstances, then, parliament responded to public opinion. But does that mean it was representative? Obviously, measured by late twentieth-century criteria it was not. However, such criteria are unhelpful. Judged by twentieth-century standards eighteenth-century electoral practices, the geography and variety of constituencies and styles of parliamentary management, were corrupt and irrational. Insofar as hindsight seems to endorse the arguments and proposals of the reformers, it obscures the sophisticated position of the conservatives and distorts contemporary perceptions of parliament's functions. Except for the advanced radicals of the 1790s, parliament was seen not as a means to popularly accountable government, but as a bulwark against arbitrary power, as a check or balance in the finely-tuned, historically-tested and much-sung British constitution. The hard-won liberties of the free-born Briton, not the rather dubious blessings of democracy, were held to be the chief glory of that constitution. Since popery served as a metaphor for arbitrary power, conservatives and radicals alike could justify the continued exclusion of catholics from the political nation. The almost talismanic quality of the words 'British constitution' to which defenders of the status quo appealed, is illustrated by the radicals' claim that they simply wished to 'renovate' it, to restore the balance between king, lords and commons by rolling back undue ministerial influence.

Increasingly the radical strategy for renovation hinged on widening and rationalising the franchise. They hoped to check ministerial power, in Ireland called 'English influence', by making parliament more representative and MPs more accountable to the electorate. According to this theory an MP's dependence on public opinion would insulate him from government patronage. The logic of radical critiques of parliament shines through in retrospect, but again, the eventual triumph of reform, the fact that in the long run the radicals 'won' the argument, does not *prove* that the conservative position was ideologically untenable. After all, the radicals did not win the argument in the eighteenth century. Indeed, it has been suggested that the failure of the English reform movement in the 1790s was due as much to its losing the argument as to repression.[22] Similarly, if the challenge to the Anglo-Irish ascendancy was more formidable and its repression more brutal, this did not preclude an ideological defence.

Because it acted as the focus of the ideological debate which did occur, it will be useful at this point to outline the structures of parliamentary representation.[23] The 300 members returned to the commons sat for several different kinds of constituency: 64, two for each, represented the counties, two were elected by the fellows of the university and the remaining 234 sat for 117 boroughs. The size of electorates varied enormously, ranging from that of an 'open' county, like Down, with up to 6,000 voters, through the pot-walloping boroughs in which all (protestant) inhabitants were enfranchised, to the numerous 'close' corporation boroughs with an average electorate of 13 to the entirely uninhabited boroughs of Clonmines, Bannow and Harristown. An estimated 107 of the 150 constituencies were to some degree 'close'. Borough seats, a species of property owned by landlords, were more often inherited or sold than contested. Thus those borough-owners whose boroughs were abolished by the act of union in 1800–1 received financial compensation.

'Parliament' of course had two chambers: lords and commons. The Irish house of lords consisted of judges, an episcopal bench of eighteen bishops and four archbishops, and a fluctuating number of lay peers – 126 in 1725.[24] Like the lower chamber the legislative role of the upper house was circumscribed by Poynings' law. In addition the supreme appellate jurisdiction of the Irish lords was transferred to its British counterpart by the declaratory act of 6 George I (1720–82).[25] Yet even after 1782, when the declaratory act was repealed along with Poynings' law, and the legislative functions of the lords increased, it 'did not become a second chamber of remotely similar importance to its British opposite number'.[26] An air of political desuetude hung over an assembly marked by large scale non-attendance and debased by the elevation of absentee Englishmen to the Irish peerage. Certainly, judging by its absence from parliamentary reform schemes, late eighteenth-century radicals considered this institution unimportant. If so, their estimate was not completely accurate. The earliest catholic relief measures were in fact stalled in the lords in the early 1770s. More surprisingly perhaps, a Draconian measure directed at journeymen combinations in 1792 was thrown out by the upper house.[27] Peers were well represented on the privy council. But the real power-base of individual lords rested on their control of parliamentary seats. Approximately half of the 236 borough members were returned by peers.[28]

The justification for the influence of borough-owners and for so seemingly irrational a patchwork of constituencies was simple: parliament represented property not persons. And, like 'constitution', the word property had acquired virtually talismanic resonances. Some conservatives appeared to think that the mere incantation of these tried, self-evidently beneficent formulae provided sufficient defence of the status quo. Others were prepared to elaborate. The great virtue of a property-owning electorate was its supposed independence. Even certain radicals believed that domestic servants should not be trusted with votes because they were wholly dependent upon their employers. Moreover, because the men of property had a 'stake in the country' property acted as the sheet-anchor of social stability. Finally, property, and its inevitable concomitant, social hierarchy, were part of the natural order of things: parliament reflected, represented, and secured that order. Like the constitution the natural order of society was seen as the product of a long historical evolution and was not, therefore, to be lightly tampered with. Gradualism, argued conservatives, worked.

Why subject the real, tested achievement of the British constitution, the envy of the world, to experiment or abstract speculation? This position was sharpened by the contrast with the perceived calamities visited upon France by its revolution. As Edmund Burke warned, the French experience offered a fateful lesson in the dangers of hasty innovation.

All of these arguments will be familiar to students of English history. Insofar as the Anglo-Irish elite shared access to a common British political culture, and common political assumptions, it is scarcely surprising that they advanced the same ideological justifications. But the Anglo-Irish confronted different political realities. For example, it would be difficult to exaggerate the role of the established church in England, 'the ubiquitious agency of the state,'[29] in inculcating social and political conformity. The Church of Ireland, on the other hand, reached only a small proportion of the population. The political message of English and Irish anglican sermons might be the same. The size of the audience was not. Catholic priests could generally be relied upon to preach social deference and loyalty to the crown, but could hardly be expected to issue blanket endorsements of a political system from which their flock was excluded. Religious demography and the ancestral divisions of Irish society constricted the ideological hegemony of the Anglo-Irish governing elite. By English or Scottish standards the Anglo-Irish were handicapped by an unfavourable political context, although this did not precipitate ideological retreat. Nor did conservativism totally lack popular support. On the contrary, the Irish protestants' sense of cultural superiority over his 'superstitious' and servile catholic neighbours underscored a robust defence of the established order.

The vitality of the conservative cause is evident from the adoption and articulation of the term 'Protestant Ascendancy'. Although its use has been identified at earlier dates, 'Protestant Ascendancy' first enters the language of politics in a pamphlet, *The present state of the Church of Ireland . . . ,* written by the bishop of Cloyne, Richard Woodward, in 1786. Woodward employed the term in defence of the rights of the established church, which were being challenged at the time by the Rightboy campaign in Munster against excessive tithes. In these circumstances its coinage has been described by one historian as a 'sophisticated', 'aggressive' 'symbolically and rhetorically potent' addition to the 'ideological vocabulary of protestant conservatives'. It was more precise, resonant and effective than the comparatively bland 'protestant interest'.[30] Woodward's pamphlet sold well and went into nine editions, but it was not until 1792, the year of the Catholic Convention, that the term gained popular currency and assumed the character of a rallying-cry. In that year 'Protestant Ascendancy' begins to appear with some frequency in official correspondence between Dublin

Castle and London, it is defined, redefined and counter-defined on the floor of the commons (and consequently reported in the press), and, crucially, is taken up and elaborated by Dublin corporation.

However the claims made for Woodward's use of the term, or 'slogan', are assessed, the rhetorical force of the corporation's declaration published in September, 1792, is not in doubt:

> One hundred years are just elapsed, since the question was tried upon an appeal to heaven, whether this country should become a Popish King-dom, governed by an arbitrary and unconstitutional Popish tyrant . . . or enjoy the blessings of a free Protestant government . . . The great ruler of all things decided in favour of our ancestors . . . and Ireland became a Protestant nation enjoying a British constitution.
>
> Every Irish Protestant has an interest in the government of this Kingdom, he is born a member of the state and with a capacity of filling its offices, this capacity he derives from that constitution which his ancestors acquired, when they overthrew the Popish tyrant, it is guaranteed by that constitution, it is secured by the law, he is in possession of it, and we know of no power under heaven authorised to alienate our most valuable inheritance.

The declaration goes on to define Protestant Ascendancy as:

> A Protestant King of Ireland, A Protestant Parliament, A Protestant Hierarchy, Protestant electors and government, the benches of justice, the army and the revenue through all the branches and details Protestant; and this system supported by a connection with the Protestant realm of England.[31]

Catholic demands for admission to the political nation, specifically for the right to vote in the counties, prompted the corporation's rhetoric. Conservative protestant opinion was particularly outraged by the election of delegates to the Catholic Convention to be held in December. This was interpreted as a challenge to parliamentary soverignty, and the commit-tee's circular letter outlining electoral procedures met with condemnation from sixteen county grand juries. Although the grand jury campaign was orchestrated by Dublin Castle, the strength of protestant feeling should not be underestimated. Indeed the formation in 1795 of the Orange Order confirmed the popular appeal of 'Protestant Ascendancy'.

These unofficial loyalist societies, which originated in county Armagh, represented a popular initiative in defence of the crown and constitution.

They rapidly spread across mid and south Ulster and, by 1798, into Leinster and Munster. The Orange presence in Wexford and Carlow was not some phantom of the rebels imagination. Recognising the usefulness of this counter-revolutionary movement in the dangerous conditions of the late 1790s, the gentry quickly assumed leadership.[32] In the absence of direct control the authorities were wary of publicly supporting orangism, but soon extended *de facto* approval. Again, the contrast with England is illuminating. Loyalist associations were formed there in response to the French revolutionary crisis, the war and home-grown radicalism. Like the orange societies these associations registered popular support for the estabished order,[33] but while the social composition of both movements was heterogenous, in Ireland the lower-class social base was much narrower. The reason is simple. The Orange Order was an ostentatiously sectarian organisation, and in Ireland protestants were a minority. English loyalism drew on popular patriotism; Irish loyalism, in the shape of the Orange Order, reflected an embattled siege mentality.

This account has examined the conservative and reactionary faces of 'Protestant Ascendancy'. It was, after all, a defensive concept. And as politics in the 1790s polarised along sectarian lines 'Protestant Ascendancy' hardened in its reactionary cast. Yet for a moment, earlier in the decade, other possibilities existed. During the 1792 debates on catholic relief the celebrated orator and spokesman for moderate reform, Henry Grattan MP, proposed a definition of 'Protestant Ascendancy' which would have accommodated catholics within the political nation. It is important to remember that protestant opinion was neither monolithic nor uniformly extreme. Grattan's 'Patriot' colleagues in parliament, or men like Henry Joy, the proprietor of the liberal *Belfast Newsletter* (1789–95), represented an alternative, Whig, tradition which, although divided on the catholic question, offered different solutions to Ireland's problems. In the event it was Dublin corporation's declaration, not Grattan's pluralism, which matched the mood of the times.

While the declaration of 'Protestant Ascendancy' is best understood as a political manifesto – as a counterblast to the catholic challenge – it can also be read as a description of existing legal and political structures. What the corporation defined, and the Catholic Committee challenged, was legal monopoly in public office. This monopoly was protestant and, the commercial-bourgeois character of Dublin corporation notwithstanding, largely concentrated in the hands of a landed elite. The political system was closed. From this perspective 'high politics' appear as little more than family quarrels within the elite, or between the elite and its British sponsor. Office might change hands, London might encounter occasional obstruction, but the system – the distribution, in social and religious terms, of political power – remained fundamentally intact.

From this perspective also 'popular politics' might usefully denote that process whereby a closed political system was, in social or religious terms, challenged, breached, or compelled to redraw its boundaries. The process began, perhaps, in the 1740s with Dr Charles Lucas's attack on parliament's abuse of power, and, equally significant, with his agitation among Dublin's tradesmen. After Lucas 'politics' were no longer the exclusive preserve of a social elite, although politics were still effectively confined to protestants. Increasingly, 'opposition' politics were conducted out-of-doors and relied more and more upon mobilising public opinion. The impact of Lucas's career as a radical journalist, of pamphleteering during the money bill episode in the 1750s,[34] of the *Freemans Journal* in the 1770s and 1780s and of the *Northern Star* in the 1790s, all indicate the emergence of a more articulate public culture. The press, like the out-of-doors agitation to which it was so often allied, contributed to the politicisation of society at large.

Before the 1790s this new, wider, conception of politics, was expressed most dramatically by Volunteering. When France formally allied with the rebellious American colonies in 1778, Volunteer companies were formed in east Ulster to meet the threat of French invasion. The movement quickly spread. The parallels between Ireland and America's constitutional relationship with the 'mother country' were not lost on the Volunteers, who also drew on indigenous traditions of Anglo-Irish patriotism. In alliance with the patriots in parliament, many of whom were themselves Volunteer officers, the new citizen army soon turned its attention to domestic matters. With Britain's resources overstretched by war the patriot-Volunteer alliance skilfully exploited the imperial crisis, pressing their demands with the barely concealed threat of 'armed resistence', and by holding a national convention at Dungannon in 1782. Major concessions, 'free trade' in 1779 and the repeal of Poynings' law and the declaratory act three years later, were wrung from the British government in this way. However, after the winning of the 'constitution of 1782' as the Volunteers moved on to demand parliamentary reform, the alliance with the patriots began to disintegrate. Their political influence and membership declined. Finally, with the introduction of the divisive catholic question, Volunteering passed into virtual eclipse. After 1784, with the exception of a brief revival in 1792, the great days of the movement were over.

Up until 1783 the catholic question had stayed in the background. Indeed it is a telling illustration of how successful the penal code had been in subjugating catholics that the first serious opposition to the *status quo* originated from within the protestant community. The social bases of political participation were progressively extended by the extra-parliamentary campaigns of the Volunteers, and later, of the United Irishmen, both, in their different ways, protestant initiatives. Lucas, the Volunteers and the United Irishmen stretched the limits of politics. The catholic question, first raised as an immediate political issue in 1783–4, threatened to break the circle. The admission of catholics to the political nation – giving catholics the vote – which returned to the political agenda with a vengence in 1791, presaged the end of the protestant legal monopoly of power. Eighteenth-century politics were dominated by the narrowly-based Anglo-Irish landed elite which controlled parliament. During the earliest decades its ascendancy was unrivalled and unchallenged, but, as the public realm of politics gradually expanded, its authority faltered. With the emergence, in the last decades of the century, of the catholic question, it faced into a fight for its very survival.

II POPULAR CULTURE AND MODERNISATION

The draw-backs entailed in the above conceptualization of popular politics include a too-tight focus on parliament and the unmistakable whiff of Whiggish teleology. Even though parliament and the franchise did provide the main issues around which reformers, radicals and catholics organised, and even though we can trace the *development* of politicisation over time, popular politics can be explored in other ways and by different routes. Corkery's 'hidden Ireland' of Gaelic verse and residual Jacobitism, or Peter Brooke's Ulster presbyterian 'virtual nation within a nation', enlivened by internal theological disputes, refer to political sub-cultures remote from the mainstream concerns of College Green.[35] Futhermore, only narrow and patronising definitions could exclude Whiteboys and other rural secret societies from the realm of 'politics'. At one level popular politics in the 1790s were constituted by catholic and radical attempts to prize open a sealed political system, the self-proclaimed Protestant Ascendancy. At another level, popular politics were about the interaction of these radicals and catholics with an informal non-elite culture, represented in one of its aspects by the secret society tradition. In that sense the 1790s witnessed the politicisation of popular culture. However, this development depended upon more than radical proselytising of the common people. In fact politicisation intimately related to those wider processes of economic, social and cultural change usually described as 'modernisation'.

Late-eighteenth-century Irish society was becoming more literate, more commercialised, more urban. Dublin, Belfast and Cork all expanded during this period. The penetration of roads, canals, markets and newspapers began to erode regional and local perculiarities. Compared with Britain's industrial revolution the pace and scale of change was modest. Ireland for long remained an overwhelmingly rural society. Regional variation persisted. 'On the western side of the Shannon', observed Edward Wakefield in the early nineteenth century, 'the appearance of the people, their dress, the form of their cottages, and even the Irish language which they speak, are different from what they are in Leinster or Munster, or in any other part of Ireland'.[36] An even starker contrast subsisted between this predominantly agricultural regional economy where 'little money is to be seen in circulation', and the linen manufacturing zone of mid-Ulster. Geographically and temporally the 'traditional' and the 'modern' existed side by side.

Historical geographers and economic historians of a slightly later period have conceptualized this dichotomy as 'the two Irelands' or the 'dual economy'.[37] Like all models, which are theoretical constructs not descriptions of 'reality', the 'dual economy' is over-schematic. The concept of duality simplifies the complexity and interconnectedness of the Irish economy. Usefully, however, by positing the penetration of the 'old' – subsistence farming – by the 'new' – the market economy, cash – it does suggest transition.

Traditional economys are characterised by peasant proprietorship; by small-holders who produce for their own consumption and whose surplus is used to meet the various levies, rent, tithe and tax, of landlord, church and state. In the social or cultural sphere, 'traditional' refers to parochialism, illiteracy, the tenacity of custom and the persistence of pre-modern popular beliefs and practices. This outline of the traditional economy approximates to Irish conditions, although the blanket category 'peasant' obscures the intricate stratification of rural social structures. Located at the apex of the social pyramid were the landlords, in political terms those who composed the Anglo-Irish elite together with a small surviving catholic group. A step down the scale were the lease-holding larger tenants or middlemen, followed by their sub-tenants, the farmer class, and, at the base of the pyramid, the landless labourers and cottiers, who recieved all or part of their wages in 'conacre' – a small plot of land devoted to the cultivation of potatoes. The variation in income and status between and within these groups could be enormous. Modernisation, specifically commercialisation and population growth, did not replace this structure; it merely broadened the base. As landlords' rent rolls increased and the strong farmers became stronger, the landless labourers and cottiers became evermore numerous and less well off.

The process of commercialisation is comparatively easy to monitor. In 1684 there were an estimated 503 quarterly or twice yearly fairs in the country, just under half of them in Leinster. By the 1770s this total had risen to almost 3,000, Leinster's share of which had dropped to just over a quarter.[38] The impact of trade can also be detected in patterns of urban development. With the single exception of Kilkenny, all the large urban centres were ports. The rapid growth of Limerick, Cork, Waterford and, later in the century, Belfast, all reflect an increasingly buoyant export trade, whether provisions from Cork or linen from Belfast. All of these cities, moreover, were 'undisputed regional capital[s]'.[39] By far the biggest and fastest-growing city, another port, its 'harbour . . . crowded with ships,'[40] was the capital itself. Dublin and the other ports were also industrial centres, conduits of interregional trade and the economy's bankers. Cork and Dublin, in particular, financed a great deal of economic activity in the interior. Indeed, Dublin credit helped to sustain the linen boom in the north at least into the 1780s.[41]

The growth of the ports and the export trade, the proliferation of fairs and the spread of rural industry – linen manufacture was never confined to Ulster – are all indicators of the commercialisation of the economy. Less and less was production geared to immediate consumption, more and more to sale in the marketplace. As an inevitable corollary cash transactions increased. Commercialisation had two mainstays: cattle and textiles. The cattle trade – a form of capitalist agriculture – developed under comparativly favourable conditions. Pasture land was exempt from tithes after 1735 and British imposed legislation restricting the export of cattle was repealed in the 1750s. At the same time overseas markets improved. By mid-century the profitability of converting tillage to pasture prompted enclosures, a process which, as we shall see, disrupted the 'moral economy' of the countryside, displacing smaller tenants and encroaching upon customary access to common land. In this instance modernisation had a socially destablising effect: it eroded settled relationships and undermined traditional rural practices.

Paradoxically, the other main motor of economic change, rural industry, acted more as a demographic shock-absorber than as an agent of destablisation. Even by contemporary European standards eighteenth-century Ireland experienced unprecedented demographic growth. The population grew from an estimated 2.5 million in 1753 to 4.4 million in 1791, rising to 6.8 million by 1821.[42] Competition for land intensified, pushing up rents and the price of leases, but the sub-division of holdings generally kept up with increased demand. Proportionately, therefore, population increase was concentrated at the base of the social pyramid. In relative as well as absolute terms, cottiers and labourers multiplied. In Britain embryo industrial cities siphoned off such 'surplus' labour. In Ireland, Dublin performed this function on a more limited scale for its Leinster hinterland. In the short term the potentially disasterous consequences of the population explosion were contained by the diffusion of textile production. The more drastic and final remedies of mass emigration and mass starvation lay in the future.

Linen manufacture and the linen trade are usually, with good reason, associated with east Ulster. Indeed, during the boom years of the 1780s, rural domestic industry – weaving, bleaching (and the cash nexus) – overtook agriculture as the principal form of economic activity in the 'linen triangle' of north Armagh and east Down. Belfast merchants opened their own linen hall in 1785. But it is important to remember that the linen economy spread far beyond the borders of Ulster. In the 1770s Arthur Young was impressed by the extent of flax cultivation, spinning and even weaving in Connaught. In Roscommon he estimated that up to twenty per cent of locally produced yarn was also woven locally. Young refers to the sale of linens in markets in Mayo and to the ubiquity of spinning wheels in labourers cabins, in county Cork as well as in Connaught.[43] The general diffusion of the linen economy supplemented rural incomes and relieved the pressure on land.

Flax, yarn, and finished textiles were produced for the market and exchanged for cash. The importance of domestic industry and the spread of the cash nexus underlines the inadequacy of the term 'peasantry'. Access to land – ownership, leasehold or occupancy – remained the paramount concern of the great majority of the rural lower classes, but livings could now be made from a range of occupations in a commercialising, diversifying economy. What is striking about the rural social composition of the Defenders in the 1790s, for example, is the inappropriateness of the description 'peasant'. Weavers, bleachers, schoolmasters, blacksmiths, shopkeepers and publicans featured as prominently in its ranks as farmers or cottiers. The point is worth stressing. In this instance an appreciation of the social-structural consequences of modernisation squashes any easy equation of 'rural' with 'agriculture' or 'peasantry'.

Popular political consciousness is not *generated* or *determined* by social-structural change. But modernisation can facilitate popular political awareness by breaking down the local particularism characteristic of the peasant outlook. The market, the cash nexus, improved communications – a more efficient postal system, for instance – and the physical infrastructure of economic development, roads and canals, all tend towards the integration of local communities into larger regional or national units. And in the second half of the eighteenth century Ireland, in Cullen's phrase, witnessed 'nothing less than an environmental revolution'.[44] This included enclosures and house-building but, above all, more roads. Young considered Irish roads of superior quality to English ones, and by 1780 every town of any size was linked to an extensive road network – financed by county cess – crisscrossing the whole island.[45]

Of course a considerable imaginative leap is involved in relating road-building or increasing numbers of handlooms to the politicisation of popular culture. Perhaps the most that can be said is that by undermining traditional society such developments helped to create a popular audience potentially more receptive to political ideas than a traditional peasantry. According to this thesis, modernisation facilitates politicisation by eroding traditionalist impediments, like localism and habits of social deference, and through the destructive impact of social-structural change upon a custom-bound, inward-looking, peasant *mentalité*. Popular culture is exposed to the influence of 'outside' agents, such as the press or radical (or conservative) elites. If it is a thesis which asigns a too-passive role to the popular culture side of the relationship and underestimates autonomous lower-class agency, it is also one which may be adapted rather easily to Rudé's explanation of popular ideology as a compound of 'derived' (from an elite) and 'inherent' (or surviving traditional) ideas.

These processes are complex, interrelated, subtle, gradual, uneven over time and place, and difficult to trace or demonstrate, let alone verify. At one level, however, the relationship between modernisation and popular politicisation is both close and fairly clear-cut: literacy. In fact, some measure of popular literacy is a necessary, though not a sufficient, precondition of mass politicisation. High levels of literacy can subsist independently of politicisation; it is more difficult to imagine popular politics developing without some degree of literacy. In the 1790s the radical elite, the United Irishmen, skilfully employed non-verbal techniques – ritual, symbol and public demonstrations – to mobilise popular support,[46] but ultimately most of their energies were devoted to the dissemination of propagandist literature. This required a popular audience, a sizable proportion of which could read. Others could be read to: not only the literate were exposed to the printed word.

Social and cultural historians have generally identified increasing popular literacy as a key variable in the modernisation process. The causes of literacy have been usefully described – drawing on an analogy with economics – as the 'pull' of social prestige and economic utility, (which

created demand) and the 'push' of education (supply) and religion.[47] The
ability to read became more important as the written word advanced alongside economic development. Tenants might have written leases; receipts
and promissory notes changed hands in the marketplace; employers, as in
Belfast's *Northern Star*, advertised for apprentices in newspapers. In short,
the practical incentives for attaining basic literacy multiplied. Parents had
good reason to see to their children's education.

The causes of literacy – ultility, religious imperatives and so on – are
reflected by the patterns of literacy in early modern Europe. Generally
speaking protestants were more literate than catholics, craftsmen, especially weavers and cobblers, than peasants, urban dwellers than country
people. While it is believed that 'a substantial minority of ordinary people'
were able to read, an estimated seventy-five per cent of Lyons silk weavers,
for example, were literate in the eighteenth century; Paris and London at
this time achieved literacy levels of about forty or fifty per cent. Men
were more likely to be able to read than women, and more people, though
perhaps not many more, could read than could write.[48]

These conclusions which historians have drawn about the structures
of literacy are largely based on the quantitive analysis of signatures.
The witnessing of wills, court records and parish marriage records, all
generated evidence of this sort. Irish society appears to conform to
European trends, although the available evidence is more fragmentary,
impressionistic and inconclusive. In addition the problems of measuring
literacy are complicated by the extent to which Irish was still spoken.

Not surprisingly, the most literate region in Ireland was also the most
presbyterian and the area closest to lowland Scotland: east Ulster. In
the 1790s the United Irishman, Arthur O'Connor, described the common people of this region as 'probably the best educated peasantry
in Europe'; a view endorsed by Sir Richard Musgrave, who wrote of
the 'counties of Down and Antrim, where the mass of the people are
presbyterians, can read and write, and are fond of speculating on religion
and politics'.[49] Protestantism, with its emphasis on 'the word', on teaching
scripture, and on biblical knowledge, provided a major impulse to literacy.
Thus the emphatically protestant cultures of Scotland, New England, and
Sweden are commonly held to have been the most literate societies in the
eighteenth-century world.[50] Early-modern Scotland provided for a unique
system of state-aided, statutory, parochial schools, and like their lowland
kinsfolk who thereby pioneered the first 'general system of popular
education',[51] Ulster presbyterians placed a high premium upon learning.
Their vigorous religious life gave rise to a prolific 'polemical theology',[52]
and by the late eighteenth century east Ulster had developed a vernacular

culture rich enough to to produce John Hewitt's 'ryhming weavers', a Sunday school movement, local academies, circulating libraries, book clubs and reading societies, centres of the 'most advanced views of the age'; producing, it is claimed, a stratum of 'rural *philosophes*'.[53] Sixteen reading societies have been identified in Antrim and Down alone.[54]

The two eastern counties seem to have been highly literate even by Ulster standards. As we move beyond the boundaries of Antrim and Down evidence of literacy begins to thin. However, the province's comparatively buoyant newspaper market implies the existence of a wider literate audience. Before 1814 newspaper presses were hand-operated and print technology limited each issue to 4,000 copies. But the readership of the typical eighteenth-century newspaper was much larger as copies were passed on after use, read aloud to groups, and purchased by coffee houses and by joint subscription. The *Belfast Newsletter* estimated that each of its copies reached an average six readers.[55] With its eighty-eight agents and its retail outlets in virtually every town and village in Ulster and some beyond,[56] the twice weekly *Northern Star*'s audience was even bigger. Groups of workers in bleachgreens were said to have bought it or to have been 'treated' to it by 'their master's who were disloyal'.[57] Alongside the two Belfast papers, both of which enjoyed a healthy provincial market, late-eighteenth-century Ulster also managed to sustain a variety of smaller-scale local papers. *Gorden's Newry Chronicle*, *The Strabane Journal*, the *Strabane Newsletter* and the *Londonderry Journal* all found a commercial niche.[58]

The circulation of newspapers is the kind of 'supply-side' evidence which does not permit the quantification of rates of literacy, or the detailed mapping of regional variations. At best we may conjecture that the demand for the printed word, in the form of newspapers, suggests that at least a 'significant minority' of the adult population could read. Almost certainly that minority was larger in the north than in the south; among protestants than among catholics. Nevertheless, the contrast should not be too sharply drawn. The predominantly catholic south and west had a lively provincial press of its own. Four newspapers were printed in Cork at various times in the late eighteenth century and elsewhere Munster was served by the *Waterford Herald* and the *Limerick Chronicle*. The midlands were served by the *Westmeath Journal* and the *Athlone Herald*, while for the west two papers were based at Sligo. The most successful of the southern provincial newspapers, which, after all, had to compete with those Dublin papers which had national circulations, was *Finn's Leinster Journal*. Printed in Kilkenny, its proprietors built a smoothly run distribution network and it was available in 'Waterford,

Clonmell, Carlow, Cashel and several other towns on the same days of publication'.

Another kind of 'supply-side' evidence is available in the shape of the ubiquitous schoolmaster. In eighteenth-century Ireland, aside from the conversionist charter schools, children were generally taught by non-official, entrepreneur 'hedge' schoolmasters, funded by small sums out of the parents' pockets. Young remarked upon 'every child of the poorest family learning to read, write and cast accounts'.[59] There were 'several thousand' schoolmasters, who, argues Cullen, helped to create, as well as to meet, the growing popular demand for literacy. A rudimentary education might also be supplied in the home. The United Irishman, James Hope, who received only fifteen weeks formal schooling, learned much more at the firesides of the farmers who employed him.[60]

Unfortunately, harder, more precise, data, only becomes available with mid-nineteenth-century census reports. It is possible, however, to draw certain conclusions from these statistics. The 1841 census figures reveal that fifty-four per cent of catholics could read and that thirty-five per cent could both read and write. The age structure of the literate indicates that the percentage of the catholic population which could read and write in the 1790s was lower – less than fifty per cent – but that it was steadily rising.[61]

Contemporary evidence that a 'significant minority' of lower-class catholics could sign their names is provided by the success of the Catholic Committee's mobilisation of popular support in 1792. In March that year the Committee issued a 'Declaration of principles' which it asked all its coreligionists to sign. 20,000 signatures were reportedly secured in county Wexford, and the following year a newspaper referred to 'the numerous resolutions and declarations which were sent up from the south and western counties, signed by thousands of the poorer classes'.[62] The only lists which seem to have survived are from west Ulster. These record approximately 8,500 names, on parchment or in booklets, from eighteen parishes mainly in Tyrone or Armagh. Most are lists of names rather than collections of signatures, but some do offer fascinating glimpses of high levels of popular literacy.[63] The evidence of popular subscription to the declaration is patchy, but, significantly, it comes from several different places: Ulster, the 'south and west', Wexford, and Meath. Again, it is impossible to quantify, yet it is clear that Lecky's 'peasantry, sunk in poverty and ignorance', is a pale caricature of reality. On the contrary, the evidence, patchy, anecdotal and inconclusive though it may be, strongly suggests that literacy kept pace with other aspects of modernisation.

Modernisation, it is argued, and in particular mass literacy, facilitates, if it does not actually prompt, politicisation. In Ireland, however, literacy was attained almost exclusively through the medium of English. In that sense modernisation meant anglicisation. The decline of the Irish language – already accelerating in the last two decades of the eighteenth century – represents a profound cultural change, intimately linked to the advance of literacy. English was the language of commerce, local administration, the court room and the printed word, Irish the language of an overwhelmingly oral culture. Gaelic literature was mainly preserved and transmitted by manuscript. In Ireland, as in the Scottish highlands, and for the same reasons, Gaelic literature and the Gaelic vernacular were major casualties of modernisation.

The utilitarian reasons for acquiring literacy were reasons also for abandoning Irish. The typical schoolmaster was bilingual, indeed a number were Gaelic poets and transcribers of Gaelic manuscripts, but their pupils invariably received instruction in English. Since English, like literacy, helped children to 'get on' in an increasingly anglicised and commercial world, English is what schoolmasters were paid to teach. Among the estimated 1,500,000 households whose language was Irish in 1806, a mere 20,000 were reportedly capable of reading Irish.[64] The correlation between modernisation and English is confirmed by the linguistic map of Ireland in the late eighteenth century. Working back again from the age structure of mid-nineteenth-century census figures, it appears that the most anglicised province in Ireland was Leinster. Most Irish, rising to eighty per cent of the population in counties Galway and Clare, was spoken in Connaught and Munster. The parallels between the rough east-west linguistic dichotomy and the so-called dual economy is obvious. Irish tended to be stronger in the more rural, less economically developed regions. In 1792 a pamphleteer observed that 'the inhabitants of Forkhill [south Armagh] and its adjacent neighbours are very illiterate, from their mountainous situation, that scarcely affords them potatoes and goats milk, of course the English language in many families, is scarcely known'.[65] Anglicisation was also a function of longer term settlement patterns. In this period Irish was still spoken in the relatively 'uncolonised' western mountain areas of Wicklow. Even closer to Dublin, as late as 1800 magistrates in south county Meath employed translators.[66]

If literacy facilitated politicisation, did the Irish language block or slow it down? There is some evidence that in the 1790s some radicals attempted to bridge the linguistic divide by proposing to translate Paine's *Rights of Man* and, in county Cork, to produce and Irish language newspaper. Since so few Irish speakers could read in that language, these proposals had limited tactical value. Moreover, the failure of the United Irish organisation to penetrate the predominantly Irish speaking west – county Clare, for example, scarcely features at all in the events of this troubled decade – might suggest that language difference did indeed act as a brake on politicisation. But there are other, more likely, explanations for conditions in Clare, such as physical remoteness from the urban centres of radical activity. Such explanations are more likely because the Irish language patently did not act as a brake on politicisation elsewhere. It was essentially a bilingual society. Monoglot Irish speakers were rare, and as we have seen, illiteracy in Irish did not preclude literacy in English.

Late-eighteenth-century Ireland was a society in transition. Linguistic, social and cultural change interacted with economic development and demographic explosion. The strains of modernisation – population pressure, the relative and absolute growth of the landless and cottier classes, the breakdown of deference – produced new social tensions. A less stable society was more vulnerable to the impact of the French revolution and the stresses of war; it offered more opportunities, too, to the enemies of the status quo. This brings us back squarely to the original conundrum: late-eighteenth-century Scotland and England also experienced profound economic and social-structural change, but these societies, put to the test of French ideological 'contamination' and war, proved more stable and resilient. Why?

The crisis of the 1790s was primarily a political one. In Ireland social *change* proved combustible because of the stubborn *continuity* of legal and political structures which institutionalised sectarianism and were based on historic animosities. Inevitably, as soon as those legal and political structures were challenged, the animosities resurfaced. This process was referred to as the 'catholic question'. The French revolution served as a catalyst, activating politico-religious tensions which had been simmering for one hundred years. It was the United Irishmen's misfortune that no amount of forward-looking rhetoric or sentiment could overcome the burden of the past. In the late eighteenth century Ireland may have undergone 'modernisation' but the passions, aspirations and outlook of many of its inhabitants were still doggedly stuck in the seventeenth.

2 Agrarian Rebels, Secret Societies and Defenders, 1761–91

Shortly after Earl Fitzwilliam took up office as lord lieutenant in 1795, he was shocked to discover that the Defenders, a militant catholic secret society, were appearing every night in arms in county Meath. He had never, he remarked, heard of such a thing in Northamptonshire.[1] His exasperation now seems almost comic, his ignorance of Irish realities lamentable. Yet the contrast between Meath and Northamptonshire is an instructive one. Although eighteenth-century England (and Scotland) witnessed their share of agrarian unrest, food riots and political agitation, they furnish no example of lower-class secret societies engaged in sustained, systematic campaigns of violence and intimidation. It is a significant contrast too, because, as Charles Tilly has pointed out, 'the nature of a society's collective violence speaks volumes about that society'.[2] Whatever it might say to us, the persistence of collective violence in eighteenth-century Ireland certainly raises questions about the image and structures of that society. An examination of the forms of popular protest should therefore provide insights into the general political and social history of the period. More directly, some understanding of these forms is essential background to any discussion of popular politics in the 1790s, particularly to any discussion of Defenderism – the prime expression of lower-class disaffection during that decade.

I WHITEBOYISM: A PATTERN ESTABLISHED

An account of the secret societies could begin with the Elizabethan 'woodkerne', with the Tories and Rapparees at the Restoration period and the early eighteenth century, or with the Connaught Houghers of 1711–13.[3] This account takes a more conventional starting-point: 1761 and the appearance of the Whiteboys. Indeed some historians, notably George Cornewall Lewis in the nineteenth century and Michael Beames today, have perceived so many recurring patterns of behaviour among the multitude of rural popular protest movements in pre-famine Ireland

(c. 1760 or 1780 to 1845) that they use the generic term 'Whiteboyism' to cover them all.[4] Whiteboyism, according to this thesis, was southern and agrarian, while the Defenders (and their successors, the Ribbonmen) are seen as northern-based, sectarian and quasi-political.[5] The distinction is valid, but it has been drawn too sharply. Each secret society had unique characteristics and specific origins. Defenderism *was* special. But the similarities between it and its southern cousins are at least as important as the differences. The Whiteboys provide an appropriate starting-point for the purposes of this discussion because the Defenders of the 1790s tapped into the Whiteboy tradition. The Whiteboys shaped a popular culture of protest which evolved modes of organisation, techniques of direct action and, most importantly perhaps, a communal ambivalence towards the law and civil authority, upon which the Defenders drew. Thomas Crofton Croker recognized the formative political potential of agrarian unrest when he observed of the 1798 rebellion that 'two generations of the peasantry had been trained up to become actors in this event'.[6] Croker referred to the Whiteboys, Oakboys, Steelboys, Rightboys, Peep O'Day Boys and Defenders. But he overstated their impact upon popular consciousness. He assumed too direct a relationship between the history of agrarian disturbances and the rebellion. Nevertheless two generations' cumulative experience of organised illegality and violent protest did condition the mass politics of the 1790s.

The styles of protest action which stretched into the 1790s and the first half of the nineteenth century originated with the Whiteboys, in Tipperary in 1761. The name derived from their practice of wearing coarse white linen overshirts, and the movement grew out of local resistance to the enclosure of common land. With the suspension of the restrictive cattle acts in 1758–59 and rising demand in Europe, investment in pasture became more profitable. Landlords re-let to graziers who in turn curtailed traditional access to commons by smaller tenants. The Whiteboys attempted to defend these customary rights by tearing down – or 'levelling' – fences, hedges and walls, by filling in ditches and digging up pasture, and by maiming or 'houghing' cattle. As the movement spread into most of the rest of Munster its programme widened. The primary grievance was the payment of tithes to the established church. The tithe was usually paid in kind – corn or potatoes – and, after 1735, pasture was exempt. These exactions were inflated, moreover, by the machinery of collection: a corps of tithe-proctors and farmers which administered the system on behalf of the clergy, at a price.[7] Such 'middlemen' were a constant Whiteboy target. The Whiteboys also tried to regulate conacre rents, by unilaterally and publicly setting 'fair' rates, and by punishing those tenants who dared pay more.[8] Between 1761 and 1765 Whiteboys were active in counties Waterford – where five of them were hanged in 1762 – Cork, Limerick and Kilkenny. The scale of the outbreak is indicated by the introduction of the Whiteboy act in 1765. The key provision of the act made the administration of oaths by threat of violence a capital offence. This went to the heart of the problem. Oaths binding members to secrecy was the defining characteristic of Whiteboyism.

Although the Whiteboys sometimes turned out in contingents of five hundred or more, some mounted on horseback, others marching in military array, the scale of violence was limited. Even so, the disturbances were labelled an 'insurrection'. Insofar as he was rejecting contemporary allegations – repeated, predictably, by Sir Richard Musgrave forty years later – of French intrigue and popish conspiracy, Lecky correctly depicted the movement as 'unpolitical and unsectarian'.[9] Since the Whiteboys drew their members and support from lower-class catholics, and since most of the bigger landlords and the established church were protestant, allegations of sectarian motives were almost inevitable. These charges, made against the background of the Seven Years War (1756–63), betrayed fears of French invasion. Local protestant paranoia ensured that the agitation of social and economic questions was quickly sucked into the political arena. In Tipperary gentry reaction to the Whiteboy troubles was sharpened by a bitterly contested county election in which the successful candidate, Thomas Matthew, a member of a convert family, had been stigmatised as a representative of the 'catholic interest'. The local detail is crucial because the Dublin government at this time disregarded reports of the Whiteboys as papist insurgents. It is in the area of local or regional politics, for example, that the explanation lies for the trial and execution of the Clogheen parish priest, Nicholas Sheehy. Sheehy had 'probably [been] mixed-up' in the disturbances in Tipperary, but it seems clear that he was the victim of sectarian animus and judicial murder.[10]

Two years after the Munster unrest erupted a brief tumultuous spasm of popular agitation burst out in mid and south Ulster. The Oakboys or Hearts of Oak – a reference to the sprigs of oak which these agrarian rebels wore on their hats – first appeared in 1763 in north Armagh. On this occasion the main grievance was an increase in county cess (or tax) for road-building. As with the Whiteboys, the movement quickly spread. Oakboy incidents were reported in counties Derry, Tyrone, Fermanagh, Monaghan and Cavan. Again the payment of tithes was opposed. The movement differed from other protest movements in the period, however, in the openness of its tactics. Mobilising at the signal of blowing horns, the Hearts of Oak marched with military precision, to the accompaniment of fife and drum.

'Visits' were paid to local gentlemen and episcopalian clerics, who were then compelled to make public pledges to reduce the rate of cess and tithe. Large detachments of troops were sent to the region and after a number of skirmishes, in which all the casualties – fifteen killed and one capital conviction – were on the Oakboy side, the movement collapsed. The next Ulster-based popular movement was the Hearts of Steel or Steelboys. The Steelboy disturbances, which ran from 1769 to 1772, were triggered by the re-letting, at higher rates, of farms on the great south Antrim estate of the marquess of Donegall. Increased rents, some evictions and local taxation – cess – were the principal sources of the disorders, which focussed on Antrim and Down but also infected the adjoining areas of Armagh, Derry and Tyrone. The Steelboys used threatening letters and nocturnal raids to pursue their objectives. The parallels with the Whiteboys are obvious.[11]

In fact, the unrest in Ulster coincided with the re-emergence of the Whiteboys in the south. This second agitation lasted from 1769 to 1776. Tipperary and Kilkenny were once more affected, as were Wexford, Carlow, Queen's county and Kildare. Among the targets now were those catholic clergy who condemned Whiteboy outrages from the pulpit. Pastoral letters and the ultimate ecclesiastical sanction, excommunication, were ignored.[12] Anti-clericalism of a sort was an even more pronounced element in the Rightboy movement of 1785–88.[13] Named after the fictitious 'Captain Right' who set the rate of tithe by public notice, the agitation began in county Cork, then fanned out through the rest of Munster and into south Leinster. The early stages of the Rightboy troubles provide a striking example of how 'agrarian' movements could intersect with politics. John Fitzgibbon referred to 'the independent gentlemen . . . who set them in motion',[14] an allusion to Sir John Conway Colthurst and other 'independent gentry' who had clashed with Lord Shannon and his allies in the established church during the 1783 election. By colluding with the catholic lower classes in Cork these 'gentlemen Rightboys' succeeded in embarrassing Shannon and vented their own hostility to tithes. The gentry resented tithes, reasoning that money in the pockets of the anglican clergy was money out of theirs. As the Rightboy campaign widened and they began to direct their attacks against cess, hearth tax, high rents and so on, gentry involvement faded. Catholic Church fees – for baptisms, marriages, funerals and the twice-yearly dues payable at Easter and Christmas – were rising during the 1780s and were regarded by the Rightboys as yet another unjust exaction. However, the priests escaped comparatively unscathed. While the Rightboy campaign had essentially run its course by 1788, the clandestine structure remained in place, reactivating, for example, in 1791, when tithe-proctors were visited by 'Capt. Right's light dragoons, well mounted and armed'.

Attempts were made to regulate wage rates and houses were raided for arms.[15] As protestants alone were entitled to bear arms, this 'disarming of the protestants' provoked the usual fulminations about catholic plots. Such 'insinuations', as he called them, were rejected by the county high sheriff, (borough) MP, and future United Irishman, Arthur O'Connor. With the national catholic revival under way the local accusations were more politically pointed than ever, and the Catholic Committee in Dublin publicly welcomed O'Connor's intervention.[16]

II THE PECULIARITIES OF THE IRISH

What 'volumes', in Tilly's sense, does the collective violence of the secret societies speak about the nature of eighteenth-century Irish society? What needs to be explained is the pervasiveness and persistence of organised agrarian protest: the secret societies proved remarkably durable. How, in the end, do we account for the contrast between the disturbed condition of, say, Tipperary, and the comparative social tranquility of Northhamptonshire, or for that matter, Midlothian? At least two caveats should be entered immediately. Firstly, as Sean Connolly has suggested, the comparison is perhaps a misleading one. Although historians and commentators have understandably sought parallels and drawn contrasts with Ireland's nearest neighbour, a more legitimate standard of comparison may be offered by contemporary Europe. Viewed in this light it is the exceptional character of English stability, not the distinctive nature of Irish collective violence, which stands out most strongly.[17] Secondly, the extent of English public order should not be exaggerated. The systematic poaching in Windsor forest which led to the Black act in 1723, or the Sussex smugglers' war of the 1740s, remind us that England was not immune from organised or structured social violence.[18] Nor did it escape 'ordinary' crime. According to Lecky, in the early eighteenth century 'the neighbourhood of London swarmed with highwaymen, and many parts of England were constantly infected by bands which hardly differed from the Irish raparees'.[19] Nevertheless, the increasing effectiveness of the modernising English state had largely quelled the banditry of highwaymen and smugglers by about the 1750s. Thereafter, urban and food riots became the characteristic form of public violence.

Ireland had a different experience. The peculiarities of the Irish, which seemed obvious to numerous contemporary commentators, are somewhat cautiously acknowledged by historians. The historian has good reason to be sceptical. The evidence of commentators – foreign travellers, for example –

is impressionistic. Moreover, in Ireland a great deal of evidence of this sort is tainted by the authors' prejudices. Many of these social commentaries were written in the early nineteenth century, not as cool sociological surveys but as moral-reformist tracts. Some, like Robert Bell, pressed their case for social or educational reform by painting lurid sketches of a volatile, unregenerate peasantry. Others, like Edward Wakefield or Thomas Crofton Croker exhibit a kind of exasperated anthropological curiosity. Significantly, their observations were advanced not long after the trauma of the 1798 rebellion. Thus when Wakefield writes of the 'disposition to revolt, which form[s] so conspicuous a feature of the character of the catholics in Ireland',[20] it can be assumed that this judgement was coloured by his own memories of actual rebellion. Finally, these commentators casually resorted to racial and religious stereotypes which are now totally devoid of analytic credibility. Wakefield's description of the Irish as 'a people ardent in their pursuits, accustomed to act without foresight, and to determine without reflection' tells us much more about Wakefield and the tradition – which stretches back through Edmund Spenser to Giraldaus Cambrensis and looks forward to the Victorians[21] – in which he wrote, than it does about the 'Irish', catholic, peasant, or otherwise. Such confident summaries of the 'national character' are about as conceptually valuable as A. T. Q. Stewart's wry suggestion that 'the Irish have been made violent by some noxious element in the potato'.[22]

It would be a mistake, however, to dismiss the evidence of social commentary in its entirety. It is difficult to believe that this voluminous literature and the remarkable unanimity of opinion and perception which it reveals, rested on nothing more solid than the fantasies, prejudices and moralism of hostile witnesses. The zeal and presuppositions of the reformers did undoubtedly distort their accounts, but these men were witnesses, and they did, at some level, describe social realities. In short, the fact that so many observers noted the lawlessness or disaffection of the Irish lower classes provides some grounds for supposing that this was so. As we have seen their perception is partly explained by post-rebellion jitteryness. On the other hand, similar perceptions can be identified *before* the rebellion. In 1796 John Fitzgibbon, earl of Clare, referred to 'the natural disaffection of the Irish', while in the more peaceful 1770s Young was struck by 'a general contempt for law and order'.[23]

The recurrence of words like 'natural', 'rooted' and 'hereditary disaffection' imply the existence of a popular *mentalité* inherent in the structures or history of Irish society. Again, to contemporaries this seemed obvious. In the late 1790s the chief secretary, Thomas Pelham, ascribed popular support for the United Irishmen to 'the religious distinctions which will always make the lower classes of the people more open to seduction than the same class of men in other countries'.[24] Wakefield attributed the rebellious character of Irish catholics to 'the low and degraded state in which they have been kept', or in other words, to the penal laws. Presumably this is what Lecky had in mind too, when he wrote that catholics had been 'educated through long generations of oppression into an inveterate hostility to the law, and were taught to look for redress in illegal violence or secret combination'.[25] Ireland was divided along religious, 'racial', cultural and linguistic lines, and these divisions, entrenched in folk memory and perpetuated by the country's legal, political and institutional structures, effectively prevented the evolution of a more integrated, deferential and stable society.

The contrast with Scotland is illuminating. This was a more homogeneous society in which, in the eighteenth and nineteenth centuries, 'specifically agrarian discontent [was] . . . notable by its absence'. Compared with Ireland, Scotland enjoyed social 'tranquility'. T. M. Devine sees part of the explanation for these contrasting experiences in the different levels of social control. As an 'hereditary elite' the Scottish landed class exercised 'inherited authority'.[26] Ireland's landed class was of more recent vintage, and Ireland, as Cullen points out, was 'above all . . . a colonial society. Settlers were resented more than landowners'.[27] Of course, in the eighteenth century the distinction between 'settlers' and 'landowners' could be next to non-existent. The Scottish landed elite also commanded the 'vertical loyalty' of its tenantry by virtue of their shared protestantism. Religion and history reinforced deference and elite hegemony. In Ireland, religion and history undermined those ideological scaffolds of social control. And if religion – and this might equally be applied the presbyterian Steelboys – *separated* the Irish lower classes from the (predominantly anglican) landed class, it at the same time helped to forge a common sense of identity – a lower-class solidarity which facilitated organised protest.[28]

There were, then, what may in the broadest sense be termed cultural determinants of the oft noted Irish 'disposition' to lawlessness or open disaffection. However, most modern historians, although they are usually prepared to incorporate a cultural dimension in their arguments, analyse the causes of rural disorder primarily by reference to economic change. For example, after summarizing the different cultural bases of social control in Ireland and Scotland, Devine goes on explicitly to discount 'the popular myth of an historic struggle between catholic peasant on the one hand and an alien class on the other' as an adequate explanation for the high incidence of agrarian unrest in Ireland.[29] Ultimately he relates unrest to changes in the rural economy. Similarly, Connolly states that every major outbreak of agrarian protest from 1760 on was 'linked in each case to major shifts in agricultural circumstances, most commonly a deterioration in market conditions'.[30]

The advantage of such approaches over the 'unregenerate peasantry' school of analysis is that economic changes, whether rising prices or enclosures, are more precise and measurable categories than shared 'dispositions'. The problem with such approaches is that although they may often – though not always – explain the *origins* of rural protest, they cannot account for the peculiar *forms* these protest movements then took: the secret societies. Economic change occurs in society. It affects men; men with values, expectations, ideas and aspirations. And it is these shared assumptions and beliefs, variously conceptualized as the 'moral economy', 'popular culture' or collective *'mentalité',* which condition popular responses to economic change.

The pervasiveness and durability of the secret societies reflects and relied upon a popular *mentalité* not unlike that decried by Fitzgibbon or Wakefield. It is axiomatic that the 'social bandit' or insurgent cannot long survive without the active support of some, and the tacit consent of the majority, of the community within which they operate. To lower-class catholics the Whiteboys came from 'us', while tithe-proctors, landlords and magistrates belonged to 'them'. In this respect, it has been observed, the recurrence of the word 'boys' in the names of so many societies was not accidental. The expression 'the boys', which is still used in reference to the IRA, implies a certain tacit approval.[31]

'Us' and 'them' attitudes were embedded in the Irish 'peasant's' notorious disregard for the rule of law. This phenomenon found expression in a number of ways. One striking manifestation of contempt for authority was the 'rogues and rapparees' *genre* of popular literature. The classic text of Irish social banditry, which went through numerous cheap editions during the eighteenth century, is Cosgrove's *A genuine history of the lives and actions of the most notorious Irish highwaymen, Tories and Rapparees.* The social bandit, familiar to several peasant societies, has been depicted as a Robin Hood-style figure, usually of gentlemanly birth, launched onto his outlaw career as the victim of official injustice. These colourful characters may have been robbers, but they were invariably friends to the poor. Criminals in the eyes of the law, they were often folk heroes in public opinion.[32] Cosgrove's case-studies fit this pattern. One of these, Redmond O'Hanlon, was the 'son of a reputable gentleman' who 'frequently [gave] share of what he got from the rich to relieve the poor'. Significantly, he 'had a much greater antipathy to the English than to the Scotch or Irish'.

That is to say he preyed on anglican settlers but left local presbyterians and catholics unmolested. Significantly too, O'Hanlon operated with a band of 'fifty effective men' in south Armagh,[33] an area plagued by Tory activity well into the eighteenth century. The Tories were dispossessed catholics who carried on a guerrilla campaign against the settlers, whose effect in legitimizing popular violence Lecky considered inestimable.[34] It seems likely that books such as Cosgrove's *Genuine history,* hawked around the country by pedlars and used by hedge schoolmasters, complemented a vibrant oral tradition or folk memory, endorsing and celebrating Tory resistance to confiscation. According to Michael Davitt, the Tory heroes, recalled in song and legend, perpetuated a popular belief 'that Cromwell's clan would one day loose again the lordship of the land'.[35] Thus the Irish social bandit tended to be more politicised than his European counterparts. One pamphleteer, writing from the vantage point of the early nineteenth century, thought the effect of 'rapparee literature' pernicious in the extreme, claiming that 'the transition from theory to practice was but short'. However, a modern writer who argues that the *genre* was more a symptom than a cause of lawlessness, is undoubtedly closer to the truth.[36] In either case the popularity of the *genre* suggests the prevalence of attitudes sympathetic to banditti such as the Whiteboys.

Closely related to Tory folklore was the hold which Jacobitism retained on the popular imagination. There were, of course, no Jacobite risings in Ireland in 1715 or 1745, and by the 1750s Jacobitism had vanished as a realistic political option. Nevertheless, the imagery and symbolism of Jacobitism persisted. The first Whiteboys sported white cockades and marched to Jacobite tunes. Remarkably, as late as the 1790s, a renegade Defender claimed that some of his erstwhile comrades were attached to 'the old family of Stuart's'.[37] This claim is unlikely but intriguing. The long survival of a, necessarily covert, popular allegiance to the Jacobite cause, and a Jacobite dimension to the rediscovered Tory 'party' before the 1750s, is now persuasively argued by a number of English historians.[38] Regrettably, as one of these scholars has noted, the history of Irish Jacobitism after 1714 is still 'almost *terra incognita'*.[39] However, one area of this uncharted territory has been partially explored: the politics of the *aisling* (or vision) poetry of deliverance in Gaelic Munster. Cullen insists that the Jacobite aspirations expressed by the *aisling* had little direct political consequence, but concedes that the poetry 'suggests alienation and may even have helped to keep a feeling of alienation alive'.[40] Like Tory folklore, lingering Jacobite sentiment served as a reminder of dispossession.

A current of muted disaffection ran through popular beliefs, although its strength and significance are hard to evaluate because it did not translate into active political discontent. 'The general contempt for law and order' noted by Young, usually manifested itself in other, less dangerous ways, illicit distilling for example. Whereas by 1760 the social bandit had already passed into the realm of popular mythology, those other outlaws, the illegal poteen or whiskey makers, were very much a part of everyday reality. Indeed the golden age of illicit distilling roughly coincides with the Whiteboy era. Whiskey emerged as a commercial product around the mid-eighteenth century and peaked in terms of commercial activity in rural Ireland about 1800.[41] Government policy, designed to regulate the liquor trade, inadvertently encouraged the proliferation of unlicensed stills. From 1779, in an attempt to make the revenue officers' task more manageable, the number of stills were officially limited to those with a capacity of two hundred or more gallons. After 1785 the excise duty on spirits rose steeply. In practice these measures promoted a thriving unlicensed cottage industry.[42] The colourful image of the poteen maker ought not obscure the fact that this was an important and widespread economic enterprise, particularly in the west and in south Ulster. For instance, between 1802 and 1806, 13,439 unlicensed stills were seized.[43] How many continued to function? Illicit distilling was normally carried on in remote and defensible woodlands and glens. 'Ferocious' 'gangs of sixty or eighty men' operated, posting look-outs and employing elaborate early warning systems, using horns and torches to signal the approach of the 'revenue'. During the 1780s detachments of cavalry were 'stationed all over the country for no other purpose than that of still hunting'.[44] The intractability of the unlicensed trade in the face of such official determination to extirpate it provides a spectacular demonstration of how impervious to the writ of law the common people could be. And the retailers of spirits were no more respecters of the law than the manufacturers. Unlicensed taverns seem to have been as numerous as unlicensed stills. Again, evasion of the 'revenue' was not merely condoned by the drinking public, but 'considered . . . most meritorious'.[45]

The distiller's ability to function depended upon a conspiracy of silence in the community he served. The position of the poteen maker as a law-breaker endorsed by the community parallels that of the secret society. In fact the activities of the two sometimes merged. Perhaps the single most violent Defender incident during the 1790s – the murder of eleven policemen near the village of Drumsna, county Leitrim, in April 1795 – was sparked off by a raid on an illegal still. Two years later the seizure of another still, near Ballybay in county Monaghan, precipitated serious clashes in which fifteen local people and six soldiers were reported killed.[46]

Illicit distillers functioned with impunity and the social bandit was celebrated in popular tradition. The collective *mentalité* thus revealed facilitated the operation of secret societies. In 1796, for instance, a newspaper attributed 'various robberies and burglaries' in the countryside to felons, to whom the common people, assuming that they were 'connected with Defenderism . . . readily allowed asylum'.[47] However, while the *mentalité* facilitated organised, illegal protest, it could not cause or activate it. An historically-rooted popular alienation from 'legitimate' authority merely helps account for the resilience of the secret societies. It cannot explain how, or why, they came into being. The best answers to those questions are the answers which, by their actions, the societies gave themselves. These were protest movements, actuated by immediate concrete grievances like tithes, high rents, and the erosion of customary rights. The first Whiteboy movement arose as a response to the enclosure of commons. The Steelboys reacted against *new* high rents, *new* leases and evictions. Significantly, before the Defenders, none of these movements challenged the system of land ownership, or sought to abolish rents or tithes. Rather they agitated for a reduction of those exactions to levels sanctioned by custom as 'fair'. Moreover, the scale of violence against people – as distinct from property – was comparatively modest. According to one count, in thirty years of agrarian unrest only fifty or so people were killed.[48] The Whiteboys sought to regulate the local economy. Whiteboyism was informed by a vision of social justice – Thompson's 'moral economy' – not social revolution. Pre-famine agrarian protest movements were what social scientists call 'reactive'. Their motives were conservative, or backward- looking, their aims limited, their tactics pragmatic.

The conventions, patterns and purposes of direct action were thus clearly defined and adherence to those conventions required effective organisation, underpinned by a popular ideology. The rhetoric of justice, fairness and customary right expressed an alternative legitimacy to the laws of courts and magistrates. In their self-perception, and in the perception of the communities from which they sprang, Whiteboyism enforced a rough popular or 'natural' justice.

Oath-taking – a defining characteristic of the secret societies – had a parallel self-legitimizing function. Oaths were pioneered by the Whiteboys in the 1760s, and this is one reason why they provide a logical starting point (and a generic label) for any discussion of these movements. The first Whiteboy oaths instructed members 'to be true and faithful to each other'. They were also enjoined 'not to drink any liquor whatsoever whilst on duty'.[49] Oaths, when obeyed, gave the perpetrators of 'outrages' security against detection and punishment, and offered the societies a sense of cohesion, solidarity and mystique. By laying down stiff penalties, including transportation and execution, for taking and administering oaths, the various Whiteboy acts and the insurrection act of 1796, acknowledged the centrality of this practice for illegal organisations. It is difficult, however, to assess how effective oaths actually were. William Farrell of Carlow recalled that after they had taken the United Irishmen's oath, 'the people were as merry as crickets, for every man that joined it as soon as he got the signs and passwords, thought there was some magic in it that would make them happy the rest of the day'. The United Irishman, James Hope, was more sceptical, and more succinct. 'Oaths', he observed, will 'never bind rogues'.[50] Certainly, the casual manner in which William Carleton was sworn into the Ribbonmen in 1813 – almost without his realising it was happening! – illustrates how not everyone considered oaths solemnly binding.[51]

If oaths did not always guarantee secrecy or the commitment of the initiate, they did represent an attempt to impose *rules* of conduct upon a society's members. The Whiteboys acted according to self-defined standards. A sense of legitimacy, distinct and opposed to civil authority, is evident also in the use of military terminology: the Steelboys 'Captain Justice' and 'Captain Firebrand', for example. Finally, the fairly strict conventions governing violence suggest conformity to an unwritten code. In fact, as the low levels of personal violence indicates, more reliance was placed on the threat of force – the threatening letter, or public notice, usually given specious authority by the signature of some mythical 'captain' – than force itself.

Collective violence and intimidation were more readily accepted in a pre-democratic age. What were the alternatives? Peaceful forms of protest – appeals to the courts, political pressure or civil disobedience initiated by the lower classes – are all products of later, more sophisticated societies. Although some Defender lodges later operated an economic boycott, intimidation, personal violence or attacks on property were the most common and effective means of redressing grievances. Up to a point the authorities expected, indeed tacitly licenced, food riots and other types of direct action.[52] Up to a point also – the point at which the military had to be called in aid of the civil power – the authorities proved unable to control rural protest. As local, unpaid amateurs, magistrates were as vulnerable as anyone to intimidation, and in every outbreak of unrest after 1760 the magistrates faced accusations of 'supineness'. Nor could the authorities expect protesters to be squeamish in their methods. As Thomas Paine observed, 'it is over the lowest class of mankind that government by terror is intended to operate, and it is on them that it operates to the worst effect. They have sense enough to feel they are the objects aimed at, and they inflict in their turn the examples of terror they have been instructed to practice'.[53]

The Defenders, and after them the Ribbonmen, diverged from Whiteboy patterns. Defenderism was 'proactive' and 'associational', as in the maelstrom of the 1790s it developed revolutionary aspirations. But just as the Defenders shared tactics and organisational forms with the Whiteboys, so they shared many Whiteboy concerns. Politics and sectarianism did not replace traditional socio-economic grievances: they fused with them, the precedence of each varying from place to place. The behaviour of a group of Meath Defenders, 'or as they now call[ed] themselves, regulators,' who in 1796, 'frequent[ed] each fair, market and ale house threatening to knockout the brains of every protestant, and to regulate the price of labour, rent of land and value of provisions,'[54] illustrates how agrarianism and politics could merge. It is that combination of assertive anti-protestantism (and of the crude nationalism or republicanism which often lay behind it) and standard Whiteboy objectives which gave Defender ideology its peculiar adaptability and appeal during the 1790s. It was a revolutionary movement certainly, but it carried within it thirty years experience of agrarian unrest. A Whiteboy leader in the 1760s was known as 'Captain Fearnot'; the Meath Defenders in 1797 were led by a 'Captain Fearnought'.[55] There were even some continuities in personnel. A prominent rebel in south Antrim in 1798 was identified as a former Steelboy captain.[56] The popular movements of the 1790s, the Defenders and the clandestine, militarized United Irishmen, continued the Whiteboy tradition as they were politicising it.

III   THE ORIGINS OF THE DEFENDERS

Before turning to a detailed investigation of the origins of Defenderism it will be illuminating to look briefly at an eighteenth-century secret society of another kind: the free masons. The oaths and catechisms employed by the Defenders were more elaborate and esoteric than those of the Whiteboys and suggest a strong masonic influence. The craft, moreover, served as a model for other political secret societies. Dr William Drennan proposed that the United Irishmen (as they were to become) should have 'much of the secrecy, and somewhat of the ceremonial attached to freemasonry'.[57] While masonry was in one sense secret – members were oath-bound never to divulge anything concerning the craft's ritual or business – it was not clandestine. Nor was it socially exclusive. Lowly servants might be members, and in the 1790s some lodges engaged in 'thumping matches' with United Irishmen, Defenders and Orangemen, a recreation which places them all squarely in the same faction-fighting social milieu.[58] The sheer number of lodges, particularly in Ulster, points to the popular character of masonry in this period. Figures available for 1804 list 104 lodges in county Antrim, 92 in Tyrone and another 151 in Armagh, Derry and Down. In spite of papal bulls excommunicating masons in 1738 and 1751, the official historians of the craft claim that the majority of its members were catholic.[59] It can therefore be assumed that many ordinary people had first-hand experience, or had at least come into contact with, freemasonry, and were aware of its powerful mystique. Public visibility may account for its influence. There were, for example, masonic Volunteer corps, bedecked in masonic regalia, in Tyrone, Louth and Dublin.[60] A Volunteer funeral at Loughall in 1784 – the year, and the place, north Armagh, where the Defenders originated – was attended by 'twenty three bodies of free masons, in regular procession in number 300'.[61] Although specific and direct 'influences' are often impossible to trace, the masonic complexion of Defenderism is undeniable. The passwords and secret hand signals, the biblical language and deliberate mystification of the tests, oaths and catechisms, the use of the terms 'lodge' and 'brother' and, in at least one case, 'Grand Master',[62] all suggest the Defenders' debt to masonry.

According to a contemporary account the first Defender lodges were formed after a brawl near the village of Markethill in Armagh in 1784. These lodges resembled other pre-famine factions which engaged in pre-arranged, ritualised 'challenges' or fights, at fairs and markets. Initially, the political and religious elements in the rivalry were muted. Catholics and protestants mingled in both the Nappach and the Bawn 'fleets', as they were called. However, in the 1780s, the unique social, economic and demographic structure and denominational geography of the county ensured that the contest soon underwent 'a thorough reformation from a drunken war to a religious one'.[63]

In fact, the precise chronology of events leading to the formation of the Defenders and their rivals, the Peep O'Day Boys, is in some doubt. Although the account cited above pinpoints their origins in the quite specific circumstances of 1784, Young mentions Peep O'Day boys in the area in the late 1770s.[64] The Markethill affray, in other words, should not be blown out of proportion. The incident, minor in itself, only triggered such repercussions because it occurred in the already unstable conditions of late-eighteenth-century Armagh.

Armagh was the most densely populated county in Ireland, and the most complex. Each of the three major religions was represented in

roughly equal proportions. Anglicans of English settler stock were concentrated in the north, presbyterians of Scottish origin in the middle
and the indigenous Irish, often Gaelic-speaking, catholics in the south
of the county. As the use of the Irish language demonstrates, time,
intermarriage and acculturation had not obliterated racial distinctions.
Racial differences buttressed differences of religion. Presbyterians were
commonly referred to by the Defenders as 'Scotch'.[65] Linguistic, religious
and racial diversity created, to use Cullen's phrase, 'cultural frontiers',
lines of tension where catholic Irish met protestant settler. Cultural frontiers
criss-crossed Armagh: sectarian animosities could quickly surface. These
animosities were exacerbated by population pressure and, paradoxically,
by the prosperity of the county.

The population explosion which was affecting the whole rural economy
was particulary acute in Armagh. Competition for land became stiffer.
As new leases came on to the market catholics began to outbid their
protestant neighbours. It has been argued that the theory, most clearly
formulated by Hereward Senior, that land competition fuelled sectarian
rivalries, overstates the importance of land in a proto-industrial economy,
(of which Armagh at this time provides a classic example). Nevertheless
there is contemporary evidence to support the view that the granting of long
leases to catholics, made possible by the repeal of some property-related
penal legislation in the 1770s and 1782, aroused protestant resentment. For
example, although the Steelboy troubles were supposedly free of sectarian
rancour, one of their declarations announced that they were all 'Protestants
or Protestant Dissenters', and complained of 'lands given to papists, who
will pay any rent'.[66]

The acquisition of property was one aspect of rising catholic prosperity, participation in the linen trade another. Irish domestic textile
production was most intense within the so-called 'linen triangle' of north
Armagh and west Down. This zone accounted for fifteen million of
an average forty-nine million yards of linen manufactured in Ireland
in the mid-1780s. 'Between 16,000 and 20,000 weavers' worked in
county Armagh alone.[67] Not surprisingly, the Peep O'Day Boys – the
name refers to the tactic of raiding at dawn – were nearly all 'journeymen weavers'.[68] So, presumably, were their neighbours and rivals,
the Defenders. On their earliest excursions to seize arms from local
catholics the Peep O'Day raiders were instructed to 'cut the webs in
the looms' belonging to their victims.[69] Some of the most substantial
linen merchants and manufacturers such as Bernard Coile in Lurgan,
the Lisburn Teelings and the Armagh Coiglys, were catholic. All were
targets for Orange mobs or official persecution after 1795. Catholic

wealth and property was easily construed as a threat to Protestant Ascendancy.

The Armagh troubles, comprising about 100 separate incidents between 1784 and 1791, have been attributed to a break-down of social control. According to Professor Miller the linen boom and the consequent changes in Armagh's economy produced a stratum of young, independent wage earners. As the financial importance of land relative to income accruing from weaving, spinning and bleaching, declined, generational and social discipline based on land and its inheritance collapsed. Miller presents an intriguing, closely-argued and well-documented thesis. Certainly the rapid economic changes are not in doubt. At the Lurgan linen market 'nothing but ready money was taken', and Armagh at the time was described as a 'hotbed of cash'.[70] As an explanation, however, it is insufficient. The emphasis is misplaced. The main motor of the disturbances was political.

Some penal legislation had been repealed in 1771, 1778 and 1782, and by the early 1780s sections of the Volunteer-reform movement had placed the catholic question on the political agenda. It was a fiercely divisive issue. The Volunteer commander-in-chief, leading whig and Armagh grandee, Lord Charlemont, himself opposed concessions to the catholics. Some of the more politically advanced Volunteer corps nonetheless actually recruited catholics and – in contravention of the penal laws – armed them. Another reported source of firearms, which seem in any event to have been readily available, was Lord Gosford. Gosford, 'tired of having his orchards robbed, placed armed men to guard them. These happened to be catholics. This was immediately laid hold of'.[71] By seizing catholic-owned firearms the Peep O'Day Boys unilaterally enforced the penal laws. Arms raids re-asserted Protestant Ascendancy. From the outset of the disturbances, right up to the mass expulsions of catholics in 1795–6, the magistrates were accused not merely of 'supineness', but of complicity with the Peep O'Day Boys and Orangemen. If the Peep O'Day Boys are seen as a political phenomenon rather than a law and order problem, then the reason for the partiality of the wholly protestant magistracy becomes clear. The leniency of the county assizes towards alleged Peep O'Day offenders strengthened local suspicions of official bias and signalled to catholics that little protection could be expected from the civil authorities. The name Defender (the first lodge was founded at Bunkerhill near Armagh City) signifies the self-protecting vigilante role which the movement initially saw itself as fulfilling.[72] The formation of secret societies was also virtually a reflex action. Some of the captains of the fleets had been veterans of the Oakboy and Steelboy episodes.[73]

A minor sectarian vendetta, punctuated by a few more serious clashes, continued for the rest of the decade. A marked escalation occurred in 1787, when two troops of dragoons had to be stationed in Armagh City. On 1 May, 1788, the Defenders publicly paraded from Blackwaterstown to Moy, and the rumour spread of an intended attack upon the barracks at Charlemont. Their new assertiveness received an instant reply with the establishment of new, aggressively protestant, Volunteer corps at Benburb, county Tyrone, Tandragee and Armagh. On 21 November the Benburb company, accused by local catholics of being nothing more than a 'pack of Peep O'Day Boys', was attacked by Defenders. Two of the attackers were killed. As a sequel the funerals of the two dead men were 'attended by immense multitudes of catholics from many miles around' and a week later a large, heavily armed force of Defenders attempted to 'apprehend and take' two Benburb Volunteers at the bleach green where they worked.[74]

The tensions which these incidents vented were sharpened by a mutual economic boycott and by rumours of planned massacres. A contemporary pamphleteer accused a 'set of vipers', including a 'divine', of 'poisoning the minds of the unwary peasants with the dregs of the forty-one rebellion'.[75] In Ireland the fear of massacres was activated by political crises and during the 1790s catholic belief in the existence of an Orange 'extermination oath', played a considerable part in the genesis of the rebellion. These fears were prefigured in Armagh in the 1780s when local communities posted precautionary sentinels after dark.

By 1789 the focus of unrest had shifted to the south of the county and beyond, into south Down, north Louth and Monaghan. Already the new lodges were numbered, suggesting that Defenderism had at this stage a federal structure, if not yet a centralised, regional leadership.[76] South Armagh's environment was particularly suitable for Defender-style organisations. Almost bereft of a resident gentry to police it, its terrain rocky and barren, the bandit could move with ease through the countryside and among the overwhelmingly catholic, Gaelic-speaking population. Citing the standard index for lawlessness, more than one observer called attention to the widespread 'private distilling and selling of whiskey' in the area.[77] It is against this background that one of the most horrific episodes in the whole ugly catalogue of sectarian strife – the murder of a protestant schoolmaster at Forkhill in January, 1791 – should be understood.

At the beginning of 1787 a Forkhill landowner, Richard Jackson, died, leaving 3,000 acres to be 'colonised by protestants'. Some catholic 'squatters' were subsequently evicted from waste land on the estate. The will also provided for the free education of local children, and four schoolmasters were appointed. This improvement scheme was administered by Lord Charlemont's correspondent, the Rev. Edward Hudson. But one man's improvement is another man's intrusion, and at one point Hudson's horse was shot from under him. It was Hudson too, who reported that the Defenders controlled 'a great expanse of country to the south and east of Forkhill . . . [and] could assemble almost in an instant on signals given by whistle'.[78] This well-drilled group was spurred to action by the appointment of a protestant schoolmaster, Alexander Barclay, in place of a teacher prepared to give catholic instruction in the Irish language. They were also provoked by the alleged involvement of Barclay's brother-in-law in an attack upon Forkhill's parish priest at the end of 1790.[79] A month later a group of fifty or sixty Defenders struck. Barclay's tongue was torn out and his fingers cut off. His wife and brother-in-law were mutilated. Their grisly work complete, the assailants held a torch-lit procession through the district. It was afterwards claimed that Barclay had been killed to prevent him appearing as a witness against some Defenders.[80] This episode had a profound impact on protestant opinion and inflamed the bitter opposition to catholic relief which followed.[81]

By the close of 1791 the Defenders were still a localized movement centred in Armagh and the adjoining areas of Down, Louth and Monaghan. After the Forkhill murders sectarian feuding had continued much as before. Two Defenders were killed during a riot at the Forkhill fair in August and in November protestants came under attack at a fair in Monaghan.[82] Viewed from Dublin Castle, the Defender troubles at this point probably looked like a sectarian variant of the by now familiar Whiteboy-style disturbances. They presented, it seemed, merely a law and order problem of manageable proportions. By the beginning of 1793, however, the scale of violence had escalated dramatically. Defenders were active in Meath and Cavan and were viewed by many protestants as an instrument of the Catholic Committee. Lord Hillsborough called the committee and the Defenders, 'Dublin papists and country papists'.[83] His suspicions were shared by the government. 'As yet we are not at the bottom of the plot,' wrote Under-Secretary Cooke, in February, 1793, 'which certainly is connected with the levelling factions of all parties and formed part of the plan which would have taken place if the catholics had not been gratified'.[84] How, during the course of 1792, had the Defenders broken out of their parochial confines and become entangled in national politics?

Conspiracy theories, such as that advanced by Cooke, proved seductive because they offered simple explanations for discontent, attributing it to identifiable human agents. It is always tempting to dismiss such theories as paranoid and simplistic. Nevertheless historians would be negligent if, in their pursuit of more complex and convincing 'underlying causes', they automatically ruled out the possibility of actual conspirators. It is unlikely that the Defenders were being manipulated by some sinister coterie of Dublin merchants, but the contacts, the collusion, between the Defenders and the Catholic Committee remains intriguing. Equally important was the indirect effect upon Defenderism of the massive mobilisation and proselytising of the lower classes conducted by the committee. As the lord lieutenant, Westmorland, informed his superiors in London, 'the precise points which are selected [by the Catholic Committee] as the great objects . . . are particularly calculated to strike the popular mind'.[85] Simultaneously, as Plowden suggests, when the Paineite 'democratic rage' began to grip Ireland in the last months of 1791, the 'several seditious and inflammatory papers published in Dublin, and dispersed through the country seemed to have countenanced and encouraged the Defenders in their proceedings'.[86]

Such extraneous influences had an impact, but Defenderism also had a logic and momentum of its own. Most likely some principle of contagion operated: one parish being infected by, or copying the next. Moreover, the spread of Defenderism exhibited a definite pattern, a pattern which corresponded with the sectarian geography of the region. For over 100 years small numbers of Ulster presbyterians had been moving into north Leinster and north Connaught. In the 1740s the process began to accelerate as these generally more skilled people followed the linen industry which was expanding in the same direction. This was a potentially explosive process because, in a colonial society, 'settlers were resented more than landowners'. Cullen's insight appears to be borne out by the distribution of Defender flashpoints. In Louth 'a strong pocket of protestant settlement had been created around Dundalk', while Collon (the Speaker, John Foster's seat) was 'perhaps the most protestant parish in the county'. In north Meath and 'the adjacent parts of Cavan, there reside[d] numerous tribes of presbyterians, called by the common people Scotch', the object of 'hereditary animosity'.[87] The grim logic of this cycle of ever-widening inter-communal conflict was given added impetus by the popular excitement generated by the catholic agitation. Rising expectations and the extravagant benefits anticipated in the wake of emancipation fuelled a premature catholic triumphalism. Local sectarian quarrels were infused with an almost millenarian zest. 'Spirits were high in expectation of the change. Treasonable songs, scurrilously abusive of the protestant religion were publicly sung by drinkers in tipling houses and ballad-singers in the streets. A ferment prevailed which seemed to announce an approaching insurrection . . . '[88] There was no insurrection in 1792, but the rumours of impending civil war did stimulate and condition the new 'political' Defenderism.

3 'Rumours of War': the Catholic Agitation, 1791–3

Between 1783, when it was raised by certain Volunteer reformers, and 1829, when emancipation was finally won, the catholic question remained the central issue in Irish politics. The 'question' concerned the admission of catholics to, or put the other way, the continued exclusion of catholics from, the political nation. The political nation, the 'Protestant Ascendancy' as it was defined in response to the catholic agitation in 1792, rested on legal exclusivity. The repeal of those penal laws which related to political, as distinct from civil or property, rights, would therefore, many believed, endanger the state itself. The catholic question thus raised issues of first principle and of the first importance. It is not surprising that when the question was re-opened in the summer of 1791 (and again at the start of 1795) it produced a sharp reaction from the ascendancy. This conflict is the theme which runs through the whole political history of the 1790s. Catholic agitation provoked a crisis in Anglo-Irish relations in 1791–3. 1792 witnessed rumours of civil war. Catholic politics proved the undoing of a lord lieutenant, Fitzwilliam, in 1795. Nor is it too much of an exaggeration to describe the unrelenting violence and the expanding clandestine organisation which followed Fitzwilliam's recall and led to rebellion as a continuation of the catholic question by other means. Any account of Irish politics in the 1790s, popular or otherwise, must come to terms with the politics of catholic emancipation. And in the history of the 1790s, indeed in the history of the struggle for emancipation generally, 1792 stands out as the critical year.

The crucial innovations of the Catholic Committee's campaigns of 1791–3 were the alliance with the radical dissenters and the mobilisation of a mass movement. Catholic strategy relied, at several decisive stages, on popular participation and support, and much of the committee's propaganda was directed to that end. Public opinion now embraced the lower classes. None – except, perhaps, women – were considered too humble to add their signatures or marks to petitions or to cast their vote for delegates to convention. These campaigns represent the key moment in the process of popular politicisation. It is no coincidence that this was the moment too, when Defenderism began to catch the attention of newspapers and of politicians. In 1792, remarked Thomas Addis Emmet, Defenderism began 'to spread through other parts of the kingdom, and not a little to connect itself with more general politics'.[1] The high politics of the catholic question, the manoeuvrings between London and Dublin Castle, the role of Edmund Burke and the heated parliamentary debates, have been recounted elsewhere in great detail.[2] What follows does not neglect high politics. It does, however, consider the catholic campaigns as a popular movement, and examines the role which these political agitations had in stimulating the growth and shaping the character of Defenderism.

I   CATHOLIC REVIVAL

The origins of the Catholic Committee can be traced to the Catholic Association, founded in 1757 by Charles O'Connor, Dr John Curry and Thomas Wyse. Although organised pressure 'out-of-doors' played little or no part, penal legislation relating to religious toleration and to property rights was relaxed during the 1770s and in 1782. The position of the catholics first became a major political issue in the context of the Volunteer-reform movement of 1783–4. It was the reformers, such as the bishop of Derry, the presbyterian minister, William Steele Dickson, the Dublin barrister, Peter Burrowes, and William Todd Jones, MP for the borough of Lisburn, who took the initiative. But their overtures to the catholics were not endorsed by the movement as a whole. Prominent reformers like Lord Charlemont and Henry Flood were opposed to granting the franchise or the right to bear arms to catholics.[3] It is important to remember that to eighteenth-century radicals, particularly those, such as the Anglo-Irish, in the British tradition, catholicism, or 'popery', was associated with poverty – 'wooden shoes' – idolatry and despotism. A founder member of the United Irishmen, Dr Drennan, wrote in 1784 that 'the catholics at this day are absolutely incapable of enjoying political liberty, or what is the same thing, political power . . . it must require the process of time to meliorate their hearts into a capability of enjoying the blessing of freedom'.[4] Conversely, in the same year Burrowes asserted, in true enlightened idiom, that 'Popery is decaying and likely to decay all over Europe'.[5] In other words – and this was an argument later used to great effect by Wolfe Tone – the old equation between catholicism and tyranny was now outmoded. These differences of opinion, represented by Burrowes and Drennan, were echoed by English reformers at the time.[6] In the short term the catholic question proved so divisive, even among the most radical Volunteers, that it had to be shelved.

That experience of abandonment provided a sharp lesson in *Realpolitik* for two catholic reformers of the 1780s, Richard McCormick and John Keogh.[7] The public intervention by McCormick and Keogh – the latter wrote a pamphlet, *Thoughts on borough representation* – in the politics of reform was emblematic of a wider intervention. A catholic, Matthew Cary, edited the *Volunteer Journal*, and catholics, although strictly forbidden by the letter of the law to bear arms, enrolled in Volunteer companies as early as 1780. The expense of purchasing a uniform must have excluded the poorer catholics, but the size of this citizens militia – 80,000 by 1781 – indicates popular participation. Moreover, there is no reason to suppose that the practice of arming lower-class catholics, which sparked off the troubles in Armagh, was restricted to that county. Indeed government intelligence in 1784 detected a substantial catholic presence in Volunteer companies throughout the country.[8] In the spring of 1784 the politically advanced section of the Dublin Volunteers, led by James Napper Tandy, admitted catholics, 'low mechanicals', to their ranks, thereby confirming Grattan's distinction between the socially respectable 'old' and the beggarly 'new' Volunteers.[9] In September a requisition to the sheriffs to summon a city meeting to appoint delegates to a national reform convention had twenty-six catholic signatures out of a total of sixty-one.[10] Composed mainly of small tradesmen and shopkeepers, this Dublin-based group represented in embryo a fairly typical cross-section of the activists of the 1790s. Leadership, also Dublin-based, was provided by McCormick, a big employer in the textile industry, Keogh, a wealthy silk merchant, and other successful businessmen such as Edward Byrne, Randal McDonnell and Thomas Braughall. By 1784, then, middle-class, 'middling' and even lower-class catholics were playing a role in national political life unimaginable earlier in the century. And that, presumably, was another lesson learned by McCormick and Keogh.

For the time being, however, the Catholic Committee was still dominated by the aristocratic-hierarchy faction of lords Kenmare, Fingall and Gormanston and Archbishop Troy, supreme practitioners of the traditional, and ineffectual, strategy of supplication. The catholic question revived in 1790. There seem to have been two reasons for this: the new political climate created by the French revolution and the rumours and intimations of the British government's favourable disposition towards the English catholics. On 26 January the committee deemed it a 'proper time for exertion on behalf of the Roman Catholics of Ireland towards the attainment of a repeal of the penal laws'.[11] The administration did not concur. Not a single MP could be persuaded to present the subsequent catholic petition to parliament. Later that year at Cork, the lord lieutenant, Westmorland, refused to accept an address unless the last section, requesting a relaxation of penal legislation, was expunged.[12] Meanwhile the Catholic Committee had initiated new delegate elections, extensively broadening its base and enhancing its representative character.[13] The balance of power within the committee shifted, away from the aristocratic-ecclesiastical old guard towards the more assertive and 'democratic' merchant and professional catholics. The new committee members included Edward Lewins, Richard Dillon, Dominic Rice and Dr W. J. MacNevin, all, later, active United Irishmen.[14] In February 1791 the Committee determined to make another application, 'for a redress of grievances', but Kenmare and Fingall, no doubt at the Castle's behest, refused to co-operate.[15] Already then, by the spring of 1791, there were clear signs of internal class-based tensions. The application was eventually suspended pending the passage of the English relief bill. The Mitford act, which became law that summer, further encouraged the catholics. It was available in cheap pamphlet form in Dublin by 11 July, the same day on which Westmorland wrote that the act would 'produce much mischief', and urged Pitt to consider its repercussions in Ireland.[16] The campaign began to stir. Soundings were taken of the whig opposition, and on 16 July a delegation from the committee met the chief secretary, Major Hobart, to inform him that the committee intended to petition parliament. Most significantly, a catholic-dissenter alliance appeared to be in the making.[17]

The mere prospect or threat of catholic-dissenter political co-operation was enough to jolt the British government into action. London favoured concessions not least as the best way of 'effectually counteracting the union between the catholics and dissenters'. 'I may be a false prophet,' declared Lord Grenville, 'but there is no evil that I should not prophecy if that union takes place.'[18] The authorities' extreme wariness of 'the dissenters', by which they usually meant radical, Belfast-centred presbyterians, rested on a perception of them as disaffected and prone to 'levelling', republican doctrines. 'The town of Belfast', a Castle official informed Whitehall in 1784, 'has ever been infected with disloyalty and is so still.' To Sir Boyle Roche the northern presbyterians were 'a turbulent, disorderly set of people, whom no king can govern, or no God please'.[19] The presbyterians in turn felt alienated from the Dublin anglican establishment. A correspondent of the United Irish *Northern Star* compared the catholic's position to that of the dissenters during the reign of Anne, a reference to the test act (1704–1780), which excluded them from public office. He then urged his co-religionists to support the catholic cause. 'Neither let presbyterians be afraid or

ashamed to speak, having suffered themselves, severely suffered for many
years, under the galling restraints of a proud Ascendancy.'[20] That sense of
alienation, combined with their concentration in Ulster, made the dissenters
a potentially formidable and disruptive political force. The pro-colonist
sympathies which they had displayed during the American war and their
role in the Volunteer movement, which had been strongest in north-east
Ulster and Dublin, helps explain government alarm at the possibility of
a catholic-presbyterian alliance. From the presbyterian radicals' point of
view, an alliance with the catholics, aside from considerations of natural
justice, offered the best means of revitalising and broadening the campaign
for parliamentary reform. Their strategy was simple: to link the two issues.
'We will support you', they were telling the catholics, 'if you will support
us.' Westmorland reported contacts as early as March 1791,[21] but the
relationship, which was never smooth, had to be carefully cultivated.

The first public attempt to integrate the catholic and reform issues came
at the Belfast Volunteer Bastille Day celebrations on 14 July. Three
resolutions, composed by a young Dublin barrister, Theobald Wolfe
Tone, were put forward. The first identified English influence as the
great national grievance. The second proposed a reform of representation
in parliament as a counterbalance. The third argued that no reform would
be 'just or efficacious' which did not include the catholics. However,
even the heartland of the radical reform movement was not yet ready to
embrace the catholic cause. The third resolution was defeated.[22] Tone's
famous pamphlet, *An argument on behalf of the Catholics of Ireland*, was
written to break the resulting deadlock. Aimed, essentially, at a northern,
dissenter audience, a very large edition was printed in Belfast and widely
distributed throughout Ulster.[23] In the event the July meeting proved to be
only a temporary setback. In August Belfast Volunteer corps exchanged
addresses with catholics at Elphin and Leitrim, although the tentative
quality of these exchanges underscored the fragility of the developing
relationship. As Drennan warned the Belfast men:

> At present the catholics are cautious. They think you are squibbing on
> in the paper without any serious intent of doing them service; they think
> you are a divided body like themselves, and it is only the minority that
> talk it well . . . they meet as they are met. A few companies hold out
> terms of amity and a few meetings of their own return them thanks for
> doing so. All this is on a par.[24]

The mistakes of 1784 would not be repeated. Keogh advised Charles
O'Connor, one of the organisers of the catholic addresses, and grandson

of the founder of the original Catholic Association, to 'Go on; but call on them to show that they extend their liberal principles thro' the north as you extend yours thro' Connaught. At the same time, keep clear of deciding about reform or other political questions, they must feel that you can answer only *all Ulster* on such subjects.'[25] The catholics and reformers were playing politics with each other. Although some radicals, Tone and Thomas Russell for example, exhibited a genuine commitment to catholic emancipation, and some catholics to reform, a strong element of *Realpolitik* operated on both sides.[26] Drennan's interpretation of catholic strategy sounds convincing. 'The truth was and is', he wrote, that:

> the catholics wish to have two strings to their bow – *a part* to treat with government, *a part* to ally with us – and if one string cracks, why, try the other. This is good, and *perhaps* fair archery. None pledge, but those who come among us, and it is easy for the body at any time to disclaim them, if government is gained, and to back them if government holds out; but at any rate to use them as a bugbear to the minister who is alarmed, not surely at what is, but what may be.[27]

The alliance may have been uneasy at times, but from the catholic standpoint it was clearly effective.

Undoubtedly, conservative catholics like Archbishop Troy or Lord Kenmare viewed contacts with the dissenters with as much alarm as the Castle. But the pace was now being set by the Dublin middle-class leadership and by a group of small landed families from north Connaught. In October, the Dublin faction, Dr Theobald McKenna, Braughall and others, established a club, the Catholic Society, distinct from the Catholic Committee, and free from its constraints. Westmorland thought it consisted of 'fifty or sixty of the most violent agitators'. To Drennan it represented a cabal designed to counteract 'aristocratic influence' within the committee.[28] On 21 October the new society issued a declaration, written by McKenna, calling for the abolition of the *entire* penal code. The language and arguments of this declaration, which advocated 'a spirit of harmony, and sentiments of affection' between Irishmen,[29] bear a striking resemblance to the first public pronouncements of the Society of United Irishmen, which was founded in Belfast the same month. A Dublin Society was then established in November. The primary objective of the United Irishmen was parliamentary reform, and they drew much of their inspiration from the French revolution, but the society was also a response to the political ferment and possibilities opened up by the catholic question. Two of the founder members, Tone and Russell, were warm partisans of the catholics. The former, of course, had written the *Argument*, the latter corresponded with Charles O'Connor.[30] The name of the new radical club, United Irishmen, was carefully chosen to symbolise the strategy of uniting catholic, protestant and dissenter, which it would pursue. The role played by the United Irishmen in the catholic agitation – as 'bugbear' to government, as campaigning partner of the committee and as a militant pressure-group within it – was crucial. The formation of these radical and catholic clubs in Dublin and Belfast, together with the broad sweep of McKenna's declaration were the opening shots of the most formidable challenge to 'Protestant Ascendancy' yet mounted.

The ascendancy was determined to resist catholic demands, but the ultimate decision rested with the British government. To lobby its case in England the committee appointed a London agent, Richard Burke. On the face of it, he was a shrewd choice. As the eloquent critic of the French revolution, his father Edmund's prestige was at its peak. The Burke name virtually guaranteed ready access to the upper echelons of government and distanced his catholic clients from the 'levellers' at a stroke. Edmund Burke, moreover, was sympathetic to the plight of his catholic fellow-countrymen and hostile to the ruling 'junto'. It seems likely, although hard evidence is lacking, that he used his considerable influence and extensive political connections in London on behalf of the Irish catholics. Early in 1792 he publicly intervened in the debate with his *Letter to Sir Hercules Langrishe,* and was apparently in contact with Keogh via the chaplain of the Spanish embassy, the Rev. Thomas Hussy. Keogh himself was in London for three months at the end of 1791.[31]

Richard Burke's disastrous performance as agent – perhaps the only point upon which the Catholic Committee, Dublin Castle and the British government agreed – has obscured his real achievement *before* he came to Ireland. Between October and December, 1791, he met with Grenville, William Pitt and Henry Dundas to press the catholic case.[32] As home secretary with responsibility for Ireland, Dundas instructed the Dublin administration to sponsor a relief bill in parliament. 'Liberal' on most matters Irish, when lord advocate of Scotland (1775–1783), Dundas had resisted political pressure to support a bill copperfastening catholic disabilities.[33] He possessed a clear-headed view of the ascendancy mentality. 'I am aware,' he informed Westmorland, 'how difficult it is to persuade persons in the exclusive possession of power to admit to a participation of privileges a description of men whom they have been accustomed to look upon as justly excluded from that participation'.[34] For the British government, however, – and there is no reason to doubt Dundas's assertion that 'from the beginning of this business [Pitt] and I have never had a shade of difference in our opinion'[35] – the admission of catholics to a 'participation of privileges' represented a way of disengaging them from the embrace of the radicals and of securing their loyalty. London was more concerned with resolving a political problem (a concern which assumed greater urgency as the prospect of war with France loomed) than with defending the protestant monopoly of power.

Nothing demonstrates more clearly what Malcomson has called the 'lovelessness' of the Anglo-Irish relationship than the manner in which the British browbeat the Irish protestant 'friends of government' and the English civil servants in Ireland into conceding some of the catholics' demands. Dundas warned the lord lieutenant not to encourage the 'protestant interest' to rely upon 'the support and protection of Great Britain', because:

> it is necessary that the publick and parliament of Great Britain should feel that the object for which their aid is demanded is one in which they are interested . . . If it is a mere question if one description of Irishmen or another are to enjoy a monopoly of pre-eminence, I am afraid that it is not a question on which they would feel either their passions or their interests so naturally concerned, as to justify the application of the resources and force of Great Britain in the decision of it.[36]

The implications of this letter were devastating. By categorising protestants as 'one description of Irishmen', Dundas signalled that in London's opinion this was a question of politics, not, as Dublin would have it, of first principles. Secondly, by raising the issue of 'force' he alluded, as early as December, 1791, to the possibility of armed conflict. The British ministry's position was pragmatic, reasoned and clearly articulated. In the end they did not need Richard Burke to persuade them. More important than the substance of Burke's contacts with the ministry were the rumours which these fuelled in Ireland. Reports circulated through the protestant community that he had received assurances of the British government's 'favourable disposition' towards the catholics, occasioning such alarm that Westmorland – unsuccessfully – requested a public denial.[37]

As protestant confidence was shaken by Britain's hard-headed approach, it was assailed simultaneously by the combativeness of the newly militant catholics. Protestant opinion was particularly offended by the tone of McKenna's widely distributed declaration.[38] Hobart directly asked the Catholic Committee to disown the document, while Westmorland used his influence with the 'moderates', specifically Archbishop Troy, to obtain a public rejection.[39] Disingenuously, the committee argued that as the

Catholic Society was a separate body the committee could not be held
responsible for its pronouncements. Lord Kenmare then distanced himself
from the strident style adopted by the 'democrats', by issuing a traditional
loyalist address on behalf of the catholics of Kerry.[40]

The tensions between the aristocratic and democratic factions culminated
at a meeting on 17 December, 1791. The aristocrats seceded from the
committee.[41] The split was extremely bitter. According to one account –
which does not, it should be noted, tally with the minutes of the meeting
– Randal McDonnell entered the room, 'walked up to the chairman, told
him he was an old woman, unfit to sit there, and desired him to leave the
chair and make room for one more fit to occupy it. He then seized his
lordship by the arm to thrust him out. Lord Fingall did not resist; he rose
and immediately withdrew, followed by all his party. Thomas Braughall
was then placed in the chair, and put all the resolutions they desired.'[42]

The aristocratic secession had immediate political reverberations across
the country. Indeed the conflict between the Kenmarites and the Dublin
middle-class leadership provided the occasion for the first full-scale mobilisation of catholic public opinion. The factionalism and manoeuvering
which the dispute generated at provincial level drew an ever-widening
circle of people into the political arena. It would have been difficult
for any catholic in the winter of 1791–2 not to have taken sides in the
debate. During late December and early January a flurry of meetings
produced resolutions in favour either of Kenmare or, much more often,
the Dublin leadership. Significantly, the most vociferous support for the
Dubliners came from Connaught. John Keogh had acquired extentive
property and had numerous tenants in Sligo, Leitrim and particularly
Roscommon, and at least seventeen people from this region, including
the prominent catholic activists, Joseph Plunkett and J. J. McDonnell,
were members of the Dublin Society of United Irishmen.[43] Myles Keon
and Charles O'Connor, one of the first Connaught United Irishmen, had
already been engaged in mobilising public opinion in the province. In
November they had travelled through each county procuring addresses 'to
the Belfast people and . . . propagat[ing] the national spirit'.[44] In January
meetings at Drumsna, Carrick-on-Shannon, Jamestown and Ballinamore
issued resolutions endorsing the committee in Dublin as the 'only organ'
entitled to represent them. Effigies of Kenmare were burnt in 'almost every
market town in Roscommon and Leitrim'. Pro-Dublin resolutions came
from Drogheda and Limerick.[45] In Dublin itself Kenmare was censured
at a series of parochial meetings and, as 'Lord Lickspittle, the Kerry
traitor', burned in effigy.[46] An attempt to shut the doors of a parish
chapel to one meeting was abandoned when it was pointed out that 'a

sledge would remove that difficulty'. Keogh then proceeded to publicly castigate Archbishop Troy.[47]

The Kenmarites were no less busy. Three addresses supporting Kenmare, and signed by, among others, the bishop of Kildare and Leighlin, were organised at Carlow (a county in which Kenmare owned land).[48] Others were drawn up at Kilkenny and Wexford. In Wexford the bishop presented the Kenmare address to a 200-strong congregation and proposed that it be adopted verbatim. But he was challenged by the local committee activists, Edward Hay and James Devereux, and in the end only eleven signatures were secured.[49] The small number of signatures collected by the Kenmarites generally, sixty-three in Kilkenny, forty-two in Carlow, illustrates the weakness of the faction.

The campaign against Kenmare was brief, intense and victorious. It consolidated the position of the Dublin leadership and had a major politicising impact upon its constituency – the common people. Firstly, the middle-class led frontal assault upon the aristocratic political camp dispensed with traditional codes of deferential conduct. The lesson was clear: the authority of the nobleman or bishop was neither sacroscant nor immutable. And secondly, as T. A. Emmet recalled, 'in the course of the meetings, where these counter-resolutions were passed, the condition of the catholics was the subject of universal discussion; and thus the sense of their rights, and indignation at their wrongs, were exceedingly increased'.[50] In effect the Kenmare episode opened the first chapter in the story of popular politicisation in the 1790s.

At the British government's behest a bill for the further relief of catholics, proposed by Sir Hercules Langrishe and seconded by Major Hobart, was introduced to parliament on 25 January, 1792. Hobart and Sir John Parnell had managed to persuade Pitt and Dundas to withhold the rights to vote and to bear arms.[51] The main provisions of the intended legislation admitted catholics to Trinity College and to the bar. But the temper of the ensuing parliamentary debates, the violence of the language, and the extreme positions adopted by the protestant 'ultras', actually sustained the high levels of political excitement already aroused by the Kenmare controversy. Even before the debate had commenced the explosive potential of the issue was evident from the press. The pro-catholic *Morning Post* alleged that 'a certain belligerent sec.' had advocated 'gunpowder and the bayonet [as] the only specific remedies' to catholic agitation, while the administration-controlled *Faulkners Dublin Journal* wrote of 'protestants of spirit . . . cleaning their firelocks'.[52] The chancellor, Fitzgibbon, predicted that civil war would inevitably result if the catholics attained power.[53] Language of this sort – language largely ignored by historians – became commonplace as the year progressed.

Considering the concessions on offer at this point, the ferocity of the protestant reaction might at first sight appear hysterical. In fact the arguments advanced by ultras such as George Ogle, Sir Boyle Roche and Dr Patrick Duigenan, reflected majority sentiment in the house. The catholic bills of 1792 and 1793 were only carried because the British government, through the medium of patronage dispensed by its Irish 'cabinet', controlled parliament. Most of the 300 MPs voted against their wishes, better judgement and, they believed, their own best interests. However clouded by pseudo-theology or apocalyptic rhetoric, the ultra's argument also possessed sound logic. Ogle in particular had a gift for slicing through the verbiage to the fundamental issues. 'Let the real or affected liberality of gentlemen disguise the matter as they please,' he declared during the 1793 debates, 'let them turn it and twist it into what forms or what shapes their ingenuity can invent . . . it is a question of power.'[54] Protestant opposition was uncompromising because of what might be called the 'thin end of the wedge' theory: the belief, characteristic of conservatives, that concessions, however small, would lead inexorably to more and yet more, culminating in a transfer of political power and the undoing of the act of settlement. 'The steadiest friends of the British government,' Westmorland wrote, are 'apprehensive that such trifling indulgences will give the catholics the strength to press for admission to the state and in that foreseeing the ruin of political power for the protestants and (trifling as you [i.e. Dundas] may consider the danger), a total change of the property of the country.' Ogle was more concise. 'Nor can I think it within the power of human wisdom,' he said, 'to do anything for the Roman Catholics without endangering [the] Ascendancy in Church and State.'[55]

Protestant fears were real. Langhrise's bill eventually became law, but the debates preceding it did little to encourage reconciliation. James Cuffe, for instance, urged the king's ministers to 'tell all men of all religions "we have power enough to protect our establishment in Church and State. We will protect them on the principles of the Revolution, and we will punish those who seek to disturb the peace and tranquility of this growing country."'[56] A petition for catholic relief presented to parliament on behalf of the citizens of Belfast was curtly rejected.[57] So too was the petition which Richard Burke had foolishly attempted to introduce by walking on to the floor of the house. A third petition, presented on 18 February by John Egan, MP, was turned down by 208 votes to 26. Though the outcome of the debates was never in doubt, the ugly demeanour of the house stripped the concessions of the conciliatory effects which the British government had intended. The stormy passage of the legislation actually raised the political temperature. Most offensive to the Catholic Committee were the aspersions cast upon its representative character. As the main Castle paper put it 'they are a small *popish faction* in Dublin, who by fraud and cabal, have attempted to give themselves an importance to which they have no claim'.[58]

That accusation had far-reaching consequences. The committee resolved to press on for the franchise and to rebut the jibe of unrepresentativeness. Miles Keon of Connaught suggested the nationwide election of delegates leading to a national convention,[59] thereby vindicating the committee's claim to speak for all catholics. Delegate-elections were the central element in the catholic agitation of 1792, and the most controversial, provoking a protestant backlash. Yet these represented only one aspect of the mobilisation of public opinion, which had already been set in motion by the campaign against Kenmare.

On 17 March the committee published a declaration of catholic principles. The declaration was designed to lay to rest assertions about the incompatibility of catholicism with liberty and had been suggested some months earlier by Drennan.[60] It disavowed such notions as that princes excommunicated by the pope could be deposed by their subjects, that 'no faith is to be kept with heriticks' and so on.[61] Importantly, in the Irish context, the declaration renounced 'all interest in, and title to, all forfeited lands resulting from any rights of our ancestors, or any claim, title or interest therein'.[62] This was meant to quieten fears about the alleged circulation of 'maps, pointing out the property of the old popish possessors',[63] and to counteract the powerful argument that granting the franchise would eventually lead to a catholic restoration and the overturning of the act of settlement. The declaration was dispersed throughout the country. In April the tiny 'Belfast Roman Catholic Society' alone had 5,000 copies printed as handbills.[64] Here was an attempt, no less, to get the entire catholic community to subscribe to the committee's profession of liberal doctrine, including a denial of papal infallibility.

Inevitably some efforts were made to frustrate the process. In September it was reported that the 'peasantry are informed by busy protestant agents that the paper contains a renunciation of the religion of their fathers and absolute condemnation of the pope and holy Church'.[65] The parish priest of Duleek, near Drogheda, opposed the declaration. Nevertheless 250 of his parishioners signed, and the response from county Meath in general was 'considerable'.[66] The Duleek priest's action was far from typical. The catholic clergy were in fact the main organisers of the collection of signatures at parochial level. And the evidence from other parts of the country suggests that this aspect of the committee's strategy was a brilliant success. 20,000 signatures were collected in county Wexford and tens of thousands more in Ulster, Munster and Connaught.[67]

Although most of the evidence is second-hand and of limited statistical value, its import is clear: in the spring and summer of 1792 the Catholic Committee went to the people for a mandate, and got it. Like the anti-Kenmare campaign the collection of signatures involved large numbers of lower-class catholics in active politics. The practical effect of the declaration was probably small: it preached only to the converted. Its true significance lay in the mobilisation of popular support and popular support was ultimately a stronger argument that the profession of liberal doctrine.

A great deal of energy and expense was devoted to the making of public opinion. On the same day on which the delaration appeared the committee ordered the printing of 10,000 copies each of Burke's *Letter*, Tone's *Argument,* a digest of the popery laws prepared by the Dublin United Irishman, Simon Butler, a pamphlet by Todd Jones, Grattan's speeches, and an intended petition. 60,000 items in all, 'to be circulated thro the kingdom at the rate of print and paper'.[68] In an illuminating example of the United Irishmens' role in the campaign, the Clonmell Society in Tipperary distributed 10,000 copies of the digests and other pro-catholic literature sent from Dublin.[69]

The efficient country-wide dissemination of printed propaganda is a reccurrent feature of the catholic, radical and revolutionary agitation of the period. Catholics and radicals distributed greater quantities of political literature in the 1790s than conservatives and consequently their arguments had greater exposure. They also had greater effect because they were more closely attuned to popular grievances. But it was never simply a battle of ideas. Experience is often a better teacher than propaganda. The public meetings called to censure Kenmare, or the collection of signatures to the declaration of principles amounted to a practical education in politics. And if the lower classes learned their politics by doing, then the decisive experiences of 1792 were the delegate elections.

The plan for the election of delegates, printed as a circular letter signed by Edward Byrne, found its way into every corner of Ireland. Of Byrne, one of the wealthiest merchants in the country, it was claimed that 'his influence, extend[ed] through almost every trading town and city in the Kingdom, [he] wielded at will the commercial interest of the Irish catholics'.[70] Business contacts, the organisation which the committee had built up over the decades, and extended in 1790–1, and the parochial structure of the Catholic Church, all facilitated the fairly rapid and efficient implementation of the plan. Arguing that mass county meetings might be imprudent, the plan called for meetings at parish chapels at which one or two 'respectable persons' should be appointed to vote at the county election. Each county was to elect one to four delegates with corresponding associates resident in Dublin. Lastly, 'every endeavour [was] to be used to cultivate and improve the friendship of [the] clergy'.[71] At a meeting on 21 April a number of the Dublin leaders were appointed to tour the country to oversee the collection of signatures to the declaration of principles, the raising of subscriptions and the election of delegates.[72] The task of nationwide organisation was carried out by Keogh, Braughall and Tone. In July, for example, Braughall and Keogh visited Tipperary, Carlow and Kilkenny. Later that month and in August, Keogh was in Louth and Down with Tone. In September they went to Ballinasloe, Mayo, Tipperary again, and Limerick.[73] Their industry paid off and the catholic organisational structures proved effective. As we have seen, tens, possibly hundreds of thousands of signatures were collected. The committee also raised £4,280 in subscriptions, almost half that figure, £2,022, in Dublin alone.[74]

One of Keogh's primary objectives was to enlist the support of the hierarchy. Archbishop Troy and Kenmare had returned to the committee and the explicit endorsement of the whole hierarchy would clearly strengthen the leadership's hand. Keogh's success in wooing their support bears testimony to his considerable political skills. One senior Castle official described him as 'extremely plausible', another as 'cunning, insidious and deep'.[75] As they were returning from an expedition to Rathfryland, county Down, Tone noted in his diary, '18th July, Gog [i.e. Keogh] converts a bishop at Newry, another at Downpatrick . . . 19th July, Drogheda, leave Gog converting another bishop . . . '[76] He attended meetings of the bishops of Connaught, Munster and Ulster, and in his own estimation succeeded in winning their confidence. In a revealing passage from a letter written in October, Keogh referred to certain bishops as 'old men, used to bend to power, mistaking all attempts for liberty as in some way connected with the robbers and murderers in France . . . '[77] The contemptuous tone and the caustic allusion (by a United Irishman) to the French revolution suggest a self-confident, adroit politician. Nor did he rely solely upon 'cunning' and 'plausibility'. According to the lord lieutenant he threatened the Munster bishops with a withdrawal of laity funds if they did not co-operate in the election of delegates.[78] By whatever means, Keogh managed to swing the full weight of the Church behind the campaign.

The elections continued throughout the summer and autumn. John Foster reported a large gathering, probably for that purpose, at Drogheda on 1 June. By mid-August, in Westmorland's opinion, elections had been completed 'in most places', although he complained that they were conducted in such secrecy that it was impossible to be sure. Keogh, a more reliable source in this matter, confirms that eighteen counties and four towns had chosen delegates by the beginning of October. A month later twenty-five counties and all the bigger towns in Ireland had voted.[79] In short, the committee had succeeded in mobilising virtually the entire catholic adult male population. Moreover the lower-classes not only participated in politics, but did so in the teeth of protestant landlord opposition. In the early months of 1792 catholics generally had supported the middle-class challenge to aristocratic authority. In the summer they defied the authority of the protestant gentry. To some worried observers it seemed as if the traditional restraints of deference and social control had broken down. Westmorland complained of the 'agitation and impertinence of the lower catholics everywhere'.[80] More worrying still, the new spirit of defiance or 'impertinence' appeared to have taken up arms in the guise of Defenderism.

II DEFENDERISM AND 'MORE GENERAL POLITICS'

The relationship between Defenderism and the catholic agitation of 1792 is neither direct nor clear. In an increasingly polarised and tense situation the political or sectarian dimension of Defenderism became more sharply defined. In many protestants' minds, and arguably *in fact*, the upsurge of Defenderism in 1792 was connected with the process of electing delegates, holding parochial meetings, collecting signatures, raising funds and distributing literature. As a contemporary pamphleteer noted, 'parochial meetings, county meetings, Catholic Committee, Societies of United Irishmen and Defenders were all jumbled together in one enormous mass of vice and wickedness'.[81] Four years later during a court case in Meath reference was made to the Defenders originating 'in the parochial meetings' in 1792. Indeed, Leonard McNally believed that this had been sanctioned by the committee in order 'to carry through parliament, by influence of terror, the catholic bill'.[82] What seems likely is that during the heady days of 1792 at least some Defenders came to think of themselves as the 'armed wing' of the Catholic Committee. If, as Hobart claimed, the 'lower order of papists' were 'universally impressed with ideas (however vague) of considerable advantages to be gained to them by some convulsion in the state', then the disarming of protestants – in 1792 there were 180 Defender arms raids in Louth alone – takes on fresh significance. Was this practice part of 'the intimidating system of the Committee'?[83] A more plausible, and less conspiratorial, explanation is that the Defenders, swept along on a rising tide of catholic euphoria, unilaterally – and by direct action – engaged 'Protestant Ascendancy' at a local level.

Certainly Defenderism was invigorated by the diffusion of propaganda, catholic and Paineite, and by the eruption of political activity. 'Keogh', remarked Dr Drennan, 'has the nature and had the wish to excite the people.'[84] He explicitly linked catholic emancipation to concrete social benefits. The vote, claimed Keogh, equalled security of tenure, because 'for want of the protection of the elective franchise, the poorer catholics are turned-out of their little farms, at the expiration of their leases, to make room for protestant freeholders, who can assist their landlords by votes'.[85] Westmorland thought that 'Political discussions ha[d] raised very much the expectations of the lower catholics. They have been taught that the elective franchise will improve their condition and they connect it with the non-payment of rents, tithes and taxes'.[86] These expectations assumed almost millenarian proportions as the anticipation of some form of catholic 'restoration' took hold.

The sudden expansion of Defenderism in 1792 can be traced to a further source: popular perceptions of the French revolution. In July it was reported from Meath that the common people were sworn 'to be true to one another, to their religion and the king, George the third, till there should be an invasion' (from France). A number of Defenders tried at the Louth assizes in the spring of 1793 also stood accused of administering that oath.[87] Revealingly, the author of the Meath report linked local Defender activity to the catholic agitation, and urged that a stop be put to 'private proceedings and to prevent the election of' the convention, or as he called it, in a pointed reference to France, the 'National Assembly'.[88] The revolution inspired Defenderism in two ways. Firstly, as catholic Ireland's traditional ally, France continued to figure in the popular imagination as 'deliverer'. This quasi-Jacobite folk-memory explains how the Defenders could embrace the prospect of a French invasion *before* the war. Moreover, Defender oaths and catechisms are shot through with a messianic concept of deliverance, expressed by a blend of French, biblical and masonic imagery. Secondly, the new revolutionary doctrines found a responsive audience. The Defenders 'talked of the famous system of liberty and equality in the most extravagant manner. Why should others have land and property and they want it?'[89] Characteristically, 'levelling principles' fused with much older catholic resentments rooted in seventeenth-century dispossession. It has even been suggested that the Defenders made contact with French agents in London in 1792, and that they had adopted a crude version of republican ideology independent of, and antedating, the United Irish movement.[90]

Defender violence offered the Catholic Committee's enemies rich opportunities to discredit them. In February Drennan mentioned a Defender riot near Dundalk and wryly commented, 'government will probably make it out a rebellion'.[91] In May and June, just as the committee's nationwide campaign was getting under way, Defender troubles burst out in Louth and Down. Typically, the first major riot in Louth occurred at a fair. According to Westmorland's account the fairs in Louth were attended by northerners for the purchase of wool and other raw materials. At one of these the northerners (protestant weavers) were attacked and beaten by Defenders, their sacks ripped open and the contents scattered. At the next pattern or public feast day in the area the crowd, which allegedly included several Defenders, was dispersed by a company of light horse, led by local magistrates and by the Speaker, John Foster. Two men were killed and a number wounded.[92] Although Foster privately acknowledged that the disturbances did 'not seem to have the smallest connection with the Catholic Committee',[93] both the Catholic Committee and the ascendancy party sought to make political capital from the unrest. In a letter, written by Keogh (probably to Richard Burke) he enumerated 'the desperate and unprincipled proceedings of certain monopolists' in stirring up sectarian clashes, the most telling of which, he suggested, be relayed to the English ministry. Keogh also took an ironic swipe at 'our Speaker [who] is wonderfully alert in procuring the peace of the country'.[94] At a public meeting in Dublin in October he renewed the accusation: 'we know the goading in Louth; we know the military excursions, when the people were warm at their merriments, and many guess the design.'[95] The design, in Keogh's view, was to link the catholic agitation to popular disturbances. As one newspaper complained, 'certain jobbing gentlemen . . . have for some days past taken much pain to magnify some petty quarrels in a country fair near Dundalk into open rebellion – and poor Popery! as usual, comes in for the principal blame'.[96] During 1792, Thomas Emmet later observed, Defenderism and 'more general politics' began to converge.

Recognising that their opponents could use Defenderism to embarrass them politically, (suspecting indeed that Defender unrest was deliberately fomented for that purpose), the Catholic Committee tried to defuse the situation which had developed in south Down. The United Irishmen too had a vested interest in ending sectarian strife. The trouble there began on 6 May near the village of Rathfryland in the Mourne mountains. Some young men were killed in the clashes and a local presbyterian minister, Volunteer and United Irishman, Samuel Barber, arranged a 'peace treaty' between the Peep O'Day Boys and the Defenders.[97] But the potential for large-scale conflict remained. 'From three to four thousand' were said to 'regularly assemble every day and night in arms', and one of the local grandees, Lord Downshire, asked the Dublin administration to send troops.[98] Troops were dispatched and stationed at Banbridge and Castlewellan.[99] But like nearby south Armagh, this was difficult terrain to police.

At the beginning of June Lord Annesley bitterly complained that 'the papists are getting more insolent every day' and that people were afraid to attend Castlewellan fair, 'as the town is mine and the papists treat them ill'.[100] The troubles appear to have stayed on the boil during June as later that month a meeting of the sheriffs and magistrates was summoned to discuss the disturbed condition of the county.[101] Once again Keogh laid the blame squarely at the door of the ascendancy, whom he accused of arming the poorer protestants, 'the very wretches who are reported to be the Peep O'Day Boys'. He also alleged that 'idle and artful reports' were circulated, 'to inflame the minds of the rabble' and singled out Annesley, 'a nephew of the Beresfords', as the chief culprit. These accusations were repeated in a handbill, signed 'Commonsense', and probably written by Keogh.[102] For its part, the ascendancy did not hesitate to extract political advantage from the strife. At the height of the campaign for catholic relief, Foster, it was claimed, sent a list of individuals killed in the riots in Down, to the prince of Wales. 'Their names were marked "protestant" and opposite there was a note – "killed by a catholic"'. The prince was then asked to show the list to the king.[103]

On 14 July, the third anniversary of the fall of the Bastille, and in marked contrast to the previous year when the pro-catholic resolution had been rejected, several of the leading catholics and Dublin radicals, including Keogh, McKenna, Tandy and Tone, attended the Belfast celebrations. On the 17th, Samuel Neilson, editor of the *Northern Star,* proposed that a delegation be sent to Rathfryland to restore the peace. 'The restoration of tranquility', noted Tone, (soon to replace Richard Burke as agent to the committee), 'is to us of the last importance'.[104] The next day Tone, Neilson, Keogh and a local linen merchant, Alexander Lowry, met with clergymen, magistrates and gentry at Rathfryland. All agreed that in this instance the Peep O'Day Boys had been the aggressors, although a local priest shared the blame. The catholics at the meeting promised to see to the offending cleric's transfer. The delegation also decided to draw up an address calling upon the Defenders to desist from violence. 1,000 copies were printed and distributed throughout Down and Louth.[105] On 7 August a second expedition to the Mournes, joined this time by Leonard McNally, took place.[106] On the 12th Tone met with some Defenders at Newry who requested that he represent them at the forthcoming assizes. On the 16th Lord Hillsborough informed the delegation that the Defenders were in possession of 4,000 stand of arms and a tantalising entry in Tone's dairy reads 'The ambassadors . . . admit the 4,000'.[107] The 'ambassadors', in other words, were in a position to know how well armed the local Defenders were.

Did Tone commit a political blunder by meeting the Defenders at Newry? Similarly, what did Keogh hope to achieve at this point by visiting Defender prisoners in Dundalk gaol, or the Catholic Committee by exploring the possibility of feeing counsel at certain Defender trials? These contacts left them open to charges of complicity; charges duely made by a lords secret committee in 1793.[108] By the testimony of friend and foe alike Keogh was a gifted and astute politician; nor are Tone's diplomatic and political talents in doubt. Perhaps the explanation for their apparent tactical misjudgement is that they wished to harness, or at least wished to have the option of harnessing, Defenderism to the catholic cause.

A strategy of this sort might explain Napper Tandy's association with the Louth Defenders. Tandy, who took the Defender oath at Castlebellingham, was probably introduced to the lodge there by the Rev. James Coigly, and Coigly was already at this stage connected with the Belfast United Irishmen.[109] Tandy distributed money and the handbill 'Commonsense', a forceful attack on the ruling 'junto'.[110] In October, shortly after this expedition, an association was formed for the non-consumption of Castlebellingham beer. It seems more than coincidental that at the end of September a leading Dublin United Irishman, Simon Butler, 'proposed a non-consumption agreement against the Ascendancy'. Butler's proposal was not adopted, but the Catholic Committee were nevertheless suspected of being behind the Castlebellingham boycott.[111] Richard McCormick and Thomas Warren, prominent in both radical and catholic politics, were reported to be in correspondence with the Defenders.[112] While insufficient evidence exists (for this early date) to support a grand Catholic Committee-United Irish-Defender conspiracy theory such as that posited by Musgrave, there is enough to suggest a network of contacts. Possibly these contacts were established as insurance against the danger of armed conflict, a danger which seemed increasingly likely as the campaign, and opposition to it, became more intense.

III   A 'POPISH PARLIAMENT': THE IMPACT OF THE CATHOLIC
      CONVENTION

Protestant reaction to the steep escalation of the Catholic Committee's political activity was swift and vociferous. They were angered and unsettled by the claim made in the preamble to Byrne's circular that the committee had assurance from the 'first authority' that a petition for further relief would meet with a positive response. The 'first authority' transparently referred to the British government. Whether true or false the claim unnerved the upholders of ascendancy.[113] The legality of the proposed 'popish parliament' was also questioned, on the ground that it challenged actual parliamentary sovereignty and was therefore unconstitutional. Indeed, in Westmorland's view the committee had 'already exercised most of the functions of a government'.[114] In anticipation of that line of attack the committee submitted its plan for elections to the scrutiny of two barristers, both of whom confirmed its lawfulness. The Dublin administration was at first uncertain how to respond – Westmorland actually used the phrase 'wait and see'. Predictably, Fitzgibbon was more bullish, insisting that the authors of the plan were liable to criminal prosecution. Perhaps fortunately for the lord lieutenant he did not act on his lord chancellor's advice, as the attorney and solicitor generals' eventually concurred that the plan was, in fact, legal.[115] The county grand juries were less constrained. Beginning with Derry, grand jury after grand jury issued resolutions denouncing the Byrne circular. Sixteen counties in all condemned the document. This counter-campaign seems to have been carefully orchestrated by Dublin Castle in an attempt to intimidate the catholics, mobilise protestant public opinion and, most importantly, impress the British government with the strength of opposition to more concessions. At this stage the protestant position was best defined by Dublin corporation's declaration of 'Protestant Ascendancy'. The hermetically-sealed political system, which this statement sets out, left little room in which to practice the 'art of the possible'. Its unflinching tone vividly conveys the bitter polarisation aroused by the catholic agitation, and betrays the extent of protestant insecurity. Confronted by an aggressive Catholic Committee allied to a revived reform movement, the ascendancy could no longer assume automatic support from Britain.

As preparations continued for the convention, to be held at the beginning of December, tension mounted. The threat of violence, more or less implicit in the postures struck by the ascendancy and by the committee, became more open. The omission in the secondary literature of almost any reference to the rumours of war is extraordinary. Accounts of the campaign usually refer to the election of delegates and then concentrate on the proceedings of the convention. For some reason the gravity of the crisis in the autumn of 1792 has been underestimated. Yet, because it tells us a great deal about the demeanour of both the Catholic Committee and the 'Protestant Ascendancy', it is essential that that gravity and tension is stressed. The politics and politicians of 1792 were extremist and confrontational. Once this is grasped the rapid descent into bloodshed in the years that followed becomes more explicable. On the other hand, the rhetoric of violence may have amounted to little more than attempted intimidation, and it should therefore be handled with a certain scepticism. In November, for instance, Tone reported that in Keogh's opinion 'this will not end without blows, and says he for one is ready', and then asked himself the question, 'is he?'[116]

Keogh was certainly alert to other possibilities. In a deft political manoeuvre he approached Lord Abercorn offering to support him as lord lieutenant if he took up the catholic cause.[117] The marquess of Abercorn, an absentee landlord with substantial property in Ulster and his own 'interest' in the Irish parliament, was a friend of Pitt's and a correspondent of the aristocratic United Irishman, Archibald Hamilton Rowan. As early as June 1791 he had intimated his availability for the lord lieutenancy, and rumours concerning his likely appointment circulated in April and May, 1792. In Malcomson's view Abercorn represented the only real alternative to the entrenched ruling clique in Dublin Castle.[118] In January, 1792, Abercorn had written that he was in favour of 'every equality but political equality' for the catholics.[119] However, his response to Keogh's overtures, made by Tone through George Knox, MP, was cool. But as his later 'conversion' to full catholic emancipation demonstrates, the high political route was well worth exploring.

At the time these contacts were being made Abercorn was counselling that a tough line be adopted against the catholics. 'It is time', he urged Major Hobart in October, 'for English government to proclaim themselves earnest and ready to stand by the government and parliament of Ireland, though I own', he admitted, 'I could not at once point out the manner, I hope it will be done'. The worst possible scenario he could contemplate would have been to *presume* the convention illegal, act accordingly, and then 'fail in the proof'.[120] Abercorn's uncertainty mirrors that of the ascendancy. And in the case of the ascendancy, insecurity compounded uncertainty, particularly in respect of the British government's intentions. The 'greatest of all our difficulties', declared Westmorland, 'is the suspicion that English government wish them [the catholics] to have further privileges'.[121] London's less than whole-hearted support, coupled with the increasingly strident tone of the catholic campaign induced something close to panic. Two weeks before the convention was called Hobart stated, 'as the case now stands – the Irish parliament is on the defensive, and has an unquestionable right to call on his majesty to assist them in supporting the protestant establishment in Church and State . . . which', he added, employing an argument which Fitzgibbon would later use with more success, 'he is bound by his oath to maintain'.[122]

With renewed Defender violence, the Catholic Committee's political mobilisation of practically the whole catholic community, unsureness about British support, and apprehension about the convention, almost inevitably, deep seated anxieties about 'another 1641' resurfaced (or were deliberately promoted to firm up protestant resistance and influence the British government against the catholics). On 18 September a man passed through the streets of Wexford, 'warning and foretelling that protestant throats would be cut from ear to ear'. Aware of the impact such stories could have, the local catholics offered a reward to anyone who successfully prosecuted the culprit, 'if he is not insane'.[123] Pointing out that there were insufficient troops stationed in Ireland 'to suppress a general and universal rising', the lord lieutenant informed Pitt that this was 'an event which the stories of former times and rebellions make protestants conceive to be the object of the various meetings and correspondences amongst the papists'.[124] Both sides in the unfolding drama were guilty of raising the political temperature to dangerous heights. One committeeman complained that 'the catholics speak too loudly in the porter houses of the number of armed men that they can bring into the field. Such language is intemperate'.[125] Grattan, who had been in London since September, alleged that certain ascendancy figures had 'represented the catholics as in a state of rebellion, probably to get the English to crush them'.[126] Tone noted that 'The Chancellor we hear talks big. If he attempts to use violent measures, I believe war will be the inevitable consequence', although he himself felt this was unlikely. On 9 November, the day before he made this entry in his diary, Tone paid a visit to the courts where 'sundry barristers appl[ied] to him for protection in the approaching rebellion'. All this provoked 'exceeding good laughter' and Tone's biographer, Frank MacDermot, characterised these exchanges as 'badinage' before proceeding to a broader point about catholic propaganda being conducted 'on the basis of obedience to the law and loyalty to the crown'. However, considering the extent of civil war mongering at this time, perhaps the barristers' little 'joke' was not quite so innocent as MacDermot believed.[127]

In the end it is impossible to ascertain how much all of this was merely, as Tone put it, 'big talk'. By mid-November, for example, Westmorland expressed the view that there was no immediate danger of conflict, although he nevertheless requested extra troops. A month later he was sending frantic messages to London warning that if they did not publicly commit themselves to the defence of the constitution, 'English government in Ireland is at an end'.[128] But by this he may simply have meant that conciliation of the catholics had pushed the Castle's traditional supporters in parliament to the limits of their endurance. Yet in a way the true intentions of the protagonists are of secondary importance. Even if the warlike rhetoric was only sound and fury, the alarm it caused had practical consequences.

In the north Volunteering revived in response to a perceived catholic threat to the constitution.[129] Pro-reform Volunteering revived as well, menacing the ascendancy with force from another quarter. Reports circulated of arms being imported and the northerners allegedly ordered cannon from the Dublin iron founder, and United Irishman, Henry Jackson.[130] The pervasive political uncertainty also appears to have sharpened the credit crisis of November–December 1792. Attributed by some to the panic aroused by the civil war scare, others suspected the government of stage-managing the shortage in a bid to stoke up anti-catholic sentiment.[131] And, as argued earlier, it is no coincidence that it was in these highly charged circumstances that the Defenders first entered the national political arena.

The Irish crisis, of course, had an international context. France went to war in April, 1792, and from then on it seemed only a matter of time before Britain was drawn into the European conflict. War radicalised the revolution, as the Jacobins and their *sans culotte* allies began to set the pace. The 'September massacres' of 'royalist' prisoners by the Parisian crowd particularly shocked contemporary opinion. In Britain domestic unrest and the fear of 'French infection' led to the formation of loyalist associations and the issue, in May and December, of royal proclamations against seditious writings. 'Liberty Trees' were planted in towns across Scotland to celebrate French victories at Valmy and Jemappes. In December the English militia was called out and regular troops were despatched north of the border.[132] On the face of it, these alarming developments, at home and abroad, can only have reinforced the British ministry's desire to conciliate his majesty's Irish catholic subjects. Mass discontent, even civil war, in Ireland was the last thing it needed.

John Keogh saw in Britain's difficulties catholic Ireland's opportunity. In a speech to the convention he argued that with the 'critical situation in England; stocks falling [and] . . . Liberty Tree[s] planted in Scotland', the moment had arrived to press on for their maximum demands.[133] If trouble was going to erupt it was expected that the convention, which sat in Tailor's Hall, Back Lane, from the 3rd to the 8th. December, would be the flashpoint. The catholics suspected that an attempt might be made to stop or interrupt the proceedings. If that happened, then, in the opinion of the committee's *de facto* ambassador in London, Dr Hussy, 'resistance would follow'.[134] In another speech to the delegates Keogh asked: "'Have you considered the magnitude of your demand and the power of your enemies? have you considered the disgrace and the consequences of a refusal, and are you prepared to support your claim?" The whole assembly rose, as one man, and, raising their right hands, answered, "WE ARE".[135]

In a sense the Castle was correct in attributing the assertive behaviour of the convention to the radical penetration of catholic politics. Several of the principal architects of the catholic campaign, Keogh, McCormick, and the committee's agent, Wolfe Tone, were United Irishmen, as were the editors of those catholic champions, the *Hibernian Journal* and the *National Evening Star*. The membership of the Dublin Society at this time was divided approximately equally between catholics and protestants.[136] However, in the administration's view it was a predominantly catholic club. 'Two thirds catholic', in fact, according to Hobart and to *Faulkners Dublin Journal*.[137] And that perception was perhaps not unwelcome to the catholics. It may well have been a further application of Drennan's 'radicals as bugbear' theory. Drennan certainly suspected as much. In late November he wrote, 'our society, by the bye, is growing really important. Not a night but 12 or 14 are admitted and take the test'. He then went on to argue, 'the catholic cause is selfish compared with ours, and they will make use of every means for success . . . they will send the sanguine men into our society, and the heads of their sect, for it is but a sect, though a numerous one, will not enter it, but stand off sullen and reserved'.[138]

Of the 231 elected delegates to the Catholic Convention 48 were members of the Dublin Society of United Irishmen, 18 of whom joined in November or December, 1792.[139] These radicals operated as an organised pressure-group within the committee, and in this capacity their contribution to the convention debates was decisive. The 'Back Lane parliament' passed two resolutions which finally severed catholic politics from the last traces of deference, moderation and gradualism. The first, which called for total emancipation, was proposed by Luke Teeling, Lisburn linen merchant, chairman of the committee of accounts, and representative for county Antrim. 'Citizen Teeling' had received 'instructions' from Samuel Neilson and the Belfast United Irishmen shortly before the convention met and Tone, who was also in touch with Neilson, slipped Keogh a note on the convention platform advising him to support the motion.[140] The second resolution was even more audacious. Christopher Dillon Bellew, one the representatives for county Galway, proposed that the petition for complete emancipation should be laid directly before the throne. By-passing Dublin Castle in this unprecedented manner amounted to an enormmous snub; nor did Bellew evade the implication. 'It has been said', he announced, 'my plan is disrespectful to administration. I answer, it is intended to be so. It is time for us to speak out like men. We will not, like African slaves, petition our task-masters.' Bellew's motion was seconded by a United Irishman, J.

J. McDonnell of Mayo, who, like Teeling, had consulted his radical colleagues 'off stage' before the convention assembled.[141] The interventions
of Teeling, McDonnell, and Dr. MacNevin, who made a rousing speech
from the floor, suggest a co-ordinated United Irish manouevre to seize the
initiative. In the event they carried the day. But the United Irishmen did
not have it all their own way. Although the convention passed a resolution
of thanks to the people of Belfast (and the delegation to London contrived
to journey by way of that town), it refused to receive a deputation from
the Dublin Society.[142]

After the convention passed off without incident the focus of tension
shifted to the reception of the delegation in London. Would a rebuff
detonate a popular revolt?[143] The atmosphere of crisis was palpable. The
credit shortage tightened and the military presence on the streets of Dublin
became more visible.[144] The new 'National Guard' Volunteers, sponsored
by the United Irishmen, including Keogh, and supposedly modelled on
the French example, were suppressed by proclamation on 8 December.[145]
Clearly, if the threat of armed force had tactical value for the Catholic
Committee, actual violence while the delegation was in London could only
harm their case. Both the administration and the committee understood
this. Yet Defender arms raids in Meath and Louth continued apace. This
perplexed the lord lieutenant, who considered them part of 'some scheme
of which [he could not] fathom the bottom: it certainly is very injurious
to the peaceful desire of the Roman Catholics'.[146] The committee, aware
of the political damage which the unrest might inflict, despatched two
representatives from Drogheda on 31 December to tour the chapels in the
area and, in conjunction with the local clergy, 'exhort the common people
to peace and good order'. A meeting in Dublin issued an appeal for calm
to the 'lower orders'.[147] This episode indicates that while the committee
had contacts with the Defenders, it did not exercise control over them.

The catholic delegation was favourably received. Interestingly, Grattan
had remained in London, and appears to have been lobbying on their
behalf.[148] Subsesquently the English ministry had a clause in favour of
the catholics inserted in the speech from the throne which opened the 1793
session of the Irish parliament. On 4 February Hobart introduced another
catholic relief bill. Predictably the protestant ultras at once pounced upon
the Defender disturbances. Duigenan complained on the first day of the
debate that catholics of the lower rank were 'at this moment' disarming
protestants in Louth, Monaghan, Cavan and Meath.[149] As in 1792 the
parliamentary debates were spliced with abusive rhetoric. Again the ultras
articulated what the silent majority were thinking. Under-Secretary Cooke
divided the house into three groups: 'those who would give nothing, those

who are for everything, those who are for Major Hobart's bill. The first is much the largest and would be decisive were it not for the influence and wishes of government'. The vote on George Knox's motion for total catholic emancipation, in other words, for allowing catholics to take seats in parliament, registered the true sentiments of the house. The motion, proposed at the prompting of Knox's patron, Abercorn, on 25 February, presented MPs with a delicate political problem. It was interpreted – correctly – as an opportunistic intervention. 'Gentlemen said it was a race between L[ord] Abercorn and Lord Westmorland,'[150] although this did not prevent the motion being defeated by 163 votes to 69. The government, however, got its way, and the catholic relief act of 1793, which extended the franchise to forty shilling freeholders in the counties, received royal assent in April. But, as had happened with its forerunner in 1792, the bad tempered buffeting to which the bill was subjected in both commons and lords, robbed it of the conciliatory effect for which the British government had hoped.[151]

Indeed, the course of events – the rise of an uncompromising 'democratic' middle-class catholic leadership; the routing of the more placatory ecclesiastical-aristocratic old guard; the bad grace with which the 1792 act was passed; the popular mobilisation and propagandising of the renewed catholic campaign; the bitter counterblast by the grand juries and Dublin corporation; the scare-mongering; the spread of Defenderism and the revival of protestant and pro-reform Volunteering – conspired to thwart the British government's design for knitting Ireland's religious denominations into an integrated political community. The reverse happened. The combativeness and the limited success of the revamped Catholic Committee, combined with the perceived 'desertion' of their British protectors, delivered a profound shock to ascendancy morale. In 1791–3 the supporters of 'Protestant Ascendancy' experienced political trauma. Catholics too, were aware of having passed through a major crisis, of having approached the edge of a precipice. Looking back on the autumn and winter of 1792 some months later Drennan recalled, 'the catholics were driven to great despair and were resolved to go to extremities rather than again be driven from the door of the constitution. A contest was expected'.[152] Lower-class catholics had had their expectations raised only to be dashed, a process repeated during the Fitzwilliam debacle in 1795. The bill had become law, yet they were still taxed and tithed. What, after all, had changed?

Some things had changed. Popular catholic alienation from the state had deepened, and become overtly politicised by the direct experience of challenging the ascendancy. In the history of Defenderism 1792 is the transitional year. The scale of violence had changed. The Speaker's life was threatened. And as Defender activity increased, repression became more ferocious.[153] The most dramatic episode ocurred on the borders of Cavan and Meath. In the neighbourhood of Bailieborough and Coolnahinch a body of around 600 Defenders were confronted on the 22 January by some forty local protestant 'gentlemen', members of the County Meath Association, reinforced by twenty regular soldiers. The Defenders were routed, suffering thirty-eight fatalities. None of their opponents was killed.[154] Some Defenders, trapped taking refuge in a house, died in circumstances which provoked controversy at the time. The 'innocent and guilty', according to one contemporary, 'were dragged from their hiding places and butchered in cold blood'.[155] Further evidence of harsh repression was offered at the spring assizes in Louth, when twenty-one capital convictions were handed down.[156] The upsurge of Defender violence and the forcefulness of the response were related to the euphoria generated by the catholic campaign. The Defenders openly and self-consciously defied 'Protestant Ascendancy' and in Meath the challenge was met. During October, 1792, a catholic meeting at Trim issued a statement which regretted 'the severe disposition of many of our protestant brethren'.[157] The thirty-eight Defenders killed near Coolnahinch were victims of their own enthusiasm, and of the protestant bitterness (and fears), aroused by the catholic agitation.

'Normal' politics did not survive the shock of 1792. Thomas Bartlett contends that the anti-militia riots of 1793 would not have happened, or at least not on that scale, were it not for the events of the preceding year. Lecky thought that the '98 rebellion would not have occurred, or at least would have been confined to the north. It has been suggested too, that the success of the catholics in winning the vote, 'broke down the resistance to union [with Great Britain] among Irish protestants'. As the debates on relief had revealed, the ultimate protestant nightmare was that the catholics would eventually gain a majority in parliament. A united parliament, in which catholics would always be a minority, removed that danger.[158] More immediately, the society which emerged from the high drama of the campaign for catholic relief was more sharply divided and unstable than ever, the majority of its populace more disaffected than before. The extremism which characterised the politics of the 1790s, and which found its ultimate expression in rebellion, had its roots in the traumatic events of 1792.

4 Radical Ideology, Popular Politics and Parliamentary Reform

In stressing the legal, open and constitutional character of the United Irishmen and of the Catholic Committee during the first half of the 1790s, historians have, by implication, underestimated the seriousness of the crises of 1792–3. They have failed to grasp the political extremism of protagonists on all sides. As a logical corollary of this too stark a contrast has been drawn between the earlier period and the overtly revolutionary years from 1795 to the 1798 rebellion. Catholics and radicals made a concerted appeal to a popular constituency *before* 1795, and the 'constitutional' phase needs to be re-examined in that light.[1] As the great wave of catholic agitation subsided, political tensions were sustained by an intensifying campaign for parliamentary reform. On 13 March, 1793, Under-Secretary Cooke reported to Whitehall, 'We have been on the eve of rebellion these three months and nothing but the forces of the establishment has saved us'.[2]

From the date and context it is clear that this is a reference not to the catholics or Defenders but to the activities of the United Irishmen and to the Volunteer revival. Comments such as Cooke's, by no means uncommon at the time, graphically convey the gravity and drama of the situation and the militancy of the reformers. The re-opening of the catholic and reform issues provoked a severe political crisis. Experience of crises and the deliberate courting by catholics and reformers of a plebeian audience were among the several sources of popular politicisation. Others included ideas and news from France and the opposition press. The variety of sources should be noted because of the dominance enjoyed by the United Irishmen in accounts of the radical history of the period. Yet while a preoccupation with the United Irishmen has obscured the diversity of popular politics, their pivotal role as agents of politicisation is nevertheless unarguable. To a large extent their policies and ideas contributed the 'derived' element to the new popular ideology of the period.

I THE SOURCES OF RADICAL IDEOLOGY

It is tempting to view United Irish ideology as a derivative of the 'new' ideas popularised by the French revolution and by Paine's *Rights of Man.* Such influences were undoubtedly important. It was a fiercely modernist movement. As one writer has put it, 'it had no predecessors and no successors, and it did not seek its title-deeds from history'. And that sense of modernity was self-conscious. 'We have thought little about our ancestors,' announced the Dublin Society, 'much of our posterity'.[3] But the impact of French and Paineite ideas and the modernism of the United Irishmen can too easily be overstated. In fact many of the assumptions which informed their political outlook are traceable to another revolution in another country: the Glorious revolution of 1688. They were as much the Anglo-Irish representatives of British radicalism as Irish Jacobins. Recent scholarship, by Elliott and by Wells,[4] has drawn attention to the existence of a radical network or community in the British Isles. It may often be more appropriate to approach Irish, English or Scottish radicalism in the 1790s from this perspective, than from a strictly national standpoint. This is clearly the case during the years 1797–1803. Earlier, however, United Irish delegates attended the Scottish reform conventions in 1792–3 and United Irish literature was reported to be circulating in Scotland in 1794.[5] Ideologically this radical community drew on the same assumptions and traditions. At the 1791 Bastille Day celebrations in Belfast 'many striking emblems in allusion to the revolution of 1688 were displayed'.[6] The Dublin Society lauded 'the genius of the British constitution', while the renegade United Irishman, William Paulet Carey, argued in a pamphlet that the revolution of 1688 had established the right to collective resistance.[7] The rhetoric of British radicalism was assimilated with ease into the imagery and vocabulary of United Irish publications.

The eighteenth-century background to that language had its origins in 'revolution principles' and Lockeian contract theory, of which arguments advanced by critics of government were essentially elaborations.[8] At the core of this position was the belief that all government originated in a contract between rulers and the ruled, the right to resistance if that contract was broken, and the idea of a 'balanced' constitution. Although the first two principles were occasionally reiterated, what most concerned these critics in the early eighteenth-century – the 'real' or country whigs and Commonwealthmen – were 'imbalances' in the constitution. Balances, they believed, checked arbitrary power (an eighteenth-century obsession),[9] and safeguarded civil and religious liberty. These consisted in the distribution of power between king, lords and commons and in the separation of executive, legislature and judiciary. In particular the Commonwealthmen were wary of the balance being upset by an expansion of 'ministerial prerogative' through a systematic corruption of parliament. They argued that the power exercised by the executive, which rested on patronage, could best be counteracted by place and pension bills disqualifying MPs in the ministers' pay from sitting in the house.[10] From about 1760 the emphasis shifted to a reform of representation which, it was claimed, by making parliament more responsive to public opinion, would secure traditional liberties.[11] The reform platform built up during the second half of the century was shaped by the new politics of extra-parliamentary agitation: the Wilkesite and Association movements in England and the Volunteers in Ireland. Theoretical ballast was supplied by a group of radical intellectuals, mainly dissenters, such as James Burgh, Joseph Priestly and Richard Price. The doctrines articulated by this group – natural and inalienable rights, the legitimacy of opposition to arbitrary power – dramatised and made concrete by the American revolution, provided radicals throughout the British Isles with a common fund of ideas.

A good illustration of the debt owed by Irish radicals to the British tradition was their attitude towards catholicism. When Thomas Paine observed that 'Monarchy in every instance is the Popery of government,'[12] he spoke with the authentic voice of British radicalism. To these eighteenth-century thinkers catholicism, or 'popery' as they usually referred to it, represented tyranny, poverty and superstition. Catholics, they felt, could not be trusted with political power. In the radical utopia imagined in Burgh's *Account of the Cessares* (1764), catholics were excluded from public office.[13] Despite a substantial catholic membership and an advocacy of catholic emancipation, a number of United Irishmen shared the suspicions of their English counterparts. Dr Drennan's doubts about the compatibility of catholicism and liberty have already been noted. The *Cork Gazette* denounced 'priestcraft' and, remarking on Bonaparte's victorious Italian campaign in 1796, the *Northern Star* welcomed 'the approaching downfall of the Pope'.[14] Although committed to equal citizenship for catholics, many United Irishmen viewed their religion as backward and authoritarian.

What distinguished Irish from British radicalism was its critique of Ireland's constitutional subordination to Great Britain. The Anglo-Irish constitutional relationship is the theme which runs through every major exposition of whig ideas written in Ireland. William Molyneux explicitly acknowledged his debt to Locke and dealt with contract and natural rights theory, but his primary concern was with the injustice referred to in the title of his book, *The case of Ireland being bound by Acts of parliament in England, stated* (1698). Interestingly, Molyneux was a unionist. His complaint concerned lack of representation. 'I have no other notion of slavery,' he asserted, 'but being bound by a law to which I do not consent.' The representation of the Irish people in the British parliament was for him 'an happiness we can hardly hope for'.[15] This aspect of *The case* was conveniently ignored by those eighteenth-century politicians who took up its arguments, and in the 1782 edition the offending passage was suppressed. Otherwise *The case* (republished nine times between 1698 and 1782) stands as a classic formulation of Anglo-Irish nationalism and colonial whiggery. Its influence can be traced through Swift in the 1720s – 'all government without the consent of the governed is the very definition of slavery' – and Dr Charles Lucas in the 1740s, to the United Irishmen in the 1790s. The intellectual lineage of their restatement of the definition of slavery as 'that state in which men are governed without their consent' is not hard to establish.[16] The sense of grievance expressed through this polemical tradition was directed at England and at her representatives in Ireland. Whereas English radicals identified the 'court' as the font of all patronage and corruption, their Irish counterparts blamed 'English influence'. As the first declaration of the Dublin United Irishmen proclaimed, 'We have no National government – We are ruled by Englishmen and the servants of Englishmen.'[17]

Presumably historians used to style eighteenth-century protestant nationalism 'colonial', because, although it entailed a denunciation of the unfairness of the British connection, it never questioned its ultimate legitimacy.[18] Eventually the United Irishmen sought, in Tone's phrase, 'to break the connection', thereby rendering the qualifier 'colonial' redundant. Appropriated, as they were, by romantic nationalists during the nineteenth century and perceived to this day as the 'founding fathers' of Irish republicanism, the essentially protestant-radical identity of the United Irishmen has been blurred by the mists of nationalist hagiography. However, the retrieval of that identity should not preclude consideration of the place of an ill-defined, embryonic nationalism within their ideology. This operated at three levels: middle-class resentment of commercial restrictions imposed by Great Britain, an emerging interest in Gaelic Irish culture, and a tactical-political exploitation of popular anti-English prejudices.

Most prominent at the outset were commercial grievances, and in this respect, before the adoption of an overtly republican programme, United Irish arguments did not markedly differ from those advanced by earlier 'colonial nationalists'. According to this view Ireland's commercial backwardness resulted from her constitutional subordination. By contrast, the nation's economy would flourish inside the political framework of an equal partnership with the bigger kingdom. Indeed Ireland would, 'in arts, commerce and manufactures, spring up like a balloon, and leave England behind her at an immense distance'. Such arguments were the commonplaces of several generations of Anglo-Irish politicians and it is not surprising that Tone compared his opinions with those of Molyneux and Swift.[19] Similarly, the United Irishmen employed the same tactics on the economic front as the reformers of the 1770s and '80s, promoting a non-importation campaign in response to the trade depression of 1792–3.[20] These tactics and economic theories reflect the movement's social profile. The United Irishmen began as an essentially middle-class organisation – merchants, shopkeepers, doctors and lawyers.[21] They were committed, for example, to a free market and opposed to the proto-trade unionism represented by journeymen combinations.

Such commercial grievances were unremarkable in eighteenth-century Ireland. One of the newer features of the United Irishmen was their participation in the 'Gaelic revival' of the time. They sponsored a harpers' festival at Belfast in 1792 and Irish language classes in that city were advertised in the *Northern Star*.[22] Never a prominent item on the United Irish political agenda, cultural revivalism was nonetheless important. It indicates a groping towards a profounder sense of nationhood based upon a separate cultural identity. Such a concept would have been wholly alien to earlier critics of English 'influence', like Swift, who considered himself – in cultural terms – an Englishman who happened to have been born in Ireland. Irish bourgeois cultural nationalism was part of a Europe-wide rediscovery of the 'folk', which had clear political implications.[23] Moreover, as practical revolutionaries the United Irishmen were alert to the propaganda value in appealing to popular anti-English sentiment.

Of course many historians would query the existence of anglophobia as a significant element in eighteenth-century popular culture. Elliott characterises the 'Irish peasantry' as 'essentially loyal' and Irish catholics as 'not natural rebels', arguing that popular nationalist and separatist aspirations formed in the course of the 1790s.[24] This was not how a number of contemporaries saw it. At one end of the political scale Tone referred to 'an inextirpable abhorrence of the English name and power', while at the other extreme the earl of Clare wrote of a 'rooted and hereditary hatred of the British name and nation'.[25] The speed with which so many of the apparently apolitical lower classes of 1790 came to join the revolutionary underground army of 1796–8 is best explained by the deep fissures in Irish society. Anti-English, anti-protestant and anti-authority sentiments were latent in the eighteenth century. The crises of the 1790s did not so much create as activate them. Whether a concerted policy of conciliation, like that pursued by the British government (but sabotaged by the ascendancy) in

1791–3, could ever have created a more integrated polity and society must remain a moot point. Starting from different premises the United Irishmen also attempted to integrate Ireland's various sects into a single nation: 'To make all Irishmen citizens; – all citizens Irishmen'.[26] But this comparatively sophisticated secularism had only limited impact. More persuasive for its popular audience was the invocation of nationalist symbolism: 'Hibernia's harp new strung', the wearing of green ribbons and so on. Although only a minor part of radical ideology, the effectiveness of emotive nationalism as propaganda meant that it played a crucial role in mobilising popular support.

If the United Irishmen were nationalists they were never chauvinist or parochial. They were, on the contrary, francophiles and heirs to a cosmopolitan Enlightenment. Activists drawing upon the fashionable ideas of the age rather than *philosophes* in their own right, the Irish radicals were quintessential eighteenth-century men and women. Often deists, like Tone, or like Arthur O'Connor, who 'discarded revealed religion' while at university in the 1780s,[27] they believed that 'superstition' was in retreat before the relentless march of 'reason'. They had faith in the moral perfectibility of man, the progress of knowledge and the malleability of civil society. As Samuel Barber, presbyterian minister and United Irishman, predicted, 'Before science sooner or later all tyranny will fall'.[28] We know that another presbyterian minister and radical, William Steele Dickson, read Montesqieu, while Lord Edward Fitzgerald reputedly subscribed to the philosophy of Rousseau.[29] An acquaintance with the work of the *philosophes* would have familiarised certain United Irishmen with specific political ideas such as the concept of popular sovereignty, but perhaps the importance of the Enlightenment lay at a more general level. Optimism reigned. Radicals were convinced that they were moving forward in step with history. 'The great change' confidently anticipated, was 'as natural a consequence of the present improved state of the human mind, as light is the natural consequence of the sun's appearance above the horizon'.[30]

To contemporaries it appeared that their optimism had been borne out by the American experience. The American revolution, 'the cause of all mankind', registered a strong impact in Ireland, especially in Ulster. For more than fifty years the colonies had been the destination of successive waves of Ulster presbyterians – the 'Scots-Irish' of American history.[31] Family connections then reinforced the interest and sympathy with which news of the revolt across the Atlantic was received. As important as the diffusion of democratic ideas at the time of the revolution was the power of what Palmer has called 'the myth of America' after it.[32] The new republic, with its written constitution, religious toleration and separation of church and state, was idealised. Franklin and Washington, heroes of the revolution, invariably featured in toasts at reform banquets, on banners at celebrations or even, in Belfast, on signs hung in the streets. One of the *Northern Star*'s correspondents contrasting rent, tax and tithe-ridden Ireland with an America blessed by 'the mildest and most rational system of government in the universe,' advised his readers to emigrate. A handbill distributed by the United Irishmen extolled the republic 'where they have no avaricious farmers of revenue . . . where every persuasion pays to his own peace-making clergy – and all are in harmony'.[33] America, it seemed to radicals in the nineties, was an experiment which was working, a model worth emulating.[34]

At the time the American war had direct repercussions: the emergence of Volunteering. The political complexion of Volunteering varied from locality to locality, a heterogeneity which is underlined by the fact that while the first, Belfast society of United Irishmen grew directly out of existing Volunteer structures and several members of the first Dublin society were veterans of the campaigns of the 1780s, Volunteer veterans in other areas formed the nucleus of loyalist Yeomanry corps and even Orange clubs after 1795. But, for all its diversity, in those areas, particularly Belfast and east Ulster, where the United Irishmen were thickest on the ground in the nineties, the Volunteer episode represented a formative political experience. In practical terms the reformers of 1779–84 discovered the power (and limits) of extra-parliamentary agitation, the effectiveness of the press, of popularly elected conventions and, not least, of the possibility of intimidating the legislature by the threat of force. At an ideological level Volunteering provided a civic education. The armed citizen stood at the centre of the classical republican tradition. A civil right and a public duty, the bearing of arms was the badge of a free man. The right to bear arms, secured by the constitution of the new American republic, epitomised the Jeffersonian vision of a sturdy, self-reliant and virtuous citizenry. In Grattan's phrase the Volunteers were the 'armed property of the nation'. In the eyes of radicals like Drennan or Steele Dickson, they were the nation's armed virtue.

Perceptions of America in the late eighteenth century tended to vindicate Enlightenment ideas. In Ireland these ideas were also transmitted through the medium of freemasonry. Masonry was non-denominational in character and rationalistic in tone. Its egalitarian principles and deistic God – the Grand Architect of the Universe – sat comfortably with the spirit of the age. Several well-known American and French revolutionaries and *philosophes* were masons. Benjamin Franklin, indeed, was the first Grand Master of Pennsylvania. Although the craft was officially apolitical, historians have generally assumed a connection between masonry and revolution in this period. It has even been suggested that these great political upheavals cannot be understood apart from 'the masonic milieu'.[35] During the 1790s a number of royalist writers, the Abbé Barruel, his English translator, Robert Clifford and an Edinburgh professor, John Robison, approaching the subject from a less detatched perspective, attributed revolution in France and treason in Ireland to masonic conspiracy.[36] While once again the available evidence will not uphold a conspiracy theory, the politics of masonry were certainly 'advanced'. The exception to the rule was the 'respectable' English craft. However, Irish masons, by virtue of their political activism, had a closer affinity with their American and continental brethren. In the 1780s many masons were enthusiastic Volunteers and in the 1790s some sort of interaction between freemasonry and radicalism is indisputable. During the second half of the decade lodges were often used as 'fronts' for revolutionary cells. This practice did not escape the notice of the authorities and in 1797 the Grand Master was asked to curtail the activities of those who sought to use the craft as a 'political engine'.[37] Curiously, this interaction has not been investigated by historians. In the case of Crossle and Lepper's official history of the Grand Lodge (1925) this is understandable. For them the unmasonic political entanglements of the period represent a regrettable aberration.[38] The near silence of other historians is less explicable. One possible reason for neglect, that more detailed treatment would merely be an exercise in 'turning the footnotes of history into pages of text', is not tenable. Freemasonry was an important, and in Ulster a pervasive, eighteenth-century social and intellectual phenomenon. It inspired United Irish organisational procedures and conditioned United Irish ideology.

The list of masons involved in the reform movement, the Catholic Committee and the United Irishmen is long and striking. Dr James Reynolds, the United Irishman who orchestrated the craft's most public political intervention in the winter of 1792–3 (and was consequently summoned before a lords secret committee), began his career in politics ten years earlier as a Volunteer and reformer. William Todd Jones, the pro-catholic pamphleteer, was another prominent Volunteer, reformer and mason. The fact that these men were masons, whose credo embraced 'fraternity', is not, it has been argued, incidental.[39] However, the relationship between politics and masonry is neither clear, direct nor uniform. Like Volunteer companies the political profile of individual lodges varied from place to place. The notorious Major Sirr was a mason and the craft served as a model for the early Orange Order.[40] Still, men like Reynolds, Jones or Thomas McCabe, a founding member of the United Irishmen and opponent of the slave trade[41] were more typical of the political tendency of Irish masonry.

One of the difficulties of demonstrating that tendency is the paucity of eighteenth-century masonic records – mainly membership lists for individual lodges and a frustratingly bald set of Grand Lodge minutes. Moreover, because the craft was officially apolitical, for most of the time it remained resolutely mute on political questions. This pattern was visibly disrupted by the public participation of several Ulster lodges in the parliamentary reform agitation of 1792–3. The support which these lodges gave reform, together with the numerous radicals identifiable as masons, provides a strong hint about the ideological complexion of the craft. In addition to Reynolds, Jones and McCabe, other known masons include Henry Haslett, William Tennant and William McCleary, all, like McCabe, among the 'founding fathers' of the first Belfast society of United Irishmen; Dr W. J. MacNevin of the Catholic Committee and United Irishmen; Napper Tandy's brother George, and his son, James; Matthew Dowling, John Stockdale and Hamilton Rowan of the Dublin Society; Peter Cooney, editor of the opposition *Morning Post*, and Randal McAllister, proprietor of the *National Evening Star*; Samuel Kennedy, printer of the *Northern Star*, and William Orr, the United Irishmen's first 'martyr'.[42]

Irish masonry demonstrated its potential political muscle through its role in the reform campaign. Significantly, the lodges concerned were based in Ulster, the heartland of the United Irishmen. Ulster was also the region where masonry was strongest. In an intriguing reference made in 1795, Lord Abercorn called it 'the rock of the north'.[43] The strength of the craft there added to the impact of its public intervention. During December, 1792, and January, 1793, lodges in counties Derry, Antrim, Down and Tyrone held meetings to discuss parliamentary reform, almost all of which passed resolutions and issued declarations in favour of political change. These were then inserted in the *Belfast Newsletter* and *Northern Star*.[44] More controversially, the Tyrone masons, Reynolds and his fellow United Irishmen, William Richardson and Dr James Caldwell, organised a county convention. Forbidden by craft rules as they were from engaging in political activities, the thirty delegates, representing 1,532 of their brethren, neatly circumvented the restriction by dissolving the meeting and reconvening as 'masonic citizens'. This subterfuge did not, however, mollify the Grand lodge in Dublin, which promptly issued a circular instructing all lodges to desist from political discussions.[45] The statement produced by this meeting amounts to a concise formulation of the radical position in the early 1790s:

we view with pleasure the rapid progress of liberty in France, supported by reason and philosophy, and founded on the grand principles of our institution: whilst we glory in the reflection that our illustrious Brother Washington and the masons of America were the saviours of their country, and the first founders of the Temple of Liberty – are we to see Irish Masons made the tools of corruption? We are no advocates for passive obedience and non-resistance, fealty to our sovereign does not require us to support corruption.

The address goes on condemn unjust taxation – hearth money – the penal code, the game laws, places and pensions.[46]

In contrast to their neglect of masonry, historians have drawn attention to the ideological impact of presbyterianism upon Irish radicalism. A. T. Q. Stewart describes the United Irish movement as a 'presbyterian initiative'.[47] A correlation between religious dissent and political radicalism in seventeenth and eighteenth-century Britain and Ireland has long attained the status of an historical truism.[48] There are obvious reasons for this: the number of radical publicists who were dissenters – Burgh, Priestley, Price the Quaker-educated Tom Paine – and the often militantly protestant flavour of radical ideas. Protestant insistence upon the liberty (and responsibility) of the individual conscience, for example, has been commonly regarded as a theological expression of the radical commitment to the political liberties of the citizen. Put slightly differently, opposition to spiritual authoritarianism, whether in the guise of popery or prelacy, translated into opposition to civil or political authoritarianism. At a practical level dissenters had a vested interest in political reforms which would remove the civil disabilities to which they were subjected. Predictably such practical considerations reacted with singular force upon Ulster's presbyterians. Their concentration in the north-eastern corner of the island (and the links with their lowland Scottish cousins) fostered a sense of identity, sustained by the unique self-governing structure of their church and defined, in part, *against* the Anglo-Irish anglican elite, ruling from Dublin. The most recent historian of Ulster presbyterianism describes this eighteenth-century community as 'a virtual nation within a nation', 'a distinct political society'.[49] In a real sense the northern United Irishmen emerged out of that close-knit community, in tandem with the Dublin Society which drew on a different tradition of urban radicalism. While the influence of presbyterianism, exemplified by the role of ministers and church elders, and by the ideological targets and priorities of the movement (bishops were attacked as often as pensioners and placemen) must be acknowledged, Stewart provides a useful antidote when he argues that 'it is simply not true that the presbyterians *as a body* held radical opinions between 1790 and 1800'.[50] However, Stewart's insistence that 'throughout the whole period, the majority of ministers in the

General Synod of Ulster was conservative,' is questionable. This was the synod which condemned the slave trade in 1792, which welcomed reform, and which opposed the war in 1793.

Whilst recognising the existence of political divisions in the community – over the catholic question for instance – sentiments like those expressed by the synod nonetheless seemed to flow almost naturally from the history, structure and theology of Ulster presbyterianism. Certainly this was the impression of contemporaries. Emmet thought presbyterians were 'almost republicans from religion',[51] a perception shared by more hostile observers. 'It has been the cant of the greater part of the century,' complained a presbyterian 'friend to civil and religious liberty', in 1795, 'even with the governing powers, to tax dissenters with disaffection to the government; and the nature of their religion with a tendency to republican opinions'.[52] Of course at this juncture the meaning of the word 'republicanism' is in transition. By the early 1790s it could refer either to the civic virtues of 'classical republicanism' – public duty and a repudiation of luxury, vice and corruption – or to a non-monarchical system of government on the Jacobin model. Clearly the first meaning is the sense in which Drennan usually used the word, and these austere, upright values have an obvious affinity with the dour, industrious image so often attributed to the northern dissenters.

The 'friend to civil and religious liberty' also outlined the organisational structure of presbyterianism:

> The constitutional structure of the Synod of Ulster is of the most popular nature, as it consists of clergy elected by the people themselves, and double the number of lay-elders. Each of the two delegated elders is vested with the same powers as their clergymen, have a negative and affirmative on every proceeding which does not merely concern funds of the clergy and their widows. In a body so freely constituted and so purely representative, no measure can be carried against the interests of the laity unless they suffer it through their own neglect.

'Presbyterianism', in fact, denotes a system of church government conducted by meetings of ministers and elders elected by their presbyteries (congregations) and by annual general assembly. It is not hard to see why such manifestly democratic practices earned the approbation of radicals or the suspicion of conservatives: these participatory structures underlined doctrinal antipathy to hierarchy.

The transmutation of religious theology into political ideology may be a difficult process to follow or demonstrate, but the democratic programme of the United Irishmen was certainly indebted to the presbyterian commitment to 'civil and religious liberty', and to its rejection *in principle* of papal and episcopal authority. Perhaps, too, United Irish contractarian rhetoric owed as much to the Scottish covenanting tradition as to Locke.[53] The Scottish connection may also have exerted influence in other ways. A majority of ministers in the eighteenth century were trained at the university of Glasgow, an intellectual centre of the Scottish Enlightenment.[54] There many of them would have imbibed the contractarian theories and other basic assumptions upon which the radical argument was constructed.

If Ulster presbyterianism by virtue of its structure and doctrine was, in Elliott's phrase, 'inherently radical', it was the concrete political experience of this community which propelled it into the arena of political action. The sense of identity derived from self-government also drew strength from the sense of alienation from an anglican parliament and administration. The sacramental test act (1704–80) had effectively excluded dissenters from public office and the corporations (though not parliament) for most of the century. The validity of marriages performed by presbyterian ministers were not recognised by law. And the natural resentment aroused by these disabilities was deepened by the presbyterian conviction that such treatment was scant reward for the decisive role which they had played in the defeat of James II. Nor was this perceived ingratitude quickly forgotten. In 1792 a presbyterian writing in the *Northern Star* complained of his co-religionists 'having suffered . . . severely suffered for many years, under the galling restraints of a proud Ascendancy'.[55] These festering discontents ensured that presbyterians were in the vanguard of the challenge to the ascendancy which developed in the closing decades of the century. As we have seen, in the 1770s and 1780s ministers like Steele Dickson and Samuel Barber were leading Volunteers. Dickson, Barber and the Reverend Thomas Ledlie Birch were also active in the 1790 county Down election, canvassing for the successful reform candidate, Robert Stewart (later Lord Castlereagh). Stewart's election agent was Samuel Neilson, a church elder. The three ministers and Neilson all later joined the United Irishmen. Presbyterian political activism in the eighteenth century culminated in the United Irishmen. It is a measure of the alienation of certain sections of that community that it was capable of lending substantial support to a mass revolutionary movement and that at least twenty ministers were eventually implicated in rebellion.

In conclusion it may have been noticed that no reference has been made here to the various sects and sub-divisions so characteristic of Ulster presbyterianism in this period. It has been claimed that the most radical dissenters were the latitudinarian 'New Lights'; yet about half of the twenty ministers known to have been involved in revolutionary politics were 'Old Lights' or orthodox. If a meaningful correlation did exist between theological quarrels and political alignments it still awaits investigation and demonstration.[56]

Presbyterian doctrine and experience, the secular cult of freemasonry, Volunteering, the American revolution, Enlightenment cosmopolitanism and the British whig-radical and 'classical republican' traditions, crystallised in the 'revolution principles' of 1688 and given a 'colonial nationalist' inflection by Anglo-Ireland: these were some of the sources which shaped United Irish ideology. From the variety and complexity of such political roots it is clear that the concept of 'Irish Jacobins' is simplistic. Nevertheless the French revolution did act as a catalyst.

II IRELAND AND THE FRENCH REVOLUTION: POPULAR MOBILISATION AND REFORM

The French revolution changed the rhetoric of Irish politics. Old words were stretched into new meanings. 'Liberty' and 'rights' now carried a universalist as well as a specific historical and constitutional resonance. 'Republicanism' began to assume its modern connotations. 'Aristocrats', 'democrats' and 'levellers' crowded the vocabulary of political invective. The revolution stimulated public debate and provided a model, an image, around which ideas drawn from so many different sources fused into a comparatively coherent ideology. It also acted as a radicalising agent. By overthrowing the mightiest, most populous *ancien regime* in Europe, the revolution demonstrated the power of political action, injecting reformers everywhere with fresh confidence. Like their counterparts in England, Scotland and across the continent, Irish radicals were aware that they lived in an 'age of revolution', of living at an historic moment when almost anything seemed possible. The startling and welcome news from France reinvigorated radical ideology and enlivened political activity.

At the popular level the implications of the revolution were not immediately obvious nor its impact instantaneous. In Ireland the first anniversary of the fall of the Bastille passed unnoticed.[57] Public opinion was initially stirred in a dramatic way by the debate which the revolution provoked between Edmund Burke and Thomas Paine. Paine's *Rights of Man* is a passionate defence of the French revolution written, with his audience clearly in mind, in simple, forceful prose,[58] a fierce egalitarian polemic which attacked the *ancien regime* on every flank. In it he denounced the criminal code, the game laws and primogeniture, derided titles as 'nicknames' and 'gibberish', describes monarchy as a 'sinecure' and subjects the 'corrupt' aristocracy to a relentless verbal battering.[59] Above all the *Rights of Man* caught and voiced the mood of the time. 'From what we now see,' wrote Paine, 'nothing of reform in the political world ought to be held impossible. It is an age of revolutions, in which everything may be looked for'.[60] The book's influence was enormous. Paine was elected an honorary member of the Dublin Society of United Irishmen, and sometimes his language as well as his ideas were borrowed by his admirers. Compare, for example, his phrase about the 'aristocracy as a kind of fungus growing out of the corruption of society', with Thomas Russell's description of that class as 'fungus productions who grow out of a diseased state of society'.[61] Remarking on the Burke-Paine debate, Tone observed, 'This controversy, and the gigantic event which gave rise to it, changed in an instant the politics of Ireland . . . in a little time the French revolution became the test of every man's political creed and the nation was fairly divided into two great parties, the aristocrats and the democrats (epithets borrowed from France)'.[62]

The attractions of the revolution in defence of which Paine wrote, stemmed from the perception that it had swept away a range of archaic, unjust privileges. In particular, Irish dissenters must have welcomed the disestablishment of the church and both catholics and dissenters the abolition of tithes. But the revolution was looked to as more than example or model. Across Europe and beyond, radicals thought of themselves as engaged in an international revolution. One club in Belfast actually called itself the 'Irish Jacobins'. As the *Northern Star* proclaimed, 'it is not merely the fate of France that is depending, it is that of THE WORLD'.[63] And Irish francophiles did not confine themselves to rhetoric. In the spring of 1792 subscriptions in support of the French war effort were raised at Belfast, Armagh, Limavady – where the local masonic lodge contributed – Coleraine, which raised £600 and Newry, which raised £300. From Newry a local catholic activist, Hugh O'Hanlon, sailed for France with his town's gift to the National Assembly.[64]

The early 1790s witnessed a resurgence of political activity which may be seen as part of a spontaneous popular response to the momentous events in France. However, the increasing politicisation of Irish society also owed a great deal to the determined efforts of francophile radicals to educate and mobilise public opinion. In the spring of 1791 the 'Whigs of the capital' commissioned a cheap edition of the *Rights of Man* which they disseminated 'through the kingdom'. Another twelve editions came off the Dublin presses that year. At least four newspapers, including virtually every issue of the *Hibernian Journal* between 8 April and 3 June, 1791, carried lengthy extracts. The United Irishmen distributed huge quantities of Paine's book *gratis*. Copies were left at 'roadsides and doorsteps' and they may even, like the Scottish radicals, have produced a Gaelic language translation.[65]

Newspapers, such as the *Northern Star* and the *Cork Gazette*, along with handbills and pamphlets, disseminated by the tens of thousands, often, like Paine's book, at cost price or free, played an important role in raising levels of political awareness. The *Northern Star*, in particular, set the pace and tone. The second issue depicted France as 'a Temple of universal liberty', and every issue thereafter carried extensive coverage of French affairs. After the republican victory at Valmy subscribers were even circularised with an 'account of the termination of the Duke of Brunswick's career' printed on a separate sheet.[66] Popular reaction to Valmy, notably in Ulster, indicates that the paper's francophilia was in fact in step with public opinion. In Dublin and in towns and villages throughout the north, Volunteer corps held celebratory marches, windows were illuminated and at Muckamore an effigy of Brunswick was burned.[67] A letter to the *Star* offers a glimpse of how the revolution operated as an agent of popular politicisation. Drawing attention to the increasing attachment to the 'principles of freedom . . . among all ranks, even among country peasants, whose occupations in life it might be supposed, would in great measure detach them from such speculations', the letter recounts the proceedings of a Bastille Day meeting in a small Antrim village. The young men present, 'acquitted themselves in a manner that would have done honour to refined life, and given credit to more liberal education. A number of pieces from your paper and other publications, selected for that occasion, were pronounced with all the beauties of good emphasis, and elegant delivery . . . '[68]

Inspiring and encouraging radicals, reawakening lower-class catholic hopes of French intervention and democratising public opinion, to conservatives the revolution, the source of pernicious 'levelling principles', represented a threat and a warning. By challenging the fundamental assumptions upon which established order everywhere rested, the revolution polarised and 'raised the stakes' of political conflict. 'Between these two extremes' of Burke and Paine, wrote Plowden, 'no middle post was tenable.'[69] The French revolution, never far from the minds of contemporaries, formed the background against which the catholic and reform questions of 1791–3 were fought out.

The formation and rapid spread of the United Irish movement at the end of 1791 can be explained by domestic political developments, principally the opportunities for renewed extra-parliamentary agitation opened up by the revival of the catholic question. But both the United Irishmen and the Catholic Committee were also reacting to a novel situation: a mood of expectation, of imminent change, created by the French revolution. Nowhere is the impact of the revolution more visible than in the francophilia of the United Irishmen. On 14 July, 1791, the more politically advanced Volunteer corps – out of which the United Irishmen formed – held Bastille Day commemorations in Dublin, Belfast, and the Ulster provincial towns of Derry, Newry, Banbridge, Downpatrick, Randalstown and Ballymoney.[70] The first society was founded in Belfast in October that year, the next a few weeks later in Dublin. Over the coming months smaller provincial clubs proliferated. In the literature the United Irishmen in the early years are associated primarily with Dublin, Belfast and its hinterland.[71] These were and remained the core areas, but the number of new reform clubs established beyond these centres illustrates the speed and scope of political change. United Irish societies can be identified clustered around Belfast at Sixmile Water, Lisburn, Templepatrick, Saintfield, Doagh, Randalstown and Muckamore. Other Ulster clubs were set up at Newry (called the 'Union Society'), Coleraine, Armagh City and, possibly, Rostrevor. In the south there is evidence of the United Irishmen organising at Ardee, county Louth, Gorey, county Wexford, Nenagh, Tullamore and Clonmell, county Tipperary, Limerick, Cork and Navan, county Meath.[72] Presumably there were more. As early as 6 January, 1792, the *Hibernian Journal* reported 'many patriotic societies now firmly established in the principal towns of every county not under immediate ministerial influence'. Dublin and presbyterian Antrim and Down acted as the organising centres, but the movement had, from the outset, a genuinely national dimension.

Although the radicals always considered catholic relief as subsidiary to reform, in practice they had to await the end of the extra-parliamentary phase of the catholic campaign in early December, 1792, before they could move onto the centre of the political stage. The parliamentary reform campaign which continued into the spring of 1793 was similar to the catholic one in two important respects: in its popular character and in its militant tone. Like the catholics the United Irishmen argued that the franchise would reinforce security of tenure. Parliamentary reform was linked to a whole range of concrete social benefits which would supposedly follow.

Eighteenth-century reformers attributed immense importance to parliament. As the United Irishmen declared, 'with a parliament thus reformed, everything is easy; without it, nothing can be done'.[73] Significantly, what the United Irishmen claimed they wanted to do had a distinct social-radical flavour. In 1798 Thomas Emmet was asked by a lords committee which grievances he thought would be removed by a reformed legislature. He replied, 'in the first place, it would cause a complete abolition of tithes: in the next, by giving the common people an increased value in the democracy, it would better their situation and make them more respected by their superiors; the condition of the poor would be ameliorated; and what is perhaps of more consequence than all the rest, a system of national education would be established'.[74] While Emmet does not make clear the mechanism whereby parliamentary reform would translate into social improvement, the sentiments he expresses are revealing. On other occasions the linkage was more clearly articulated. Universal manhood suffrage, the theory ran, would give extra political clout to 'the people', and compel their parliamentary representatives to be more responsive to public opinion. For example, a reformed parliament would respond to agrarian unrest with enquiry into, and redress of, the underlying grievances, 'instead of making laws to punish the perpetrators with death'.[75] The unreformed parliament, moreover, because it was managed by patronage, was enormously expensive. Democratic government on the other hand, having no need to fund placemen or pensioners, was inherently cheaper. America, boasted Paine, was run at a fortieth of the cost of England. The benefits of frugal government, it was argued, would then filter down to the common man in the form of tax reductions.[76]

Champions of 'the people', the United Irishmen launched a furious attack upon 'aristocracy'. Aristocrats were men 'who wish[ed] the bulk of the nation to be kept down for the partial advantage of a few privileged individuals'. 'The spirit of many of our laws is aristocratic,' they announced, 'and by no means calculated for the protection of the poor'. Not for nothing were the game laws a frequent radical target.[77] Faddishness aside – the Dublin Society once quarrelled for 'some hours' over the addition of 'Esqr' to Rowan's name in a public address[78] – anti-aristocratic rhetoric was serious in intent and important in implication. The radical populism which would later characterise the movement is already evident in some of its early manifestos. By 1792 it is clear that not all United Irishmen were 'moderates' or solely 'political' reformers.

The social-radical dimension of United Irish propaganda appealed directly to a popular constituency. But politicisation involved more than inundating the lower classes with broadsheets and pamphlets. It was dynamic. Politicisation meant mobilisation, lower-class engagement in, and direct experience of, politics. The first major popular intersection with politics occurred with the catholic agitation, the second with the campaign for parliamentary reform. Political activity in the latter case took the form of Volunteering, petitioning, public meetings and the elections of delegates to the Ulster reform convention at Dungannon in February, 1793. A reformed legislature, the radicals believed, would counteract 'English influence', reflect public opinion, see off the whole costly phalanx of social parasites, the placemen and pensioners, and open the way to social justice and economic prosperity. Unfortunately parliament could not be depended upon to reform itself. To expect as much was as naive as 'expecting a man to cut off a rotten limb himself'.[79] It had to be reformed from without. Extra-parliamentary protest had been a feature of British politics since Wilkes, and in Ireland since the politicisation of the Volunteers at the end of the 1770s, at the latest. The strategy pursued by reform-minded Volunteers in the 1770s and early 1780s was threefold: the mobilisation of public opinion by means of public meetings and the press, the expression of the public 'will' thus mobilised in a national reform convention and the implicit threat of force – by armed Volunteers – if that will were ignored. This strategy was revived by the United Irishmen, many of whom, of course, had been active in the 1780s and who were still Volunteers in 1792. By then, however, the impact of the French revolution had dramatically altered the political landscape.

The new radical assertiveness was met by a pronounced hardening of the conservative position. Echoing Burke, the British-style 'mixed' constitution was hailed as a unique achievement, not to be tampered with lightly. All attempts at constitutional innovation were now viewed as dangerous and, potentially, as a prelude to more sweeping, destructive changes based on 'levelling principles'. In 1794 Sir Hercules Langhrise opposed a reform bill 'upon the fatal warning of France'.[80] Nor were such fears groundless. Radical analysis located parliament at the centre of the social system and equated its reform with a transformation of society. Reform therefore was not merely a question of extending the franchise, regulating electoral procedures and neutralising patronage. For contemporaries it raised the fundamental issue of the distribution of power. Reform was seen by advocate and opponent alike as the precursor of much greater, social, change. Thus the political excitement and tension generated by the campaign.

Proposals for a reform of representation were adopted at a Volunteer rally in Belfast on 14 July 1791. This measure was then tirelessly promoted through meetings, resolutions, declarations and in the pages of the United Irish newspaper, the *Northern Star*. The issue was then taken up by others, not directly under United Irish control. The independent press – the *Cork Gazette*, the *Dublin Evening Post* and the *Morning Post* for instance – supported reform. A sizable number of masonic lodges and presbyteries in Ulster also joined the campaign. Above all the political climate was electrified by a massive Volunteer resurgence. By any standards an impressive feat of political mobilisation, the reform movement assumed its full force from mid-December, 1792, after the agitational phase of the catholic campaign had ended.

The focus and culmination of this eruption of political activity was to be an Ulster reform convention, at Dungannon – not coincidentally the site of the Volunteer Convention in 1782 – to be followed by a national convention at Athlone. Conventions were first proposed in 1774 by the influential British radical, James Burgh. With their elected delegates and clear implication of popular sovereignty, conventions were arguably more representative, alternative, parliaments and became a standard weapon in the late eighteenth-century radical armoury.[81] The convention strategy was employed by the Irish Volunteers in 1782–4, on three occasions by the Scottish reform movement in 1792–3, by the Catholic Committee and now by the United Irishmen. The elections for the Dungannon convention on 15–17 February, were held in various parts of the province in early 1793. If the geography of representation was somewhat patchy, the democratic credentials of the assembly were established by the presence of 'moderate' voices dissenting from the United Irish platform. After two days debate and discussion the convention issued a declaration calling for parliamentary reform.

From the standpoint of legally constituted authority the mere act of calling a convention represented a challenge to the sovereignty of parliament. This was one reason why the Catholic Convention drew so much fire. It was part of the rationale too, behind the convention act (April, 1793), prohibiting future such assemblies. An even more direct challenge to authority was offered by the Volunteers. With the re-opening of the catholic question and the mood of political expectancy created by the French revolution the Volunteers, especially but not exclusively in the north, began to revive. The revival had an explicitly political character. In Dublin in December, 1792, a new 'National Volunteers' company was formed with regalia modelled on the French National Guard. This company, a creation of the United Irishmen, reportedly pledged 'not [to] lay down their arms until they have obtained the privileges desired by the Roman Catholics and a reform of parliament'.[82] A pro-reform masonic gathering in Tyrone announced, 'let every lodge in the land become a company of citizen soldiers – let every Volunteer company become a lodge of masons'.[83] Like the freemasons, however, the Volunteers were not unanimous in their politics. One Volunteer asked why he armed replied, '"is it not time to arm, when three million of our fellow subjects are in chains?"' Another of the same corps, asked the same question, answered that he would never 'suffer Ireland to become a

popish country'.[84] Such confusion notwithstanding, viewed from Dublin
Castle the Volunteer revival appeared ominous. Throughout the winter
of 1792–3 reports circulated of large quantities of arms being imported
from England to Ulster. The prominent Dublin United Irishman and iron
founder, Henry Jackson, was said to have received orders for cannon from
fellow Unitedman and 'National Volunteer', Hamilton Rowan, and from
the north. The reports were probably exaggerated, but at least some arms
were intercepted *en route* from Liverpool to Coleraine.[85] The Castle took
these developments so seriously, in fact, that they repeatedly requested the
British government to station a frigate or 'naval force', 'at Belfast with
a view to overawe that town and to preventing assistance from a foreign
power'.[86] With Samuel Neilson in Belfast asking 'when do we begin? Do
we refuse hearth money or tithes first?'[87] and the administration appealing
for military reinforcements, the storm clouds gathered by the catholic
agitation had clearly not dispersed; nor were they quite ready to burst.
The National Volunteers were swiftly – and effortlessly – suppressed by
government proclamation on 12 December, 1792. The projected national
convention at Athlone had to be abandoned under the new convention act
and eventually, in the spring of 1793, the Volunteer movement as a whole
was forced to disband.

The Castle responded to the radical challenge with repressive legislation
and legal harassment. Oliver Bond, Simon Butler, Napper Tandy, Hamilton
Rowan, Dr Drennan and the proprietors of the *Northern Star* all found themselves in court between 1792 and 1794. The Society of United Irishmen
was itself finally outlawed in May, 1794. This hardline stance was in tune
with the growing mood of reaction evident elsewhere in the British Isles.
Pitt's so-called 'reign of terror', the rise of 'patriotic' loyalist associations
in England and the savage judicial onslaught upon the Scottish radicals
were all symptoms of the new mood. Arguably, by closing off most open
means of protest this wave of repression forced radicalism 'underground';
it invited, as it were, conspiratorial and revolutionary strategies. A shift
something like this can be detected between 1793 and 1795. However, by
attributing the emergence of revolutionary republicanism to the operation
of official repression, historians implicitly underestimate the militancy and
radicalism of the United Irishmen in the early years. It should be clear from
the confrontational rhetoric and strategy adopted in 1792–3 that figures
such as John Sheares, Neilson or Tone did not require much of a push
from government to prompt the 'transformation' of their organisation
into a revolutionary movement. Repression may have accelerated the
revolutionary process, but it did not cause it.[88] Moreover, the popular
nature of the reform campaign, evident from the content and quantity of

propagandist literature and the Volunteer revival, denoted a politicisation of the common man, in this instance in Ulster, which prepared the way for the creation of the mass base upon which that revolutionary movement was built. The continuities between the first and second parts of the decade, in other words, are as important as the contrasts.

5 The Rise of the Defenders, 1793–5

The year 1794 has been characterised as a lull in the overcrowded history of the 1790s.[1] The reason is obvious. Coming after the catholic and reform campaigns of 1791–3 and before the dramatic sequence of events which led from Fitzwilliam's dismissal in 1795 to rebellion in 1798, this year has indeed an appearance of 'comparative calm'. Taking into account the attendance figures at meetings of the Dublin Society of United Irishmen which began to decline in April 1793, the seeming fall-off in political activity – the 'lull' – might even be extended to eighteen months. In fact those eighteen months were formative in the development of the revolutionary movement. Political activity did not diminish, rather it was rerouted into clandestine channels. For example, almost all of the evidence relating to the Philanthropic Society, a major component of Dublin's political underground before it merged into the United Irish movement, comes from 1794. In both Ulster and Dublin the United Irishmen began organising as a secret society late that year. If this decade is approached through the history of the Defenders, moreover, the notion of a lull becomes even less tenable. A major Defender riot occurred in Cavan in May, 1794, and in August Westmeath magistrates met to discuss 'the late violences' in the county.[2] In the arena of popular direct action there was no ceasefire.

Such evidence of continuing Defender unrest has so far failed to dislodge the idea of an hiatus before Fitzwilliam. Perhaps this is because the standard accounts of the 1790s have proceeded from the twin perspective of high politics and the rise of the United Irishmen: the basic narrative history of the Defenders has still to be written. In one respect this omission is surprising. A glance at any Irish newspaper over this decade or at, say, Sir Richard Musgrave's *Memoirs of the different rebellions in Ireland* (1801), immediately confirms the Defenders' contemporary impact. Yet it is only in recent years that historians have begun to glimpse their significance – to the politics of the period and as Ireland's first 'associational', 'proactive' movement.[3] Before the United Irishmen began to build a mass-based revolutionary organisation in the later nineties – a mass-base largely consisting of Defender lodges integrated into the new paramilitary structure – Defenderism represented the principal organisational expression of popular disaffection. Lecky realised this, but he did not follow through the insight.[4] No discussion of popular politics, therefore, can reasonably neglect the development of Defenderism.

I 'BEAT[ING] THE PEOPLE INTO ANOTHER OPINION': THE ASCENDANCY BACKLASH

The rise of the Defenders in this period can be read as the popular response to the application of Draconian law and order measures, ranging from the increased use of regular troops to quell disturbances to the (certainly perceived) partiality of the magistrates and courts. At one level the Defenders' story over 1793 to 1795, is the story of the repercussions of a tough 'security policy', and any attempt to explain their 'rise' must engage with the more general history of the time. But that 'rise' was not simply a mater of increasing numbers and greater geographical spread. In these years Defenderism became more ideologically complex, organisationally sophisticated and better led. A middle-class leadership emerged in Ulster. A mass revolutionary movement began to take shape.

The Defender movement expanded and politicised during 1792 as it interacted with the catholic agitation conducted at parish level. One indication of these developments was the extension of Defender activity, mainly arms raids, from Armagh along the Ulster border counties into Louth and Meath. Another was the increasing scale of violence perpetrated both by the Defenders and by the authorities. The number of capital convictions handed down at the spring assizes in 1793 was unprecedented. The aggressiveness of the Defenders and the harshness of ascendancy repression were conditioned by the crisis atmosphere generated by the catholic and reform campaigns, and, from the spring, by war with France. The former were inspired by expectations of catholic 'victory', even a reversal of the land settlement, and by the prospect of French aid; the latter felt threatened by the possibility of French intervention and by a resurgent catholic community. Protestants also felt abandoned by Britain. During 1792 the Defenders were said to have convened 'little parliaments . . . (for so they did name themselves),' and to have asserted that they would soon 'have their own again'. In February 1793, during the parliamentary debates on catholic relief, Dr Duigenan complained that:

the catholics of the lower ranks are at this moment assembled in large bodies, with arms in their hands, breaking into, robbing and burning the homes of the peaceable protestant inhabitants of the counties of Louth, Monaghan, Cavan and Meath, and even in the county of Dublin; making public declarations that they will not suffer any protestant to reside within these counties, or in the kingdom, and the contagion is spreading through the nation.[5]

Duigenan, a protestant 'ultra', had an interest, in the context of these debates, in stressing catholic disloyalty. Nevertheless his speech did voice real protestant fears, and the reality of the situation which it described is corroborated by other evidence. Irish society had become tense and polarised. Extremism thrived. The consequent escalation in violence was first witnessed on 22 January, 1793, at Coolnahinch on the Meath-Cavan border, where thirty-eight Defenders were killed. The break-down of the comparative restraint which had hitherto governed rural unrest was then confirmed by the wave of anti-militia ballot riots which swept virtually the whole country between May and August.

The militia, established by an act which became law on 8 April, was designed as a domestic defence and peacekeeping force to replace the recently suppressed Volunteers. Volunteering had been suppressed because of its political interventions, and because even 'loyalist' corps did not come under government control. The militia was organised by county, officered by the local (protestant) gentry, and composed of (mainly catholic) conscripts, raised by ballot. The element of compulsory service provided the key grievance. When magistrates began embodying regiments in May, the persons, sometimes catholic priests, who compiled the lists for balloting, were frequently targeted by the crowd. Another major grievance stemmed from the widely-held belief that militia units would be posted overseas. Popular resistance was fierce. Artillery had to be used at the town of Bruff in county Limerick, and the county as a whole was described as in 'a state of insurrection'. In nearby Kerry on 18 June troops opened fire on some 5,000 rioters in Dingle, killing at least twelve.[6] There were serious clashes also, in Connaught, in counties Mayo, Sligo and Roscommon, at the Castlecomer intersection of Carlow, Kilkenny and Queen's county, in Wexford, Meath, Fermanagh and Down. According to Bartlett, 'in just over eight weeks as many as 230 lives had been lost . . . over five times the number of casualties sustained in the previous thirty years of agrarian disturbances in Ireland'.[7]

The underlying – as distinct from the immediate – causes of the militia riots, the form which the riots assumed and their legacy, all testify to the widening gap that was opening up between the protestant establishment and lower-class catholics. In the politically fluid 1790s alienation from the ruling elite could quickly turn to active disaffection, particularly since there existed an alternative, middle-class and radical, elite, eager and ready to exploit popular discontents. Not that the division was purely sectarian. Yet politics were conducted in terms of the challenge to, and defence of, the 'Protestant Ascendancy'. All conflict whether agrarian, class or 'national', tended to intersect at some level with the catholic question. Bartlett argues that after such factors as unfavourable economic conditions and hostility to the method of recruitment are taken into account, the unique extent and violence of the militia disturbances can only be explained by reference to the previous year's catholic campaign.[8] The populist style of the campaign had stimulated general expectations of imminent change, ranging from relief from tithes to a catholic restoration. What the catholics were in fact offered was a limited franchise, reluctantly conceded amid torrents of anti-papist rhetoric and, it seemed, the militia. There were even suspicions that the catholic gentry and clergy had made a 'deal' with the Castle, engaging 'to raise 10,000' men in exchange for 'their late emancipation'.[9] Thus the insult of a 'sell-out' was added to the injury of expectations baffled. Once mobilised the catholic masses had acquired a momentum of their own. Writing at the time of the militia riots Chief-Secretary Hobart reasoned that 'the pains which have, for these last eighteen months, been taken to persuade the people of the irresistible force of numbers, has given them such an idea of strength, that until they are actually beaten into another opinion, they will never be quiet – half the country is sworn to support the catholic cause'.

Denis Browne, MP for Mayo, placed the disturbances in a broader context, attributing them to 'the new political doctrines which have pervaded the lower classes – that . . . spirit [which] has been produced by the circulation of Paine's *Rights of Man,* of seditious newspapers, and by shopkeepers who having been in Dublin to buy goods have formed connections with some of the United Irishmen'.[10] While the United Irishmen did, in classic whig fashion, condemn the militia as yet another source of government patronage, it is doubtful that they played any significant role in directly stirring up trouble. However, Queen's county magistrates blamed 'emissaries' for provoking the unrest there, and in Tyrone George Knox referred to 'the opposition fomented by the Jacobins'.[11] It would probably prove impossible to separate the facts of radical involvement from the assertions of the paranoid official imagination, but clearly popular responses to militia balloting were sharpened by the larger political crisis. Following Whiteboy precedent, the full roster of 'agrarian' grievances – wage rates, the price of provisions, rents, tithes and taxes – were soon added to the original source of contention. What was new in the 1790s was the explicitness of the political dimension. Rioters in Westmeath told a magistrate that 'it was well Lord Westmeath was not there, as he was the person who imprisoned [the United Irishman, Simon] Butler'. More ominously, some crowds invoked the cause of the French.[12]

Since the political slogans adopted by the rioters bear all the hallmarks of Defenderism, it may be useful, at this point, to draw a distinction between 'Defenderism' and the Defenders. The first denotes a loose, pro-French, anti-ascendancy, popular ideology, the second a specific organisation. While the anti-militia rioters in Meath were almost certainly Defenders, the description of their counterparts in Limerick or Wexford as such probably only reflects the contemporary habit of blaming every outrage on 'Defenderism'.[13] The political undercurrents of the disturbances and the mass experience of armed conflict with state forces – the army – which they entailed, must, however, have facilitated the spread of the Defender organisation. For instance, Connaught, the region that witnessed the most violent opposition to the militia, emerged as a Defender stronghold in 1794–5.

The extent and violence of the riots registered a shift in popular and ascendancy attitudes. This has been read as evidence of the breakdown of the 'moral economy'. Patterns of paternalism and deference had already been eroded by the Defender tactic of raiding gentry homes. For these men at least, the 'big house' no longer held any terrors. Under the stress of polarisation and the communal antagonism generated by the catholic resurgence, gentry hegemony collapsed. An analogous development was the historically unusual position in which the catholic clergy now found itself. Whiteboys had ignored excommunication in the past just as Rightboys had resisted the payment of 'excessive' church dues. But the relationship between church and people was never under greater strain than in the summer of 1793, when priests involved in compiling lists for ballot attracted the popular wrath. Chapel doors were 'nailed-up' in Connaught, Cork and Kerry. At Athlone a priest was hanged almost to death and one newspaper reported 'attacks on the persons of the clergy in many parts'.[14] Two years later Arthur O'Connor remarked, 'ask the catholic clergy and they will tell you that their power is declined. Ask the protestant gentry from one end of the kingdom to the other, and they will tell you that the superstitious power of the catholic clergy is at an end'. The key word here is 'superstitious'. O'Connor was making a case for the political maturity of the catholic masses. Nevertheless such observations as his were not uncommon at the time.[15] During the 1790s the influence of the clergy momentarily faltered. Since this was generally a law-upholding, conservative influence – 'the Defenders', it was pointed out, 'are surely in a bad way – hanged by the laws here, and damned by [Archbishop] Troy hereafter'[16] – its weakening suggests growing political self-reliance among lower-class catholics.

The political, as opposed to the direct, causes of the anti-militia riots, and the novel and dramatic form which they took, are indicative of deep and widespread popular disaffection. What were the consequences of the disturbances? The militia's historian, Sir Henry McAnally, plays down the impact of these events. They did not, in his opinion, leave 'in the popular soul any such bitter memories as remained after other episodes in Irish history. May 1793 is not one of the black months in that story; it is not the first chapter of 1798.'[17] Given the scale of the bloodshed this seems a curious conclusion. Bartlett's judgement that the riots 'helped to create that atmosphere of fear and repression that made the '98 possible and some sort of '98 inevitable' is more convincing. Indeed, in the nineteenth century, popular tradition in Wexford characterised the events of 1793 as the 'first rebellion'.[18] Coercion fuelled disaffection. As one pamphleteer observed, such measures were 'ill-calculated to inspire men with a veneration for the government under which they live[d]'.[19] The resulting disaffection was then channelled through, and expressed by, the Defenders.

If the militia riots had the effect of embittering 'the people' against the government, this process can only have been aggravated by the 'show trials' of certain catholics in 1794. The trials had their background in the troubled county of Meath, from the start of 1793 the site of the most sustained Defender activity in Ireland. Meath was religiously mixed, with 'Scotch' presbyterian settlements in the north and east, a thinly-spread anglican landlord and farmer class and an overall, sometimes Irish-speaking, catholic majority. Of an approximate population, in 1792, of 112,000, about 2,800 were 'protestants'. As well as enjoying weight of numbers, the catholic 'interest' was far from negligible in social and political terms. 900 protestant freeholders, worth £10 or more, polled at the last election before the Catholic relief act. By 1794 at least 170 catholic freeholders had registered in the county.[20] As in south Ulster this complex denominational and 'ethnic' geography led to the drawing of 'cultural and settlement frontiers'. Defenderism and the politics of sectarianism flourished.

In October 1792, at the peak of the catholic agitation, a catholic meeting was held at Trim, a town bitterly described some years later as 'remarkable for being the residence of great numbers of the descendents of the prostitutes of Cromwell's army'.[21] The meeting, at which the Navan mill-owner John Fay was secretary, publicly regretted the 'severe disposition of our protestant brethren'. A protestant counter-meeting quickly replied.[22] At the end of that year a number of protestant gentlemen, including Thomas

Butler, formed the county Meath Association to counteract Defenderism. These were the men who routed the Defenders at Coolnahinch. Butler, the chaplain to the bishop of Meath, lived at Ardbracken, a prosperous 'English' settlement, with the largest rural protestant community in the county. By February 1793, when the heavily fortified bishop's palace was likened to a 'bastille', it was a community under siege.[23] As a magistrate Butler played a leading role in combatting the local Defenders and had allegedly 'declared openly a determination of taking off as many papists heads for insurrection as there were royalists murdered in France'. Certainly he had earned a tough reputation and his life was repeatedly threatened.[24] On 24 October the threats were fulfilled.

The local ascendancy party responded immediately. County magistrates met twice in quick succession and offered rewards for information leading to the arrest and conviction of the killers. Both meetings were attended by the bishop of Meath's brother-in-law, and a landowner in the county, the Speaker, John Foster. A few days later John Fay was arrested for the murder of Butler.[25] Foster's part in these events, and the political implications of Fay's arrest, aroused a good deal of speculation (and suspicion) at the time. Fay's home town, Navan, had been forward during the catholic campaign and hosted its own society of United Irishmen. The whole affair was easily construed as an exercise in political spite, and one newspaper complained of perjurers and of paid informers, 'sheltered – we fear not for the best purposes'.[26] Other commentators noted Foster's 'new-born influence' in Meath, and both Francis Plowden and John Keogh afterwards accused him of being implicated in the false charging of Fay.[27] Whatever the truth of these accusations, they were widely credited, and Fay's acquittal in March, 1794, must have confirmed public suspicions. The incident acquired instant notoriety. Due to 'the interest which the public took', the trial proceedings were made available in pamphlet form within a month, and after the actual culprits were identified the public was pointedly reminded of the 'rancorous avidity [with which] some men in that county thirsted after the blood of innocent individuals'.[28] In the aftermath of the catholic campaign middle-class catholics like Fay were natural objects of ascendancy resentment. It is unlikely, however, that such episodes of victimisation were simple acts of revenge.[29] Perhaps the ascendancy party at county level hoped to intimidate, or to tame the political assertiveness of, their catholic rivals.

In January, 1794, three Drogheda merchants who had been active in the Catholic Committee were charged, along with four others, with instigating Defender attacks in Louth in 1792. At the trial in April John Philpot Curren, in a masterly and witty cross-examination, demolished the credibility of the chief crown witness. During the course of this confrontation the witness admitted that he had, while a prisoner in Dundalk, spoken with Foster, but denied Curren's heavy hints that he had been bribed to give evidence. Summing-up the judge pointed out 'such circumstances as tended to discredit the witness'. The jury retired for three minutes before returning a verdict of not guilty. Some years later Curren remarked that the trials were 'scenes of more atrocity and horror than he had ever seen exhibited in a court of justice'.[30] The imprint which these trials left on the popular consciousness can be imagined. As late as 1810 Walter (Watty) Cox's *Irish Magazine* alluded to Foster's less than impartial role in these affairs.[31] What was the law, radicals could now ask, only an instrument of persecution?

By reinforcing popular perceptions of the state as enemy, 'persecution', judicial and military, had 'negative' politicising effects. That interlocking process of repression and disaffection became particularly acute in the years from the summer of 1795 to the summer of 1798. One fed off the other. The ascendancy resorted to repression because it was under attack and because its representatives were themselves frequently the victims of this campaign of violence; repression stimulated counter-violence, and so the cycle continued. This relationship is illustrated by the often personalised nature of Defender attacks. Active magistrates like Butler were prime targets. Another anglican clergyman and active magistrate in Meath, George Knipe, also attracted the attentions of the local Defenders. A bullet grazed his forehead in August, 1795, when he was ambushed shortly after prosecuting some Defenders who had attacked his home. Two years later he repulsed a similar attack, killing one of the raiders. Knipe was eventually assassinated at his house on 30 April, 1797. The leader of the raiding party, John Tuite, known as 'Captain Fearnought', claimed Knipe was their target because he was a 'heretic', and 'head of an Orange lodge' and because 'along with that, there was a man shot at his home some time before'. One of the raiders on this occasion was the dead man's brother.[32] If the sheer number of outrages in the 1790s evokes an impression of random, indiscriminate violence, in practice Defender victims – government informers, crown witnesses, the more energetic magistrates, or even MPs, like Caleb Harmon, the member for Longford – were often carefully selected.[33] It would have been extraordinary if the ascendancy had not reacted with vigour against such a sustained and systematic assault. For much of the time the Defenders held the initiative in this undeclared war of attrition. They had the advantage, which all guerillas have, of choosing when, where, and at whom, to strike. The authorities' response was piecemeal and reactive; a pattern which began to change when, in 1795, the government went on to the offensive.

This tougher 'security policy' was pursued within the context of a perceptible hardening of British attitudes towards Ireland. Again the catholic question determined the situation. Shortly after the Portland whigs formed a wartime coalition with Pitt on 11 July, 1794, the duke of Portland's close associate, earl Fitzwilliam, emerged as the prospective lord lieutenant for Ireland. Fitzwilliam, a friend of Edmund Burke, had land and political connections across the Irish sea. In August Grattan and George Ponsonby were invited to London, and Dublin was soon buzzing with rumours of an impending political shake-up. Fitzwilliam did, indeed, contemplate a 'clean sweep' of the existing administration, and within three days of his arrival in Dublin on 5 January, 1795, he sacked John Beresford, the first commissioner of the revenue. This rough handling of entrenched politicans was one reason for his undoing, the catholic question the other. When it became known that this well-intentioned man would succeed Westmorland hopes of full catholic emancipation revived.[34] In December the Dublin catholics held a meeting attended by Keogh, McCormick and MacNevin, and issued a call for further catholic relief. As in 1792 the leading catholics then set about mobilising public opinion. A report of the proceedings of the meeting was circulated 'throughout the kingdom'. At the end of January Grattan presented parliament with petitions from Antrim, Roscommon, Mayo, Leitrim, Waterfort (town and county), Queen's county, the cities of Galway, Kilkenny and Limerick and the towns of Newry, Navan, Castlebar and Sligo.[35] As in 1792 an upsurge of Defender activity accompanied the rising political excitement.

The Defender problem had persisted through 1794, sometimes flaring up dramatically. In May Defenders descended upon a fair in county Cavan declaring that *'they would destroy every Scotsman or Presbyterian they should find'*. One estimate put the death toll from this riot at over thirty. Two days afterwards the army confronted 'several thousand' Defenders at the nearby village of Ballinaugh. Another fifteen were killed and the troops burned the village to the ground.[36] By this stage the focus of Defender activity was moving from Meath and from the sectarian feuding in Armagh, to the south Ulster, north Connaught region. In July and August disturbances were reported from Cavan, Westmeath, Leitrim, Longford, Roscommon and Sligo.[37] Nor did the arrival of Fitzwilliam at the beginning of January 1795, and with it the prospects of catholic emancipation, bring any respite. In fact Fitzwilliam complained that not a day passed after his arrival that did not bring news of unrest in the countryside.[38] His recall in February did, however, instantly raise the political temperature.

Fitzwilliam had handled his brief ineptly. He made powerful enemies in Beresford and Fitzgibbon, both of whom lobbied against him in London.

The king likewise left Pitt in no doubt about his opposition to further installments of catholic relief. Pitt, moreover, believed that Fitzwilliam had overstepped his authority. On 23 Feburary the lord lieutenant was sent notice of recall. A number of contemporaries later looked back to Fitzwilliam's dismissal as the critical moment in the crisis of the 1790s. Charles Teeling called it a 'national insult' and recorded the indignation which he had witnessed at the Antrim freeholders meeting called to protest against the decision. Such scenes of public outrage were repeated across Ireland and the United Irish 'system' began to assume a more 'general and imposing appearance'. In Wexford Edward Hay collected 22,251 signatures. Some years later he wrote of 'the cup of redress [being] dashed from the lips of expectation, and it cannot be wondered at that the anger of disappointment should have ensued'.[39] Levels of violence markedly increased. As early as 3 March large areas of Cavan, Roscommon and Sligo were characterised as 'actually in a state of insurrection'. The *Northern Star* suggested that 'the rejection of the catholic bill [which followed the recall] . . . gives the insurgents a plea for disaffection'.[40]

Now that the political option had been closed off – Camden, Fitzwilliam's successor, was explicitly instructed that 'a stand should be made against the further claims of the catholics' – the government turned to counter-insurgency. Within days of taking up office the new lord lieutenant informed his superiors in London that 'the quiet of the country depends upon the exertion of the friends of the established government, *backed by a strong military force*'.[41] The reasons why the British government abandoned its previous strategy of conciliation for the politics of confrontation are unclear. It has been suggested that after the relief acts of 1792–3 the British government considered the 'conciliation account' closed, or alternatively, that Pitt wished to hold concessions in reserve to barter, at some future date, for catholic support for a union.[42] Pitt may also have been reluctant to undermine England's protestant garrison in Ireland during wartime. Whatever the reasoning which lay behind the new hardline policies the consequences were disastrous: repression, disaffection and violence.

In April eleven revenue officers were ambushed and killed after raiding an illicit still at Drumsna, county Leitrim. Their bodies, 'most inhumanly mangled', were only recovered the next day. 'Whether this event gave [the Defenders] spirit,' wrote Camden:

> or drove them to desperation from an apprehension of the consequences,
> I know not. But from that period the numbers assembled were greater,
> and they proceeded with more system and appearance of order than they

had previously done. One of the first acts of violence and of system was to put all the smiths in requisition, compelling them to make pikes.[43]

In addition to worrying indications of 'system' and 'order', the authorities must also have been concerned by signs of politicisation, for instance, by the information which they had received that 'the insurgents assume alternately the appellation of Defenders – United Brothers – and French Militia,' and that there was a 'confused notion' amongst them that a 'general rising' would soon take place.[44] Large numbers of troops under the command of General Carhampton were dispatched to Connaught. Although he did not anticipate 'very strong measures,' Camden, confident of the English cabinet's support, was prepared to sanction methods 'beyond what the very letter of the law allows'. A stance endorsed by Whitehall as 'perfectly just, manly and liberal'.[45] In June a Dublin paper referred to accounts 'from various parts of the country,' 'of the most atrocious acts committed by the soldiery on the poor unoffending peasants'. By the beginning of October Carhampton, in a wholly illegal exercise, had arrested 1,300 'Defenders' without charge or trial, and sent them aboard a tender anchored off Sligo, for service in the fleet.[46] The lord lieutenant was 'a little afraid of the zeal of the magistrates carrying this too far,' but felt that 'it had frightened these fellows more than anything'. His under-secretary took a more sceptical – and as events were to show, more realistic – view of the efficacy of repression. 'Defenderism puzzles me more and more,' he confided, 'but ultimately grows more alarming daily, as the effect of executions seems to be at an end, and there is an enthusiasm defying punishment'.[47] Strongarm tactics could prove counter-productive.

After the Fitzwilliam episode and the mass arrests by Carhampton, the situation took yet another sharp turn for the worse. Remembered in Ireland as the incident which gave birth to the Orange Order, the so-called 'battle of the Diamond', which took place in north Armagh in September, 1795, and, even more so, the expulsions from the county which followed, are important in the 1790s for the effect which they had of further discrediting the ascendancy in catholic eyes and of swelling the ranks of the Defenders and United Irishmen.[48] Armagh had been plagued by sectarian feuding since the mid-1780s. In December 1794, for example, Defenders and Peep O'Day Boys, 'young boys and idle journeymen weavers', clashed at a fair. After the twelfth of July celebrations the following year a group of catholics were attacked near Portadown.[49] The tensions which such incidents revealed culminated in the set-piece battle at the Diamond, a townland appropriately close to Loughall, over ten years before the 'cradle' of Defenderism. Although heavily reinforced by contingents from the neighbouring areas of Down, Derry and, particularly, Tyrone, the Defenders were badly beaten, suffering between seventeen and forty-eight fatalities.[50] This rout was then followed by the mass expulsion of catholics. At least one church was burned down and catholic homes and property – looms, webs and yarn – were destroyed. As the attacks continued through the winter and spread into Tyrone, Derry and Monagahan, the exodus was accelerated by the circulation of a prophecy foretelling great calamities about to befall the catholics of the north.[51] Estimates of the number of refugees ran from 3,500 to 10,000.[52] Meanwhile the magistrates, many of them clergymen, displayed resolute partiality. In the opinion of General Dalrymple, then stationed in the north, 'they seem[ed] inclined to give this contest an appellation that ought in prudence ever to be avoided, a religious dispute'.[53] The county governor, Lord Gosford, addressing a meeting of magistrates there on 28 December, denounced the 'ruthless persecution' of the catholics and 'the supineness of the magistracy of Armagh'. This, he noted, had 'become a common topic of conversation in every corner of the kingdom'. If it had not, it was soon to be, as thousands of copies of the address were printed and distributed *gratis.*[54] The refugees fled in many directions: to Antrim, Down and even Scotland. But by far the greatest number, maybe as many as 4,000, resettled in north Connaught.[55] They carried with them tales of persecution and over the coming years the fear of 'Orange' massacres was skilfully exploited as a recruiting agent by the United Irishmen. The expulsions were not soon forgotten. The Defenders at the battle of Randalstown in 1798 carried a banner inscribed 'REMEMBER ARMAGH'.[56]

Undoubtedly the experience and perception of repression and injustice helped to spread and to deepen popular alienation from the government. It gave sustenance to Defenderism and the United Irishmen, just as the mounting tide of violence stiffened the ascendancy's resolve. The 'rise' of the Defenders, then, was essentially a political phenomenon, inspired by catholic agitation and the French revolution, and accelerated by repression and sectarian conflict. Yet traditionally they have been characterised, to use Lecky's words, as a 'revived Whiteboy system'. According to Thomas Pakenham their grievances were local, connected to the land and empty of political content. Although this view is no longer tenable it would be a mistake to entirely dismiss social and economic explanations. There is no necessary reason, after all, why such explanations should be incompatible with political ones. And in fact, the political and public order crisis of the 1790s was compounded by an economy and society under unusual stress. As the population explosion exerted greater and greater pressure on land, real wages plummeted against rising prices. As the government struggled to meet the bill for a hugely expensive war, taxation steadily increased. Relentless demographic pressure and severe economic hardship stimulated conflict between landlord and tenant – familiar terrain for the Irish secret society. Nor did the Defenders neglect agrarian matters. In Roscommon they even succeeded in forcing the graziers to raise wages and lower conacre rents. In another sense the movements' ultimate aim, 'to divide the land', was agrarian too.[57] Nevertheless, the classic Whiteboy grievances occupied a distinctly subordinate place among Defender priorities.

The significance of Defenderism, historically and for the politics of the period, lay in the way in which it transcended local and immediate issues – in the qualitative leap, which it represented, from rural discontent to mass disaffection. To the authorities this was a worrying and, as Cooke's remark indicates, startling development. To the radical elite it offered rich opportunities. In order to tap the disaffection produced by the sequence of events from the militia riots to the Armagh expulsions, the United Irishmen had first to work out an accommodation with the Defenders, an accommodation which altered the course of revolutionary politics. What follows examines Defenderism as it had evolved by mid-decade; at that crucial moment when it was about to 'merge' into a revolutionary coalition with the United Irishmen.[58]

II   IDEOLOGY, ORGANISATION, LEADERSHIP

Defender ideology is difficult to pin down. The Defenders did not have a set of policies, like a political party, and any discussion of their aspirations, prejudices and beliefs, runs the risk of imposing retrospective coherence on what was in reality a tangled skein of half-formed 'ideas'. Bearing this in mind, the main elements which made up the Defender mentality are clear enough. The best evidence for this mentality comes from the movement's oaths and catechisms. The symbolism employed in these documents, a protean, inchoate compound of Biblical allusions and references to Irish history and the French revolution, gave the Defenders an attractive sense of mystique. One example of obfuscation, the password 'ELIPHISMATIS', was seized upon by the government-sponsored *Faulkners Dublin Journal*, which obligingly deciphered it as:

Every Loyal Irish Protestant Heretic I Shall Murder And This I Swear

With nice irony, but equal plausibility, the rival *Dublin Evening Post* suggested a number of alternatives including:

Every Lunatic In Patrick's Hospital I Swear May Answer That Is
Silly[59]

The inspiration is probably masonic. In the early 1780s, for instance, the
Belfast Freemasons had a toast which ran 'May every Mason who stands
in need of friendship be able to say EYPHA – *I have found it*'.[60]

Fortunately, not all Defender language is quite so opaque. 'Are you
concerned?' begins a typical catechism,

> I am.
> To what?
> To the National Convention.
> What do you design by that cause?
> To quell all nations, dethrone all kings and plant the true religion that
> was lost since the reformation.
> What do you fall by?
> Sin.
> What do you rise by?
> Repentance.
> Where did the cock first crow that all the world heard?
> In France.
> What is your pass-word?
> Elishimorta.

According to another, 'The French Defenders will uphold the cause
and the Irish Defenders will pull down the British laws'.[61] Defender
'ideology' combined elements of religious sectarianism, nationalism – the
vague notion, as Emmet put it, that '*something . . . ought to be done for
Ireland*,'[62] – francophilia and millenarianism. The theme of 'deliverance'
jostles in these documents with Irish history; Saint Peter and Saint John
with Patrick Sarsfield. When this sometimes bizarre collocation of imagery
meshed with straightforward agrarian protest, Defenderism could mean
almost anything to anyone. It was not a theoretical construct but a genuinely
popular ideology, spontaneously generated from 'below' in response to the
crisis of the 1790s; a loose, fluid cluster of ideas which tapped the sources
of lower-class catholic solidarity: religion and nationality.

The use of pass-words and catechisms, as well as hand-signals, tokens
and 'certificates', enabled Defenders to identify each other, maintained
security, facilitated communication between lodges and indulged the perennial human taste for secrecy and ritual. These elaborate devices also
had a self-legitimising function. A Defender 'captain', a schoolmaster,

captured at Letterkenny in Donegal, had a 'commission, with a large
seal to it, a parchment muster roll' listing 400 names, and 'an address
to the republicans of Ireland, signed Pichergru, General of the French
Republic'. In Galway, Defenders raiding for arms first 'produced a card
signed Captain Stout'.[63]

The Defenders developed a remarkably sophisticated and flexible organisation. An expanding network of lodges had been built up through the
agencies of 'contagion' – Defender territory ran across a geographically
contiguous belt, stretching from north Leinster through south Ulster into
north Connaught – emissaries and the militia. It was inevitable, given
the system of balloting, that Defenders would be inducted into their
county militia regiments. Members of these regiments, which were then
stationed in other counties, administered the Defender oath to the locals.
Unsurprisingly the Meath militia was particularly noted for this practice.[64]
As Defenderism spread it did not, at first, evolve any formal hierarchy
or central leadership. Rather it developed a loosely federated 'horizontal'
structure. Lodges were numbered in sequence as they were established and
co-ordinated in a low-level way by masonic techniques. Once initiated any
Defender might, it was claimed, travel through the country 'free of expense
and in perfect safety, being supplied with liquor and lodged wherever they
passed'.[65]

The federated, cellular, structure was an effective form of clandestine
organisation insofar as it proved more spy-resistant (though not entirely
spy-proof) than the United Irishmen's centrally-led pyramidal one. When
an informer infiltrated a Defender lodge, he tended to stop there, whereas
penetration of a local United Irish committee could give access, up through
the baronial, county and provincial layers, to greater quantities of high
quality information. For the historian, so often reliant on the same sources
as were at the disposal of Dublin Castle, this presents more than the usual
problems. Probably we will never know as much about the Defenders as we
do about the United Irishmen, although more evidence survives, perhaps,
than was once thought.

Beames notes the 'striking omission from Defender documents . . . of
any reference to agrarian grievances'.[66] This observation, while true, is
somewhat misleading. Agrarian grievances do feature in the reports of
Defender activity. However, the ommission does provide an important clue
about the social profile of Defender membership. This was not a peasant
movement. Weavers, blacksmiths, or Dublin's urban craftsmen were as
likely to be members as small peasant proprietors or agricultural labourers.
Workers on the Royal canal, for instance, 'above 100' of them refugees
from Armagh, were organised into Defender lodges.[67] Camden thought

that the leadership was drawn from among 'Alehouse-keepers, artisans, low schoolmasters and perhaps a few middling farmers'. This corresponds with other, 'harder', information. An imprisoned Defender from Longford named the committee-men in his lodge as a shopkeeper, a schoolmaster, a shoemaker and 'two gentlemen'.[68] Another Defender prisoner, this time from Louth, described the local 'captains' as 'men of substance'.[69] These descriptions, while many remain characteristically imprecise in the eighteenth-century style, are nonetheless revealing. Defender membership represents a cross-section of rural society below the level of gentry, it attracted the 'middling sort' as well as the 'peasantry' and men of no property.

One occupational group which stands out in the ranks of the Defenders everywhere is the schoolmasters. A number who were arrested during the disturbances in Connaught in 1795 were suspected by the authorities of acting as 'the channel of communication'. In Roscommon, schoolmasters were described as 'the principal Defender-makers'.[70] This involvement in radical politics – numerous schoolmasters were also active United Irishmen – is best explained by the unique development of the profession. 'Independent of all system and control' by church or state, the predecessors of these rural teachers had been the scribes and bards who had lived by the patronage of the old Gaelic elite, and even in the nineties some were still Gaelic poets. That 'cultural background', it has been suggested, made the schoolmaster heir to 'the resentments of the leaders of the old Gaelic landed class'.[71] These ancient resentments then fused, in a way typical of Defender 'ideology', with new, French-inspired, democratic doctrines. Although most of the literary evidence relating to the incorrigible disaffection and to the political influence of the schoolmasters dates from the early nineteenth century, it can safely be read back into to the 1790s.[72] In 1795, for example, McNally referred to 'Thomas Paine, whose works are now in the hands of almost every schoolmaster'.[73]

Unfortunately, the identities of the great majority of these schoolmaster activists and of other middle-ranking Defender leaders are unknown, and most likely unknowable. Occasionally, however, it is possible to pick out faces in the crowd.

Probably the best documented of all Defenders is the Meath school-master and freemason, Lawrence O'Connor.[74] O'Connor and others were arrested in Kildare in July, 1795, for administering an oath to the country people to 'be true to the French'. Tried and executed for high treason in September, he is chiefly remembered for his spirited and articulate defence in court. Lecky's remark that O'Connor 'was said to have been the only educated person who is known to have been identified with' the Defenders, is utterly misleading.[75] In fact schoolmasters, as noted earlier, were often leaders, or committee-men, at local level; a presence which enhanced the political calibre of the movement.

Less well known than O'Connor to students of the period, although he had achieved something of a national reputation by 1796, was the 'celebrated "Switcher" Donnelly'. Arthur Donnelly, by profession a dancing instructor, came from Tyrone and acted as a Defender commander at the battle of the Diamond. In November and December 1795 rewards were offered for his arrest in connection with a shooting. According to the magistrate who finally caught up with him in south Derry five months later, Donnelly was 'by nature form'd to be a most dangerous conspirator, very great address, good choice of words and fluency of speech and great agility of body. Amazingly muscular and with desperate intrepidy'. A regional organiser in west Ulster, he reportedly circulated like 'quicksilver' through Donegal, Tyrone, Antrim and Derry.[76]

Donnelly's career is instructive. When he was captured the newspapers referred to him as a Defender *and* a United Irishman. And by this time the merger or, more accurately, coalition, between the United Irishmen and Defenders was indeed already in place, at least in Ulster. The making of that coalition carried profound implications for both movements. Like the commencement of negotiations for French military aid, United Irish efforts to assimilate Defender lodges into their new military structures signalled the seriousness of their insurrectionary designs. It also posed problems for their strategy of forging a union of Irishmen of all creeds. Defenderism represented many things to many men, among them catholic sectarianism. The experience of John Tuite – 'Captain Fearnought' of Meath – illustrates the consequent United Irish dilemma. Tuite was 'sworn to both acts' in 1795, that is he took first the Defender and then the United Irish oaths, but the Defender oath pledged him to 'to quell the nation of heresy' as well as to 'dethrone all kings, and plant the tree of liberty'.[77] The second part of the oath indicates how interaction with the United Irishmen accelerated and strengthened the politicising impact of 'French principles'; the first part shows how much more the secular radical gospel had still to do. Putting the best gloss possible on a coalition fraught with internal tensions, Emmet later asserted that the United Irishmen had infused Defenderism with 'tolerance and republicanism'.[78] Presumably Tuite's trial report had escaped his notice.

Concerted and systematic attempts to co-opt the Defenders began in the spring of 1795, but lines of communication had been established as early as 1792. As Emmet remarked, 'from the first formation of the union its most active members were extremely anxious to learn the views and intentions of the Defenders'.[79] The best documented example of contact is the United Irish mission to Rathfryland in the summer of 1792. Wolfe Tone, Samuel Neilson and Alexander Lowry were all involved in this episode. The names are important because the same individuals appear and reappear as the hidden history of the Defender-United Irish relationship is unravelled. While it is tempting to view the Rathfryland mission as an isolated attempt – in the context of the catholic campaign – to settle sectarian feuding, other evidence, patchy and circumstantial though it may be, suggests that it in fact fits a pattern. Elliott dismisses Tandy's excursion to the Louth Defenders later that year as an act of 'bravado' motivated by 'curiosity'. Yet Tandy was probably introduced to the Defenders by the Rev. James Coigly, who was in turn associated with the Belfast United Irishmen. Coigly, if not by then a Defender certainly exercised influence amongst them, and during the years 1791–3 travelled around counties Antrim and Derry propagating 'union'.[80] His activities were complemented by Emmet's 'most active' United Irishmen. For instance, Thomas Russell travelled the length and breadth of Ulster during 1793–4.[81] Not surprisingly the group reaching out to the lower classes and Defenders in this period was the northern-based, politically militant, and often socially radical faction of the United Irishmen, prominent among them Russell, Henry Joy McCracken, Neilson and Coigly. The committed, francophile position adopted by these men made some kind of convergence with the Defenders likely.

As the adversarial rhetoric and style of the reform campaign of 1792–3 had already demonstrated, certain northerners would not shirk direct – possibly violent – confrontation with the ascendancy, and the drift of events since the collapse of that campaign only served to harden attitudes. After the Dublin society's plans for parliamentary reform were published at the beginning of 1794 the *Northern Star* announced 'The question with us is not *What reform is best?* but – *How can we possibly obtain any?*'[82] The open and 'political' routes to reform were blocked. Meanwhile the revelations from the Rev. William Jackson's treason trial gave wide publicity to the possibilities of French intervention in Ireland.[83] Circumstances conspired to encourage a revolutionary strategy. Not that men like McCracken needed much encouragement. As in Dublin it is likely that a shadowy network of lower-class clubs grew up alongside the United Irishmen in Ulster in the first half of the decade. The chairman of the 'Irish Jacobins of Belfast' in 1792 was a baker, the secretary 'an obscure tinner and braizier'.[84] In November, 1793, the *Northern Star* referred to 'a society of tradesmen in this town [i.e. Belfast] which has subsisted for three years'.[85] These tradesmen, 'farmers, manufacturers and shopkeepers', formed the organisational backbone of the 'new' underground United Irish movement which began to take shape in Ulster in 1794. 'The scheme was calculated to embrace the lower orders, and in fact to make every man a politician'. The clandestine structure was so far advanced by May, 1795, that a general meeting of delegates from the various societies could be summoned at Belfast.[86] These developments ran parallel to the welding of the Ulster Defenders into a more tightly centralised organisation.

The chief architect of the revamped Defenders was a warm friend and associate of Neilson and McCracken, Charles H. Teeling. During May and June, 1795, Teeling undertook a journey up the Antrim coast, along north county Derry, down through Tyrone, Fermanagh, Leitrim and Westmeath and into Meath. The purpose of his journey can be guessed. In Glenarm, county Antrim, for example, he stayed with a priest, the Rev. D. McDonnell, who is known to have subscribed to the *Northern Star*. In Leitrim he stayed with the Catholic Committee activist, Myles Keon. At approximately the same time Charles' elder brother, the United Irishman Bartholomew, 'traversed the whole island on foot'.[87] It was no coincidence that after meeting with Robert Simms, Neilson and the younger Teeling before leaving for America in June, Tone pronounced himself competent to speak 'for the catholics, for the dissenters and for the Defenders of Ireland'. Three months later Simms wrote to the exile that 'the organisation which you were made acquainted with amongst the catholics in this neighbourhood continues to increase and has spread as far south as Meath'.[88] Teeling himself later drew a distinction between the 'regularly organised body' of Defenders in the north and their less disciplined southern counterparts, while Simms' claim about its penetration into Meath is corroborated by government intelligence about Belfast emissaries being sent to that county, by Emmet's reference to an exchange of 'deputies' between Belfast and Meath, county Dublin and elsewhere, by Tone's assertion that Belfast exercised greater influence over the catholics than Dublin and by the activities of Bartholomew Teeling by then – like Coigly – operating out of Dundalk.[89]

In many ways the politics of the 1790s, radical, catholic and Defender, crystallized in the Teeling family. It played a crucial role in co-ordinating the coalition between the Defenders and United Irishmen. The father, Luke, a wealthy linen merchant from Lisburn, near Belfast, acted as a (hardline) United Irish surrogate at the Catholic Convention in 1792. It was he who that year paid for the *Address to the Defenders*, at Rathfryland and for the insertions of the Meath catholics in the *Northern Star*.[90] Luke also chaired the county Antrim catholic meeting called to protest against Fitzwilliam's recall, and his young son Charles – then only seventeen – acted as secretary. Charles' brother-in-law, John Magennis, the self-styled 'Grand Master' of the county Down Defenders, represented that county at the Catholic Convention, handled the local Catholic Committee subscription and was in communication with the committee secretary (and United Irishman) Richard McCormick.[91] Although the Defenders have usually been discussed at a general – and nameless – level, attention to detail reveals, at first in Ulster, then radiating outwards, a compact nexus of friends and relatives at the head of the movement. This was a group which was, moreover, deeply involved with the United Irishmen. The Teelings stood at the centre of the nexus and, as prosperous linen merchants, typified it.

In contrast with their landowning co-religionists in north Connaught or the Dublin businessmen, Ulster's catholics had maintained a low political profile throughout the greater part of the eighteenth century. If this passivity was due, as Cullen suggests, to their comparative poverty,[92] then their participation in the linen-led economic boom of the 1780s and 1790s would in part explain their new political self-confidence. Commercial relations with Belfast's radical mercantile elite would also have facilitated politicisation. Bernard Coile, a prominent Lurgan linen merchant, subscribed to the *Northern Star,* and was associated with Neilson, McCracken, Coigly and Magennis.[93] Magennis, like his fellow Defender commander, the presbyterian, Alexander Lowry, was also in the linen trade. Both were intimates of Charles Teeling who attests to their social rank and 'independent fortune'.[94] This small leading group acted as a nucleus whose family, business and political connections fanned-out into an underground network spanning the northern half of Ireland. Coigly's brother in Armagh – who employed 100 weavers – was a Defender/United Irishman. Coigly's equally mobile colleague, 'Switcher' Donnelly, may have been a cousin, while his 'close friend and relation', Valentine Derry, led the Defenders in county Louth.[95] The other main identifiable Defender leaders are Burke Rice, a man 'possessed of considerable landed property' in county Monaghan,[96] and the Armagh publican, Robert Campbell. Government informants reported Campbell's presence in Cavan late in 1795, and at Balbriggan, north county Dublin, shortly afterwards, as he 'constantly travell[ed] from county to county'.[97]

Once the cloak of anonymity is lifted then, the Defenders, it becomes clear, particularly in Ulster and Meath, possessed a coherent, radical, middle-class catholic leadership. From its origins in Armagh in 1784 as the catholic faction in a local sectarian feud, the Defender movement had gradually spread along lines of religious cleavage, or 'cultural frontiers', into county Down, Louth and south Ulster. Stimulated by the news and controversy about the French revolution and encouraged by the catholic agitation, the Defenders were transformed into a politicised secret society. This process was then reinforced, and the Defender organisation expanded, from Meath across the north midlands into Connaught, by the continuing economic, political, and law-and-order crisis. The militia riots, the 1794 trials, the Fitzwilliam episode, Lord Carhampton's activities, the Armagh expulsions and the propaganda which radicals extracted from each of these affairs, all contributed to the rise of the Defenders. By 1795 Defenderism had a presence, from Donegal to Kildare, from Galway to Louth, in at least sixteen counties and in Dublin city. They had successfully infiltrated the militia and knit far-flung lodges into a co-ordinated, if not well-disciplined, organisation. Lines of communication criss-crossed the country. Emissaries, equipped with catechisms, 'commissions' and the knowledge of the initiate, travelled around carrying instructions, proselytising and recruiting. Defenderism had evolved a chameleon ideology infinitely adaptable to varying local conditions: now sectarian, now agrarian, always francophile and anti-ascendancy. With the emergence of a recognisable regional command structure in Ulster, of a catholic leadership aligned to the radical northern wing of the United Irishmen, the stage had been set for the making of a revolutionary coalition. The vast Catholic Committee-United Irish-Defender conspiracy of Sir Richard Musgrave's paranoid imagination was not, after all, entirely detached from the historical reality.

6 From Pre-Industrial Crowd to Revolutionary Underground: Dublin's Street Politics, 1759–97

Dublin's radical and popular politics represent a special case in the history of the 1790s, and the peculiarities of their development before then merit extended treatment. Despite much exciting and important work on urban riots and crowds in other countries, notably the studies of eighteenth-century Paris and London pioneered by George Rudé,[1] and in contrast with the attention devoted to rural unrest in Ireland, Dublin's crowd has been largely ignored. The explanation for this may lie in the perception that these urban disorders were episodic and minor. This was indeed the perception of certain contemporaries. In a clear reference to the Gordon riots, Henry Grattan once asked, 'What are our riots compared to those of London?' and supplied the answer, 'nothing'. At the other end of the political spectrum, Castlereagh's private secretary, Alexander Knox, made a similar point, expressing 'both surprise and satisfaction that the Dublin mob of 31 March, 1795, fell short so amazingly, both in violence and in outrage, of the London mob of 2 June, 1780'.[2] More concisely, a modern historian of 'class conflict' remarks, 'Dublin was not Paris'.[3] Although Dublin never witnessed events on the scale of the Gordon riots or the Parisian 'September massacres' of 1792, its street politics were nonetheless significant. The same historian acknowledges this when he observes that the 1779 riot probably 'galvanized Lord North into action', 'induc[ing]' the British cabinet to grant 'Free Trade'.[4]

The Dublin crowd is an important historical phenomenon because from time to time it played a major role in national politics and because, in a manner analogous to the Whiteboy/Defender relationship, it established patterns of behaviour and developed modes of organisation which were transmitted to, and adapted by, the revolutionary underground of the 1790s. The structures and style of lower-class politics during the revolutionary decade are brought into sharper relief when viewed against the background of previous disturbances and the operation of the city's crowd.

121

I 'UNLAWFUL ASSEMBLIES AND RIOTOUS COMBINATIONS'

Public disorder, 'riots' in the theatre for example, was commonplace in the
eighteenth-century metropolis. Any attempt to chronicle each and every
outbreak of collective street violence would therefore be tedious and serve
little purpose. Rather the political complexion and sociology of the crowd
is best revealed by focussing on the three major 'political' riots before
the 1790s. These occurred in 1759, 1779 and 1784. While brief accounts
have been written about each individual event, they have never been
looked at together. A thematic approach, by drawing out the differences
and similarities between the riots, should help to clarify our picture of
the pre-industrial crowd. In addition an investigation of the context,
origins, course and consequences of these episodes, which happened at
the interface between 'high' and popular politics, may illuminate other
aspects of Dublin's (and Ireland's) social history.

The interventions of the Dublin crowd were so often able to register a
national political impact because the capital city provided it with a highly
visible, strategically placed political stage. And the 'stage' metaphor is apt:
the element of street theatre or carnival in crowd actions should not be
underestimated. Eighteenth-century Dublin, a large and important metropolis, dominated Ireland's politics, society and economy, much as London
or Paris dominated England and France. With a population in 1750 of
approximately 100,000, it was the second biggest city in the British empire.
The seat of parliament, administration and the judiciary, the capital enjoyed
a national monopoly in higher education, provided the focus for 'polite
society' and attracted a numerous resident and seasonal gentry. Ireland's
busiest port, Dublin was also an interregional redistribution centre, the
hub of the country's communications network and financial and banking
facilities.[5] These social, political and commercial functions determined the
composition of the pre-industrial workforce. The presence of the gentry
in particular, shaped the city's occupational structures. In the 1790s, for
instance, an estimated 18,415 people (11,954 women and 6,461 men),
were employed as domestic servants.[6] The gentry also supported a market
for 'luxury' goods, keeping goldsmiths, watchmakers and silk weavers at
work. The prosperity and pretensions of the social (and political) elite were
reflected above all in the great public and private building boom which
Dublin underwent during the second half of the century. The construction
of Trinity College's west front, the Royal Exchange, the Custom House
and Four Courts, the new bridges and the great private developments,
the elegant, spacious streets, squares and malls on the Gardiner estate in
the north east and the Fitzwilliam estate in the south east, ensured that

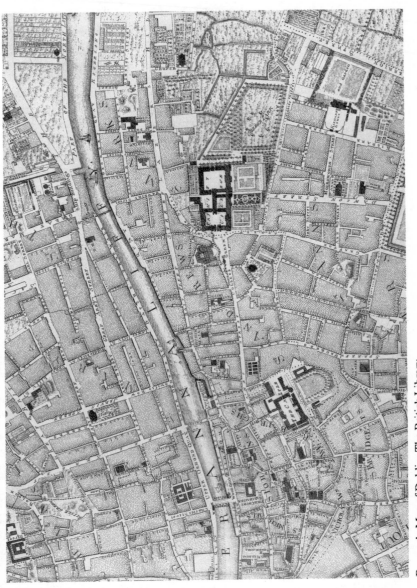

Rocque's Map of Dublin: The British Library.

the building trades were generally buoyant. The port and the Smithfield and Ormond markets north of the river Liffey, likewise provided employment in the carrying trades. Among the most ubiquitous of craftsmen was the shoemaker; a profession which, before mechanization, naturally expanded with the population. The premier domestic industry, however, was textiles. Cotton, silk, woollen and linen weavers, concentrated in the overcrowded Coombe and Earl of Meath's Liberty in the south west constituted Dublin's largest occupational group. The Liberty, 'that lawless part of the metropolis', traditional home to the 'mob', was a dense warren comprised of 'the most irregular and circuitous passages, besides narrow crooked lanes and alleys almost innumerable'.[7] As the city's population began to rise, moreover, reaching approximately 180,000 by the end of the century, the housing stock in this district remained static. In the late 1790s there were an average eleven inhabitants per house.[8] In the 1750s the typical economic unit in the domestic textiles industry consisted of a master and two or three journeymen and apprentices, all frequently living and working under the same roof. For the majority workplace and dwelling were still one and the same forty years later, but the trend was towards greater capitalisation and larger-scale production. Already by 1760 two silk mercers were 'putting-out' to between thirty and sixty looms. By 1780, Richard McCormick, worsted manufacturer, employed 200 'hands'.[9] Comparatively large scale investment and production was also becoming a feature of the sugar-refining, brewing and distilling industries. At mid-century, then, Dublin's workforce was essentially, if loosely, 'artisan' – small master craftsmen, skilled, tool-owning journeymen and apprentices – with a steadily growing component of wage-earning employees.[10]

These occupational structures underpinned the city's political life at a number of levels. The corporation consisted of an upper chamber, the board of aldermen, and a lower one, the common council, representing the twenty-five trade guilds. 'Beneath' the official guilds workmen organised in the illegal journeymen combinations; pre-industrial trade unions, seeking higher wages, shorter hours and restricted access to their crafts. The combinations tried to limit the numbers of apprentices and exhibited perennial hostility towards country workers. Their main weapons were the strike and intimidation. One, quite sketchy, list records at least sixteen strikes in Dublin between 1728 and 1759, while in 1758 the Liberty weavers proved capable of sustaining a strike over three months.[11] Combination, which sometimes performed the function of the friendly society, dispensing financial assistance to sick members or for burials, was a persistent, resilient and widespread mode of lower-class organisation, which gave cohesion and muscle to the 'craft cultures' of pre-industrial society.

Social cohesion and organisational ability based on craft and urban geography provide the analytical keys which unlock the political morphology of the eighteenth-century crowd. Contemporaries used the term 'mob' to denote collective street violence, a label which was also employed by historians before Rudé (who in fact used it himself initially). After Rudé, and E. P. Thompson's study of the 'moral economy' of rural disorder, 'mob' with its connotations of spontaneity and irrationality, was replaced by the concept of the 'crowd'. 'Crowd', in this sense, carries implications of group leadership, structure and purpose.[12] In a brief but penetrating and suggestive appraisal of what he then (in 1959) termed the 'classical mob', Professor Hobsbawm delineated its principal characteristics. It was, he argued, 'in a recognised sense, a permanent entity,' usually located 'in certain cohesive and ancient quarters of the city,' particularly those 'classical pre-industrial metropolis[es] – normally a capital – living on a resident court, state, church or aristocracy'. Furthermore, the physical proximity of the state apparatus had a politicising effect. The urban rioter tended to have 'a far more precise conception of what 'government', 'power' and the 'seizure of power' meant than peasants in remote villages'.[13] Clearly Dublin fits Hobsbawm's model in a number of ways. A capital city, site of the parliament and government buildings – the Castle – it had a resident gentry and an active crowd, the 'Liberty mob', as it was called, which was as likely to mobilise around political as economic issues.

In fact the categories 'political' and 'economic' suggest a false dichotomy. In practice politicians and polemicists tended to conflate the two. Invariably they traced economic grievances and economic distress to its alleged source: Ireland's unequal constitutional partnership with Great Britain. From Molyneux in the 1690s to the United Irishmen in the 1790s, the injustice of this relationship informed the politics of opposition. Hostility to undue English influence was first popularised, perhaps, during the Woods ha'pence dispute, in the mid-1720s, by Dean Jonathan Swift in his persona of the Drapier. *The Drapier's letters* were addressed as much to the local audience of Dublin tradesmen as to the 'political nation'. Significantly, Swift's popular reputation in the city rested on his vindication of injured Ireland's national rights. But Dublin's popular politics find a recognizable beginning in the career of the radical apothecary, Dr Charles Lucas.

Lucas first came to public attention when he attacked aldermanic privilege in the early 1740s. His critique of municipal government was then expanded into a classic whig statement of the traditional liberties of the citizen, the 'genius' of the British constitution and Ireland's equality with her sister kingdom. This phase of Lucas's career climaxed in the bitterly contested Dublin by-election of 1748–9. He canvassed the various guild halls, which were reportedly 'packed' with loud supporters, and issued a series of twenty addresses. Lucas also published the city's first regular radical newspaper, *The Censor*. It was a contentious campaign which generated at least 150 pamphlets and ended in the exile of this turbulent apothecary.[14] The Lucas affair had a major politicising impact. As his sometime running mate, James Digges LaTouche, afterwards wrote:

> From this time you might hear the lowest tradesman call themselves *free citizens . . . independent . . .* our Dublin citizens since that memorable year [i.e. 1749] have been so wrong-headed as to talk of national rights, of liberty, of worthy representatives . . . they now read newspapers, and even the votes of the commons, and have more than once been audacious enough to crowd the streets about the parliament house.[15]

Lucas confirmed the extent of his popular base when on his return to Ireland in 1761 he was elected to parliament as one of the members for Dublin. Dublin was an 'open' constituency in which 'freemen', that is guild members, were enfranchised, and Lucas reputedly 'got in [to parliament] by cajoling the very scum of the people'.[16]

Another agent of politicisation was the money bill controversy in 1753. Although in reality a self-interested quarrel between the parliamentary 'undertakers' and the executive, the undertakers contrived to represent this issue to the public as a defence of the rights of Ireland. The leading protagonist, Henry Boyle, was accused of 'inflaming the minds of the common people of Dublin', 'several dozen pamphlets' were published and celebratory bonfires on the streets of the capital greeted Boyle's eventual victory.[17]

The legacy of the Lucas and money bill affairs helps account for the depth of popular antipathy towards the idea of a legislative union with Britain. The anti-union riot of 3 December, 1759, manifested a distinct popular ideology. On 27 December the chief secretary, Richard Rigby, recalled the events of 1753 and lamented 'the national dislike of English rule'.[18] Dublin by this time had developed a lively lower-class political culture. Before the riot allegations of an intended union 'were published in coffee-houses and all places of publick resort; proclaimed by the minor orators of societies, sung at corners of streets and commented upon by coal-porters'. The volatility of the situation is underlined by a 'Heads of Bill' introduced to parliament that year which refers to a city 'grown so extensive and populous [where] such unlawful combinations and riotous assemblies are frequently formed in many parts, to the great disturbance and terror of sober and industrious citizens, that it is impossible for the most active and vigilant magistrates to preserve the peace therein'.[19] The politics of the coffee house and the street corner could assume special significance, of course, when these arenas were at the doorstep of parliament. Rigby again made the point. The 'mob', he asserted, had for many years been employed 'as an engine to carry questions in parliament'. Not a single MP, moreover, 'let them pretend what they will . . . dares support government in an unpopular question . . . and not a man in the House dares or does speak his opinion freely, if he thinks the gallery will object to it'.[20]

It is difficult to believe that the Dublin crowd exercised quite so much power over the legislature, yet the impact of 'public opinion by riot' cannot be discounted. Rudé describes the effectiveness of the London crowd in blocking the Gin and Excise bills in the 1730s as 'remarkable'. And eighteenth-century authority was acutely sensitive to urban disorder. Although policing was, for political reasons, generally inadequate, elaborate precautions were taken to keep the city 'larder[s]' stocked. Bakers were kept well-supplied and the price of bread was closely monitored in London, Paris and Dublin.[21] In the late 1750s premiums were offered on 'the carriage by land of all corn, wheat and flour to Dublin' and legislation was enacted to break price monopolies between graziers, cattle dealers and butchers and between coal merchants and ships masters. A government supporter claimed this as evidence of the Bedford administration's concern for the capital's inhabitants. 'Look', he wrote, 'at the large loaf we have' and at the moderate price of meat and coal.[22] Undoubtedly such concern applied as much to the public temper as to the popular well-being.

On 3 December, 1759, in Henry Grattan jnr.'s account, 'the people dreading a union and apprehending that their parliaments (such as they were), would be taken from them, suddenly rose in Dublin'. McDowell describes this incident as a 'startling event, a sudden, crude expression of out-of-doors interest in politics'.[23] In fact, the popular discontents which erupted onto the streets in December had been simmering since at least the spring. In 1758 the prohibition of Irish cattle exports to England was rescinded, followed the next year by that on beef and butter. These measures were criticised by the 'Patriots' as detrimental to the Irish economy. In May the lord lieutenant complained of 'the atrocious behaviour of the mob of Dublin towards those who come to Dublin to buy cattle,' while a patriot pamphleteer later attributed the ending of the December disturbances to the deployment of troops and a commons censure of 'the exportation of Irish cattle'.[24] 'The people' were restive. According to Froude, 'every day after the opening of the autumn session of 1759, a disorderly crowd hung about the doors of the parliament house'. At least one pamphlet, dated November, denying that a union was planned, is extant and at the end of that month newspapers in Belfast and Dublin dismissed reports of a union as 'without the least foundation'. The rumours were sustained, however, by the publication of other pamphlets advocating union and by the unionist sentiments publicly expressed by Lord Hillsborough.[25] They were also deliberately fuelled, 'industriously infused and propagated' by political agitators. Rigby believed the chief culprit was 'an infamous disappointed old lawyer' denied a place on the bench, who had 'been at great pains to poison the minds of the people'. Other suspects included those masters who 'over a glass inflame their apprentices and journeymen', ale-house orators and, inevitably, catholic priests.[26] There was nothing 'sudden' about the events of early December. They were months, or if the perspective is shifted, years in the making.

The proposal which triggered the crowd action was the so-called 'fourteen days' bill introduced by Rigby and seconded by the provost of Trinity, Francis Andrews. Traditionally the government was required to give forty days notice when it wished to recall parliament. The Rigby bill, modelled on similar English legislation, was ostensibly designed to meet emergencies, specifically in the event of a French invasion. With Britain then at war with France fears of an invasion were real.[27] But the proposed bill met with the scepticism of patriots and public alike. It was believed that it gave too much power to the executive, that it had been instigated by the English government and that it could be used to call a snap parliament and foist a union upon Ireland.[28] In addition to the obvious political grievance that the nation was to be stripped of its ancient liberties, union was portrayed as a harbinger of economic catastrophe for the tradesmen of Dublin. The city's domestic market, so dependent on wealthy peers and MPs, would collapse as lords and commons packed their bags for London and Westminster. 'The Castle was to become a desert [and] our men of fortune would ramble abroad after pleasure and power'. 'Trade would be lost' and 'families starve'. Indeed the rioters were afterwards upbraided for possibly having deterred the gentry from residing in the capital, 'usual at such seasons as the present, and which hath been greatly considered as extremely beneficial to the traders and manufacturers of this city'.[29] The anti-union demonstrators feared for their livelihoods as well as their liberties.

Upon a signal given by a drummer parading through the streets a crowd assembled in the Liberty about noon on Monday, 3 December. Groups, some armed with sticks, gathered at assembly-points such as taverns, then made their way to College Green, thickening into a throng several thousand strong. They then spent most of the day at the doors of parliament listening to harangues and jostling MPs. Rigby was 'hooted' and a gallows was erected as a symbolic warning of his fate should he proceed with the bill. Rigby was singled out for special attention because he had proposed the offending legislation and because of his abrasive personal style. (Even a government apologist described him as 'civil enough, though not over courtly in his way of expressing it'.) A week after the riot his servants still went armed whenever Rigby ventured out 'late at night'.[30] The lord chancellor was dragged from his carriage, a privy councillor pulled along the street, the earl of Inchiquin stripped of his wig and robe, the attorney general and others abused. MPs were stopped and obliged to swear oaths that they would oppose a union. The quality of the crowd's politicisation is evidenced by its discrimination. Rigby and other 'suspects' were targets, while 'country gentlemen of known patriot principles' were left unmolested.[31] The specificity which the rioters displayed was a hallmark of urban politics. However big or anonymous the eighteenth-century metropolis might become, to its crowd the leading administrators and politicians were never 'faceless men'.[32] Eventually the lords' chamber was forcibly entered and an old woman (complete with clay pipe) placed on the chair. Meanwhile the lord mayor, sheriffs and city magistrates had been conspicuously inactive, behaviour denounced by the lord lieutenant as 'wilful'. The mayor – Rigby called him a 'blockhead' – had in fact refused Bedford's offer of troops while the crowd was still gathered. The next day he was summoned along with the sheriffs before the commons. Examined at the bar of the house on the Wednesday he was pointedly reminded of his duty to prevent 'riotous assemblies'.[33] The deliberate non-intervention of the civic authorities on this occasion clearly indicates where their political sympathies lay. The crowd finally dispersed at nightfall after a show of force by the military – but not before they had received assurances from the Speaker, John Ponsonby, that a union would not happen.

The character of Dublin's popular politics is reflected by the composition of the crowd. Rigby's assertion that the rioters were 'of the very lowest and scum of the people' and that 'the better kind of people, the tradesmen, and the like, are ashamed and terrified at such proceedings', can be dismissed as the predictable language of an eighteenth-century 'gentleman' and government official.[34] The response of the magistrates and, afterwards, the refusal of juries to convict accused rioters,[35] suggest that the lines of social demarcation were more generously drawn than at the 'very lowest' class. This is in keeping with Rudé's findings concerning the social profile of the London crowd. For example, one element of the crowd was composed of students from Trinity College. The 'collegians' allegedly 'sent the drum' to the Liberty and students participated in the tumult outside parliament.[36] Admittedly eighteenth-century student life was more robust than it is today. In Dublin student gangs even engaged in faction fights with the Liberty and Ormond boys. Trinity students were also admitted to the gallery of the commons if they wore their gowns, a practice which might explain Rigby's claim that members always spoke with one eye fixed in that direction. Mainly, though, the crowd was recruited from a cross-section of the pre-industrial workforce. Detailed evidence is lacking, but the information which does survive can fairly confidently be taken as providing a representative 'random sample' of the rioters. Among those identified were a grocer, a 'shoemaker and watchmaker', two weavers, two other textile workers, a carpenter, an ale-seller and four shoemakers, all with addresses in the Liberty.[37] The numerical parity of textile workers and shoemakers is revealing. 'Who says cobbler, says radical,' claims Hobsbawm, and in the eighteenth and nineteenth centuries, shoemakers across Europe had a well-earned reputation for industrial and political militancy.[38] Dublin's shoemakers, it seems, were no exception.

At least eight of the ten rioters listed were 'reputed papists'. Although the denominational breakdown of the crowd remains obscure, the politics of catholic participation were combustible. The Catholic Church, alert to accusations of disloyalty in the context of Britain's war with catholic Ireland's traditional ally, France, was quick to issue a condemnation of the riot and to deny the involvement of any of its flock, 'unless some refractory and abandoned profligate[s]'. This letter was read from the pulpit of every chapel in Dublin and catholics were forbidden 'even to be spectators at such assemblies'.[39] The denial was politically expedient, yet it is illuminating that the Church thought it plausible to maintain the fiction of an almost purely protestant crowd. Similarly, Bedford noted that the riot had 'taken its rise in the Earl of Meath's Liberty, chiefly inhabited by protestant weavers', and claimed that the malcontents were 'New Light Presbyterians' with republican sympathies. Rigby blamed a 'sect among the protestants', descendants of Cromwellian settlers, who exhibited 'a dislike [of] monarchy and the Established Church'. However, this was not what Pitt in London wished to hear, and Bedford soon had a diplomatic change of mind. The papists were after all the most likely culprits.[40] Probably the most that can be said is that there was a substantial catholic contingent in the crowd and that this mirrored the city's shifting denominational balance. Dublin had a protestant majority in 1732 which, as the metropolis continued to suck in rural catholic migrants, was overtaken by about mid-century. In 1757, according to James, 'all but five of the numerous bakers in Dublin were reportedly catholic'.[41] The trend continued. Further evidence of the increasingly catholic character of the workforce can be found in

Archbishop Carpenter's condemnation of combinations in the 1770s. By 1784 contemporaries assumed a predominantly catholic lower class.[42]

Whether catholic or protestant, in this instance the crowd was successful. Rigby withdrew the bill. LaTouche states that it was rescinded on the day of the riot, but adds that the 'mob', 'for several succeeding days', continued to stop, question and administer oaths to MPs. James Kelly writes that the crowd did not actually break into parliament until 6 December.[43] Whatever the precise chronology, the important point is that the measure was *speedily* abandoned. Indeed, as the rapid publication of several pamphlets illustrates, the government was at pains to stress its responsiveness to public opinion. 'I have very good authority to say,' wrote one apologist, 'that upon mature consideration of the peculiar circumstances of this kingdom, and the dislike expressed by almost everybody of the intended alterations; all thoughts were dropped of proceeding in the proposed bill'.[44] This episode offers a classic example of the Dublin crowd in action. The urban geography, religious composition, social structures and politics of the city's lower classes are crystallized in this moment.

The parallels between the events of 1759 and the next major political intervention of the crowd twenty years later are striking. Although the specific issue on this occasion was a 'short money bill', over a month before the disturbances of 15 November, 1779, the lord lieutenant, Buck-inghamshire, reported that 'the idea of a projected union is industriously circulated as the best calculated to excite the indignation of the Dublin rioters'.[45] Again political and economic grievances were conflated. The crisis of the late 1770s originated with the American war. This gave rise to the Volunteer movement and pro-colonist sentiments in Ireland. The leaders of the 'American' party in Dublin were Sir Edward Newenham, a correspondent of Franklin's, and – at the beginning of his colourful career – the most popular city politician since Lucas, James Napper Tandy. The war also caused severe economic dislocation, resulting in a trade depression which began to bite in 1778. The capital was particularly hard-hit and the government responded to widespread unemployment and deprivation by instituting a relief fund, to which the lord lieutenant personally donated £100.[46] The patriots, now backed by armed Volunteers, responded by campaigning for the non-importation of English goods and by calling for the lifting of Britain's mercantilist restrictions and the introduction of 'free trade'.[47] The immediacy of the patriot solution had obvious attractions for Dublin's hard-pressed lower classes. It had also clear advantages for the employers, and so an unholy alliance between master and journeyman developed. Evidence later emerged that certain employers were involved in instigating street disorders during 1779.[48]

One difference between 1759 and 1779 was the role played by the opposition press. For instance, the names of a number of 'importers' whose premises were attacked on 1 June, had previously appeared on a list printed in a Dublin newspaper. Interestingly these attacks on woollen drapers' and haberdashers' shops were carried out by 'about twenty butchers'. The exact vocational designation suggests how the crowd was structured around the workplace.[49] When parliament opened in the autumn no reference was made in the king's speech to free trade, prompting the *Freemans Journal*, (at this time still in the opposition camp) to remark:

> Will any man venture to show his face who shall vote long supplies? – A six month money bill is too long. Let no supplies at all be granted; let the establishment pay for itself; the more distraction the better. The mischiefs that will arise to Great Britain will be intolerable. This is the moment when every man, in and out of parliament, should exert himself.

This amounted to an overt attempt to intimidate the executive by mobilising extra-parliamentary opposition. 'Men out of parliament' may have been code for 'Volunteers', yet the implications of a report in the same issue of how several 'persons well armed' attacked a house in Dame Street, 'crying out "the blood of importers must be shed"', cannot have been lost on the paper's readers.[50] On 4 November, the anniversary of King William's birthday, thousands of Volunteers paraded around his statue on College Green opposite the parliament house. Cannon were inscribed with the threat 'FREE TRADE, OR THIS', and banners draped around the pedestal proclaimed: 'Free Trade', 'A Short Money Bill', 'Relief for Ireland' and 'Glorious Revolution'. That day the attorney general, John Scott, asked 'whether parliament existed to register the pleasure of the Volunteers'.[51]

As the vote on a short money bill approached, the sequence of events which had occurred in 1759 was re-enacted. 'Incendiary letters', one, apparently, signed 'A member of parliament', were 'industriously dispersed'. On 15 November the drum was beaten in the Liberty and a crowd of 'between five and six thousand working manufacturers' converged on College Green. Fitzgibbon claimed that 'one of the mob being asked at the door of the House what could provoke them to assemble in that manner? replied by asking "why did you send for us?"'[52] MPs were stopped and forced to swear support for a short money bill. The crowd's slogans echoed those of the Volunteers and the lawyers corps present – the magistrates once more declined to act – 'echoed the huzzas of the manufacturers'. A group of rioters broke into the Four Courts in search of Scott and, not finding him there, proceeded to bombard his house with stones.[53] As in 1759 this was a spectacular, but not notably violent, affair. As in 1759 the crowd (this time aided by the spectre of the Volunteers) secured its objective. Much to the chagrin of its supporters, the administration did not oppose the passage of a short money bill. This decision in the opinion of the chief secretary, Thomas Waite, would 'hang about our necks like a millstone, and be for ever quoted to prove what encouragement people have to persevere and to scatter terrors'. That most experienced of civil servants, the first commissioner of the revenue, John Beresford, observed that so long as the offending lord lieutenant remained, 'we all live by courtesy of the mob,' and wryly concluded the letter, 'believe me ever, with great truth, though with broken windows, and almost a broken head . . . '[54] In the corridors of Dublin Castle Dublin's street politics could not be ignored, a troublesome fact which would be further dramatized by the events of the 1780s and 1790s.

Both these riots revealed a working relationship between middle-class patriots and lower-class crowd. Common political gaols superseded class antagonisms. Students, lawyers and merchants joined forces with shoe-makers and weavers. Indeed it might be argued that a true identity of interest existed. While the politics of legislative independence motivated patriots, Volunteers and later reformers, it is hardly accidental that union in 1759 was represented to Dublin's lower classes as a prelude to economic disaster, or that 'free trade' was portrayed as a remedy for unemployment. The undoubted importance of economic stimuli does not preclude popular political literacy. Rather the combination of the political and economic proved a highly inflammable mix. However, the cross-class coalition that operated in 1759 and during the late 1770s contained – to use Marxist terminology – 'inherent contradictions'. Class conflict had been momentarily subsumed by broader political struggles but when, in 1780, the specific political crisis had passed, class tensions resurfaced.

If Dublin had a history of labour unrest, parliament had a history of trying to curtail it. Anti-combination legislation was introduced in 1729, 1743, 1757, 1763 and 1772.[55] In February, 1780, a committee of inquiry was established by the commons to investigate the 'problem' of combination. Unlike previous legislation which was directed at specific trades, that which was framed on the committee's recommendation – and received the royal assent in August – represented a novel, because comprehensive, assault upon combination *in principle*. The fact that this act preceded a similar British one by nineteen years adds weight to Sidney and Beatrice Webb's observation that Dublin's workers were the best organised in the kingdom.[56] O'Connell interprets this inquiry and the subsequent law as a sort of strategic 'follow-up' operation by a triumphant Dublin bourgeoisie. Having recently won 'free trade', they moved to consolidate the victory of economic liberalism by eradicating those internal impediments to the free market, the trade unions. The timing of the bill gives this argument credence. Other evidence supports it as well. Speaking before the committee a Dublin employer remarked that the combinations were 'highly injurious to Trades, so as to have made it impossible hitherto even to supply the home consumption; and it seem[ed] to him it will be impossible for this country to receive any material benefit from the enlargements lately obtained for our Trade, without rooting them out'.[57]

The inquiry, which gave numerous employers a platform, highlighted the sophistication and extent of workplace organisation in the metropolis. Some witnesses attributed combination to 'the too great use of spirits'. An unconvincing explanation, this allegation nonetheless hints at the importance of the tavern as a place for conducting illegal business. Leaders were called 'committee men' and these 'committee men' were supposedly connected by a system of 'correspondence'. In 1781, when James Gandon began work on the Custom House, on a site plagued by combinations, newly-employed workers were obliged to take 'oaths of secrecy'.[58] The terminology is familiar. 'Committee men', 'correspondence' and oaths were all later to be characteristic of the Defenders and other 'underground' societies. The impression created by the testimony offered to the commons committee is that virtually the entire Dublin workforce was organised.[59] The efficiency of that organisation was demonstrated during the course of the proceedings when five journeymen petitions objecting to the proposed bill were submitted to parliament. Paid insertions were placed in the press and money was collected to fee legal counsel. Journeyman resistance culminated on 13 June when several thousand of them collected in the Phoenix Park. Coming only days after the shocking Gordon riots in London, this huge lower-class gathering must have sent shivers of apprehension through the ranks of the 'men of property'. The army and the Volunteers were called out. As the situation stayed calm, a deputation of six journeymen was permitted to deliver a petition to the lord lieutenant. Class politics were reasserted. The Volunteers, that largely middle-class body, which only seven months before had 'echoed the huzzas' of 'the mob', now mobilised to contain those same people once they rallied behind the banner of combination.[60]

The persistence and scale of combination in eighteenth-century Dublin demonstrates the independent organisational ability of the lower classes.

This capacity conflicts with any image of the crowd as dupe, activated at will by 'outside agitators', or as the 'hired mob' of the authorities' imagination. Still, in the political sphere, middle-class radicals tended to retain the initiative and leadership. The *modus vivendi* that existed between the radicals and the crowd is encapsulated in the career of James Napper Tandy. Regarded by some at the time (not always without justification), as a figure for ridicule, he was – for about fifteen years – a real force in the municipal and street politics of the capital. Self-appointed tribune of the people, Volunteer colonel and common council representative, in 1790 Drennan described Tandy as the 'real' lord mayor.[61] His influence over Dublin's lower classes was immense. In 1781 he led the crowd which occupied the Custom House site, in an attempt to obstruct work on a building opposed by the city's merchant community and reprobated by radicals as the pet project of Beresford. In 1790, together with Archibald Hamilton Rowan, he headed the 'anti-police' party in the mayoralty dispute and placed himself at the front of the crowd, 'beyond conception numerous', which celebrated the election to parliament of both the popular candidates, Grattan and Lord Henry Fitzgerald.[62] Although he went on to become a founder member of the United Irishmen, to flee the country and, in 1798, to accompany a small French flotilla on the last – farcical – 'invasion' of Ireland, Tandy's career as a city politician peaked in 1784.[63]

1784 also marked the last major political intervention of the traditional Dublin crowd. Later unrest was either minor, economic in character, or resulted from the activities of the more tightly structured 'political underground' of the revolutionary nineties. In contrast with 1759 and 1779 when mounting popular discontents were condensed into brief dramatic riots in College Green, Dublin during 1784 witnessed a near-continuous sequence of street disorders. At times it seemed as if the capital had fallen 'in great measure under the domination and tyranny of the mob'. In September the painter, Sir Joshua Reynolds, wrote to the lord lieutenant, the duke of Rutland, that he had intended to visit Ireland, but having heard from (the celebrated actress) Sarah Siddons, 'such a sad account of the Liberty boys', he had not the courage to proceed. 'She came away in a terrible fright,' he added, 'and has not yet recovered herself'.[64] The disturbances were fuelled by economic hardship. The downturn in the economy which began in 1783, exacerbated by 'the extraordinary inclemency of the season', continued into the following year. Rising food prices and mass unemployment returned. Speaking on a motion voting £3,000 relief for the distressed inhabitants of Dublin, Travers Hartley, one of the MPs for the city, referred to '21,000 poor' in the 'manufacturing parishes'. Froude records 50,000 artisans 'out of work and starving'.[65] The predictable patriot (and popular) reaction was a call for protection duties. On 19 February 'a numerous meeting of the citizens of Dublin' held at the Royal Exchange, demanded the imposition of duties on imported goods as a way of ensuring 'preference to our own fabrics'. That month one of the two MPs for the county, Sir Edward Newenham, many of whose constituents resided in suburban Dublin, tried to attach a protection amendment to the king's address. A few days later the other county MP, Luke Gardiner, introduced a bill for placing duties on wool. Rutland expected that protection would prove the 'most difficult issue' in the forthcoming session.[66]

Protection served as the leitmotiv of social and political unrest, but it was only one of several grievances agitating the public mind. In mid-January, for example, large 'aggregate' meetings of freeholders, called to petition parliament for 'equal representation', were convened in both county and city. The city meeting elected nine delegates to draft the petition, including Tandy and, portentously, John Keogh. Dublin's shifting denominational balance was beginning to register on the streets and in the committee rooms. Catholics were taking their place in the campaign for reform.[67] Other sources of discontent were the question of municipal rights raised by a paving bill and animosity towards the garrison.

Hostility between town and garrison is a perennial theme in the history of urban riot. These habitual tensions were intensified during 1784 by the presence on the streets of Dublin of hundreds or more soldiers, disbanded after service in America. Following clashes between the military and the locals the scale of violence escalated steeply when the butchers – a well-organised trade – resorted to the savage practice of houghing soldiers. Hitherto confined to cattle, 'houghing' (cutting the tendons at the back of the legs), was a technique pioneered by agrarian rebels. In August a crowd attacked a military escort guarding a public flogging in the Liberty. The troops opened fire, killing one of the rioters.[68]

Oil was then inadvertently added to the fire by Sir John Blaquerie's paving bill, which was placed on the parliamentary agenda at the same time as Gardiner's protection motion. This continued the process, begun by the Wide Streets Commissioners in 1757, whereby parliament assumed more and more responsibility for the administration of the capital. To the eighteenth-century citizen, keenly jealous of local privileges and liberties, such legislation was perceived as an erosion of 'chartered rights' by the central authority. While civic resistance to attacks upon municipal autonomy might be expected at all times, in the circumstances of 1784 Blaquerie's bill invited trouble. Sir Boyle Roche – suspecting the machinations of Napper Tandy – recounts how he was jostled by the 'aggregate body' for supporting the paving bill. Or as he put it, with characteristic bombast, how he had 'found himself engulfed in a vortex, whence he could not extricate himself'.[69]

This incident occurred during the riot of 5 April. The paving bill was one cause, protection the other. The riot and its immediate background closely conformed to the pattern set by the crowd's previous excursions into College Green. Handbills were distributed in the Liberty as the opposition press launched verbal broadsides at government. The *Volunteers Journal*, a particularly abrasive paper, threatened John Foster, the chancellor of the exchequer, and a staunch opponent of tariffs, with tarring and feathering, and described parliament as 'that den of thieves'.[70] On the morning of Monday the 5th a public meeting was summoned to protest about the paving bill. 'A very large body assembled' at the Thosel or city hall, about a half mile from College Green. After this meeting a section of the crowd moved down the road and broke into the gallery of the commons. The rioters' anger turned on those MPs who had voted down Gardiner's protection motion three days earlier, and they put the motion that 'Foster should be hanged'. Needless to add it was carried.[71] Again the magistrates 'stood idly by'. The crowd was socially heterogeneous. The chief secretary, Thomas Orde, blamed drunken, 'poor manufacturers', while a town meeting noted the presence of 'some respectable citizens in the gallery'. Rutland believed that the masters, who of course had a vested interest in import controls, had deliberately fomented discontent, in some cases actually laying-off 'the poorer weavers' and advising them 'to seek for employment and redress at the House of Commons'.[72]

Unlike those of 1759 or 1779 this riot had no purgative effect. After 5 April Dublin faced into a long turbulent summer. In 1759 the government responded to the disturbances by denying that a union was planned. In 1779 both 'free trade' and a short money bill were conceded. In 1784 the government held firm. The protection agitation continued. In imitation of the Americans, 'tarring and feathering' committees were formed to coerce or punish importers of English goods. It was the sustained violence of this campaign which fed the image of a city subject to mob-rule. In August Fitzgibbon who, in his own words, had the 'honour' of been included in a list of intended victims, remarked on the 'necessity of always carrying arms'.[73] The break-down of public order was compounded by the disarray of the Volunteers. On the one hand the merchants' corps helped to police the Liberty, while on the other, the Liberty corps – led by Tandy – armed and drilled 'the people'. The *Freemans Journal*, by mid-1784 in the pay of government, accused the Volunteers of training 'butchers basket-boys' and 'chimney sweeps'.

As if placing firelocks and bayonets in the hands of the lower classes was not sufficiently alarming, these 'lower artisans', as Under-Secretary Cooke noted, were 'all Roman Catholics'.[74] The politically advanced Volunteers attempt to mobilise Dublin's lower classes unavoidably entailed arming catholics – in defiance of the penal laws – and concentrated attention on the wider 'catholic question'. At an aggregate meeting in June, in which Tandy, Todd Jones and Keogh played prominent parts, the issue of catholic political rights was raised, provoking 'a very long and unpleasant debate'. The meeting eventually came down in favour of suffrage for catholics. In September a requisition to the city sheriffs to convene another meeting to elect delegates to the national reform convention had sixty-one signatures. On the copy which Rutland sent to Whitehall twenty-six are marked 'papist'.[75] 1784, with its alliances of catholics and radicals, Volunteer-reformers and 'the people', and in the way in which the lower classes were politicised by meetings, petitioning, the press and collective experience, anticipated the 1790s. Above all, the catholic question, now that it had been raised, could not be shelved indefinitely. Although no doubt informed by paranoia rather than by prescience, Orde was correct when, on 23 September, he wrote of 'the catholics, from which quarter after all, the real mischief is to spring'.[76]

Orde proved prophetic in another context too. On 24 June, 1784, he expressed the opinion that 'the state of the magistracy and of the police must be subjects for very serious consideration'.[77] As the events of that year had so vividly demonstrated Dublin, a populous, expanding and unruly metropolis where the crowd came face-to-face with the ruling elite, posed a huge public order problem. The Volunteers and the magistrates were unreliable; the 'police', such as it was, and the emergency interventions of the military, inadequate. One novel, if drastic, mode of social control, which the administration fleetingly considered, was the dispersal and resettlement of the city's weaving community, in 'different towns and villages at a certain distance' from Dublin. A limited policy of 'rustification' was in fact pursued by parliament during the 1780s. Subsidies were offered to cotton manufacturers who located outside Dublin.[78] But in the aftermath of 1784 a more immediate solution to the public order problem was sought by the establishment of an effective police force. Today the principal function of the police is perceived to be the prevention and detection of crime. Yet in its origins it was primarily designed as an instrument for the maintenance of social control and public order.[79] The present day police are such an accepted part of society, moreover, that it is hard to imagine how innovative an institution this was in the 1780s, or to appreciate the hostility which it encountered. In a pre-democratic age political discourse revolved around 'constitutional liberty' and its defence against the incursions of 'arbitrary power'. In the British Isles the idea of a 'police' was associated with continental, particularly French, absolutism. It was thought of as a standing army in disguise and as the very antithesis of 'liberty'.[80] The debate on the 1786 police bill was therefore conducted as much in terms of constitutional liberty and Dublin's chartered rights as of the need for public order. The bill had originated in Westminster in 1785, where fierce opposition by the Londoners had obliged parliament to retract. The 'experiment', shrewdly modified, was then imposed on the more pliant Irish legislature and on Dublin. Both capitals had until then been policed by a motley parish watch and constables. The new provisions abolished local control and *accountability* replacing it with a professional, uniformed and armed police force, responsible to the central authority, and operating within a single, unified jurisdiction. The Irish bill managed to avoid the opposition of the municipality – as had happened in London – by recruiting the new salaried police commissioners from among the aldermen. Resistance fell to the press, to the freemen and freeholders, who petitioned parliament in their thousands in 1786, 1788, 1789, 1791, 1792 and 1795, to the patriots – Grattan described it as a 'bill of armed patronage' – and to the crowd. Anti-police riots occurred in 1787 and 1790.[81] As the first recognisably 'modern' police force in the British Isles, the Dublin police experiment of 1786 has great historical significance, but as an instrument of social control or political repression it had no appreciable countervailing effect on the spread of organised disaffection in the 1790s.

II DUBLIN IN THE AGE OF REVOLUTION

The amount of attention paid by the authorities to Dublin, evident from the rustification scheme, the new police and in the official correspondence, indicates how seriously they took the city and its problems. The Dublin 'problem' was transformed by the new political agenda set by the French revolution, and in every way magnified by the crisis of the 1790s. As both the Castle and the revolutionaries realised, in the increasingly naked struggle for power, the capital possessed immense strategic and symbolic importance. The rural Defenders, for instance, 'had the greatest wish to spread Defenderism in Dublin', believing that a rising there, 'would be better than all they could do in the country'. The United Irish leader, Oliver Bond, 'seemed to think if Dublin was once taken, all the rest of Ireland would directly submit'. From an opposite political perspective General Carhampton, contemplating a French invasion, predicted that 'the city [would] be handed over to a municipality formed of the dregs of the people, who, armed with pikes and whiskey, would probably plunder and burn the town, and the whole kingdom then be undone for a century to come. It is impossible', he wrote, 'to calculate the probable excesses of the Dublin mob in such circumstances'.[82] Revolutionary victory or government survival, in other words, often hinges upon who controls the capital. Robert Watt planned to 'seize' Edinburgh in 1794, Gracchus Babuef, Paris in 1796 and Colonel Despard, London in 1802. Numerous *coup*-style plots notwithstanding, there was no rebellion on the streets of Dublin in 1798. Perhaps it is because of this – because they lack a dramatic climax – that the city's radical and revolutionary politics in this period (especially after 1795) have suffered comparative historiographical neglect. Whatever the reason, the literature does not reflect contemporary perceptions of Dublin's pivotal role in national politics.[83]

The exception to this neglect is the Society of United Irishmen. Its history, at least, is well-documented and well-known.[84] It has been depicted during its legal phase, from November 1791 to May 1794, as an advanced reform club, one of many in the British Isles – like the London Corresponding Society or the Sheffield Society for Constitutional Information – which registered the euphoria generated by the French revolution. The picture drawn by McDowell portrays it as a group of up to 400 catholic shopkeepers and doctors and protestant lawyers and merchants, with a sprinkling of aristocrats. These included Archibald Hamilton Rowan, an Ulster landowner and Cambridge graduate, and Simon Butler, the brother of Lord Mountgarret. Left-wing whigs, the United Irishmen's primary objective was parliamentary reform. In practice, according to McDowell, they functioned as a sort of debating society, issued declarations, and became entangled in a series of legal battles with the government over censorship and undefined parliamentary privilege. During this 'open' phase three members of the leadership, Butler, Rowan and Bond, were imprisoned, one, Dr Drennan, was eventually acquitted and another, Napper Tandy, forewarned that serious charges relating to Defenderism were to be brought, fled to America. After they were suppressed and 'forced underground' the United Irishmen, with an expectation of French military assistance, and in reaction to the deteriorating domestic situation, moved towards the politics of republicanism and a strategy of insurrection.

There is much to recommend this 'model'. William Paulet Cary, sometime editor and proprietor of the *National Evening Star*, who was expelled from the society in November, 1793, appeared as a crown witness against Drennan in 1794 and wrote a sour, self-justificatory pamphlet attacking his erstwhile comrades. Cary had an axe to grind, yet his pamphlet does give an insiders view. Interestingly, he criticises the Dublin United Irishmen's social elitism. They were dominated, he claimed, by an 'aristocracy of the learned professions – Physic and Law', and were subject to the baleful influence of the *bona fide* aristocrats, Butler and Rowan. McDowell identifies thirty attorneys, twenty-six barristers, sixty-seven cloth merchants and thirty-two other merchants.[85] Of course 'merchant' – as an analysis of eighteenth-century almanacs or trade directories would confirm – was a generously elastic term, readily applied to petty shopkeepers and wealthy businessmen alike. However, the 'middle-class' credentials of some United Irishmen are beyond dispute. Richard McCormick was a big employer. Oliver Bond, if the size of the warehouse at his home in Bridge Street is any indication, was a prosperous textiles merchant. Bond's father-in-law, Henry Jackson, owned an iron foundry in Church Street, 'iron mills' in the south east suburb of Clonskea and industrial plant in Phoenix Street and Sir John Rogerson's Quay. His capital investment was substantial – he introduced steam-powered machinery to the city – and so, presumably, was his workforce. In 1792 the printer, John Chambers, opened new premises in Abbey Street, described at the time as 'the completest printing office ever erected in this kingdom, with storerooms and every necessary appurtenance' where business was carried out 'on the most extensive scale'.[86] The 'middling', middle-class and professional social profile of the Dublin United Irishmen resembles the class structure of the Volunteer-reform movement of the 1780s.

Although the nineties in some ways mark a sharp break with the past, there were also notable continuities, over these two decades, in personnel, issues and tactics. Continuity is personified in the figure of Napper Tandy. Drennan, himself a United Irishman and veteran of the reform movement in the eighties, described the fledgling society in November 1791, as a club 'chiefly composed of the Tandean party in the city'. The very first United Irish declaration condemned 'the obnoxious and unconstitutional Police Act'. In 1793, in a distinct echo of 1784, they promoted the non-consumption of English goods and tried to revive the language of tarring and feathering committees.[87]

Clearly, the model of the United Irishmen as advanced, middle-class reformers, fits the available evidence in a number of ways. But it is also incomplete and too tame. McDowell, for instance, notes the 'bourgeois character of the society', its 'patronising' attitude towards 'the people' and the reservations of a considerable section of the membership about the wisdom of universal suffrage.[88] While his scrupulous scholarship cannot be faulted, his emphasis is misleading. Political before they were social reformers, the public pronouncements of the United Irishmen are nevertheless peppered with references which draw out the social implications of political reform. They state the necessity of 'giving political value and station to the majority of the people' and argue that the franchise will ensure 'a more equal distribution of the benefits and blessings of life through the lowest classes of the community, the stamina of society'. Nor were they blind to the possible consequences of such propaganda. 'Give the poor a country,' they warned 'the rich' in 1793, 'or you will loose one yourselves'.[89] Only by retrieving and re-emphasising such 'levelling' statements – and the examples could be multiplied – can a more accurate image of the United Irishmen be pieced together. Historians, eager to demolish the anachronistic proto-socialist constructions which later left-wing publicists have erected on such flimsy foundations as Wolfe Tone's oft-quoted reliance on the 'men of no property',[90] have moved too far in the opposite direction. McDowell and others[91] are right to draw attention to United Irish ambivalences about 'the people', but their choice of illustration lacks balance, it directs that attention towards the 'bourgeois' and the 'patronising'; ambivalences have two sides.

The Dublin Society stands at the close of an eighteenth-century urban radical tradition. Its links with the Volunteer-reform movement of the 1770s and 1780s was particularly strong. But under the impact of the French revolution and then the war; against a background of economic crisis and the eruption of the catholic question; and in response to ascendancy reaction and official repression, the politics of revolution overtook those of reform. As argued earlier, however, the contrast between the 'constitutionalists' of the pre-Fitzwilliam era and the supposedly reluctant revolutionaries of the later years has been overstated. Usually viewed in accordance with this two-stage theory and within a national political framework, a different picture of the Dublin United Irishmen emerges when they are placed in their immediate urban context. The society's relationship with the city's crowd, for instance, casts doubt on its alleged commitment to constitutional propriety.

The social and economic environment inhabited by the radicals of the 1790s both resembled and differed from the world of 1759. The Liberty was still the home of the crowd and when, in 1792, certain United Irishmen 'tampered with the mob', they were using well-worn channels of communication and employing standard radical tactics.[92] Yet the crowd, like the city, was changing shape. It was now more catholic, more politicised, more proletarian. In 1759 the religious composition of the crowd is problematic. By the 1790s its mainly catholic character is axiomatic. The riot on 31 March, 1795, for example, was provoked by the recall of Fitzwilliam and the dashing of catholic expectations of 'full emancipation'. In the sphere of radical politics, over half the membership of the Dublin United Irishmen were catholic.[93] While the posts of chairman and secretary, which rotated, were always held by protestants, this may just be a further example of the leading catholic politician, John Keogh's, caution or Machiavellianism. In practice a number of catholic United Irishmen played an important part in city politics. McCormick and another textile manufacturer, Thomas Warren, were instrumental in obtaining non-importation addresses from 'the working broad cloth weavers of the Liberty' in 1793. Both were allegedly in contact with the Defenders, and two years later the hand of McCormick (and of Keogh), was detected behind the Fitzwilliam riot.[94]

'Political' crowds in eighteenth-century Dublin were activated by political crises. The 1790s, which witnessed a sustained and formidable challenge to the established order, was a decade of near-perpetual crisis. The qualitative difference between lower-class politicisation in this and in earlier periods is illustrated by the network of plebeian 'reading clubs' and Defender lodges, which developed alongside (or 'beneath') the mainstream, middle-class radical, United Irish movement. Painite ideology injected popular politics with a new permanence and coherence. No immediate or major controversy was exercising either parliament or populace in August 1793, when on 'several evenings' 'a number of men, not altogether of the lowest class' (or, according to another account, 'a great number of idle persons'), assembled at the steps of the Royal Exchange 'to discuss politics after their own way'. On the 7th Richard Dry – later a key United Irish 'emissary' – was arrested, while waving a copy of the *Rights of Man*, for using seditious expressions. On the 11th another meeting was broken-up by the police 'on a presumption that [it] was formed to engender some new-fangled political opinions'.[95] This is an example of Dublin street politics in the 'age of revolution'. Indeed Dubliners were subjected to a steady flow of 'new fangled opinions' from the press. *The National Evening Star* was successively edited by Cary and by Randal McAllister and the *Hibernian Journal* by Thomas McDonnell, all, at some point, United Irishmen. The Society itself published the short-lived *National Journal* in 1792, and both the *Morning Post* and the *Dublin Evening Post*, can be classified as opposition newspapers. Even apolitical, commercial, papers such as *Saunders Newsletter*, or pro-government ones like the *Freemans Journal* and *Faulkners Dublin Journal*, carried news from France. However much the revolution might have been deplored, it could not be ignored.[96]

This was an era too, of rapid social change. Although Dublin was still a pre-industrial city in the sense that most people still worked at home, the artisan and the small workshop now existed side-by-side with the wage-earner and the factory. A glass works in Abbey Street employed

150 men in 1794. Ownership of the silk industry, which employed 'several thousand' weavers, was concentrated in the hands of about twenty master manufacturers. Not all of the consequences of economic change were welcomed. In 1796 *Faulkners Dublin Journal* attributed the spread of the euphemistically named 'reading clubs' among young tradesmen to a collapse of social control, caused by 'the abominable custom adopted by the masters of keeping only outdoor apprentices'.[97] Further recruits to the new political radicalism – which, after all, was a form of protest – must have been gained as a result of the poor economic conditions.

Seventeen ninety-three was a particularly bad year. The panic-induced credit shortage which was one side-effect of the political crisis of the winter of 1792–3, was prolonged by the outbreak of hostilities with France. Economic dislocation generated price inflation and mass unemployment. Estimates of unemployment in the textile trades ran to eighty and ninety per cent. In April one newspaper lamented 'a general decrease of demand of every species of goods than had been known since the memorable year of 1778'. All construction work on the grand canal was halted and admissions to the poor house rose sharply, due to the 'high price of coal and provisions'.[98] The popular reaction was predictable. On 8 May thousands of Liberty weavers, the women 'in a rage', looted bakers and butchers shops and destroyed English cloth goods. Shops all over the city were shut up and the army called out. At the end of the month unemployed weavers staged a 'melancholy procession' past the new Custom House and the homes of the gentry. More looting and another procession took place in June.[99] As usual, radicals sought to turn economic distress to political advantage. A sizable number of United Irishmen were involved in the textile industry and were therefore directly affected by the depression. For instance, more United Irishmen had addresses at Pill Lane than at any other street. Whatever the reason for this – and it is unclear – this group remained the nucleus of the metropolitan organisation throughout the revolutionary underground period after 1794. Fourteen of the twenty United Irishmen who lived there have been identified as either textile drapers or manufacturers.[100] Not surprisingly, the society to which they belonged advocated the non-consumption of English goods. In a handbill, written by Tone, and distributed in March, increased imports were cleverly linked to the war. By cutting off continental markets the war, it argued, would encourage the dumping of British goods on Ireland. 'What good came to the poor' from war? it inquired. What could they expect, only further taxation? In May, another handbill, this time written by Hamilton Rowan, declared: 'We do not want charity. We do want work'. War, it stated, 'begets poverty'.[101]

Perhaps because the discontent was not focused on any specific parliamentary measure, in contrast with 1779 or 1784, the conjunction of economic hardship and radical agitation did not ignite any big 'political' riot. The combinations, however, continued to disrupt public order. Journeymen weavers attempted to prevent women working at the loom and 'undertakers' who took on more than one apprentice were tied face to tail on horseback and paraded through the streets of the Liberty. In May over fifty 'combining' shoemakers were sacked.[102] Ironically, a combinations bill, designed to cope with this serious social problem, was rejected by the lords in 1792. The bill had been introduced to the commons on 9 March, carried, and sent to the upper house. On the 19th 10,000 workmen, 'principally in the building line' assembled in the Phoenix Park. They then marched along the South Circular Road, through St Stephen's Green and down Grafton Street to the parliament, where they handed in a petition. The following day the 'master builders' and other employers presented a second petition supporting the proposed legislation.[103] Counsel appeared for both journeymen and masters. The journeyman case turned on their objections to a clause which would have prevented masters employing anyone who did not have a certificate of good behaviour from his previous master. Counsel for the employers used the example of the carpenters to drive home the pernicious effects of combination. The carpenters, they asserted, had been organised since 1761 and had succeeded in reducing their hours, raising their wages and restricting the number of apprentices. These journeymen met in fields and in public houses and collected subscriptions, supposedly for sickness and burial funds, but actually for strike pay. Fitzgibbon – of all people – was unimpressed. He described the bill as 'oppressive and unjust' and said that 'it should not be countenanced in this house'. Nor was it.[104]

With the exception of Cary's *National Evening Star*, the lords' decision was loudly condemned by the opposition press. The *Star* welcomed the rejection of the bill because it spared 'the already too-much oppressed and degraded workmen of Dublin'. In other editions it attacked 'combinations of the rich against the poor' and accused the employers of being 'the principle aggressors'.[105] But Cary, as his subsequent career shows, was a maverick. Whatever their sympathies for 'the people', however much they sought to mobilise the lower classes for political purposes, eighteenth-century radicals usually adhered to the conventional wisdom that combinations artificially distorted the labour market and acted as a brake on economic growth. McCormick condemned combination before the committee on trade in 1780. In 1792 the *Northern Star* and the Belfast Volunteers, Samuel Neilson amongst them, were committed to the suppression of that town's nascent trade unionism. During the summer of 1792 when 'riotous and armed mobs paraded the streets of the Liberties, burning and destroying goods of manufacturers and levying heavy contributions on the inhabitants at large,' Richard and Thomas Dry, both militant radicals, actually prosecuted several 'rioters'.[106]

But prosecution and public floggings did little to curb the wave of industrial unrest, and in May the shoemakers lit bonfires to celebrate the winning of their latest wage rise. Some employers responded to the increasing effectiveness of the combinations by implementing their own *ad hoc* policy of rustification. Raw materials were sent to be 'worked-up' in the country. But the limits of this remedy soon became apparent when some of these shipments were intercepted by 'armed weavers' and destroyed.[107] Labour troubles continued through 1793 into 1794, when the *Dublin Evening Post* complained that combinations in the capital 'had arrived at an alarming pitch of audacity'. Publicans who permitted their premises to be used by these illegal associations were threatened with the withdrawal of their licenses.[108] In April the city sheriff, John Giffard, raided an ale-house in High Street and arrested a number of shoemakers for 'conspiring together in a club or society called the Crispin Union'. Books and papers were seized which provide an insight into the sophistication of the craftsmen's organisation. The combinations had formal 'regulations' administered by an elected committee known as the 'superior council'. The shoemakers were also said to have had their 'committees of safety, of secrecy, of correspondence and of visitation, their president and secretary, their convention and delegates'. According to Carhampton they had 'in a manner organised (if not disciplined) themselves, so that they can assemble in forty minutes in one body of two thousand men, by concerted signals, from one house of call to another, and have been in the habit of doing so'.[109]

Combination was important because as the commonest form of illegal, autonomous, lower-class organisation it probably served as a model for the urban Defender lodge and for the plebeian 'Jacobin' clubs. It is likely that many Dublin Defenders were already, through their experience of combinations, well-versed in the techniques and ethos of the secret society. Journeyman combinations and political underground operated in the same urban sub-culture and shared the same terminology and practices. Both had their committee-men, subscriptions and oaths. Although in the current state of our knowledge the relationship between the two must remain speculative, occasionally a duplication of personnel can be glimpsed. In August, 1795, magistrates surprised a group of fifty journeymen nailers, to whom oaths were been administered, in a field in the northern suburb of Drumcondra. Three were arrested and charged with combination. Five were later identified as Defenders.[110]

The popularising of 'French' democratic ideology and the wider political crisis of the 1790s accelerated the transformation of traditional forms of lower-class association and direct action, the crowd and combination, into an underground network. The revolutionary decade informed the politics of this underground. Tailors and shopkeepers met to discuss Paine's *Age of Reason*. William Lawler, the treasurer of the Philanthropic Society, had previously joined the London Corresponding Society. Other activists included a French man named Le Blanc and a Trinity student, John Burke. In 1794 the Reverend William Jackson was arrested as a French agent and tried for treason. Le Blanc conspired to assassinate the key crown witness. Less sinisterly he proposed to teach his comrades the French language. Fashionably, both Le Blanc and Burke were atheists. Indeed Burke, who sometimes wrote for the *Dublin Evening Post*, was expelled from the college for blasphemy.[111]

Although the extent and activities of Dublin's lower-class underground have yet to be fully uncovered, its trail leads deep into the subterranean world of the city's revolutionary politics. Because they featured so largely in the Defender trials of 1795–6, most is known about the Telegraphic and Philanthropic societies, but there are references also to a 'sixpenny Jacobin club held in one of the lanes off Castle Street', in December, 1792; to another 'Jacobin club' in July, 1794, and to a Shamrock Society.[112] Some members of the Telegraphic and Philanthropic societies had earlier been members of reading clubs. The reading matter was Painite and the clubs were later called 'preparatory schools for the fraternity of Defenders'.[113] The Philanthropic was characterised in court as oath-bound and republican, with between 100 and 140 members. It attracted tradesmen and apprentices, both catholic and protestant, distributed handbills – one was entitled 'The cry of the poor for bread' – plotted to seize Dublin Castle and the magazine in Phoenix Park and to assassinate the sheriff, John Giffard.[114] At a time when the United Irishmen were still legal and ostensibly constitutional, the political extremism of these clubs is intriguing. Yet at least one member of the Philanthropic Society, Thomas Dry, was also a United Irishman (and later, a Defender), while Lawler was in contact with Hamilton Rowan – after Tandy the best known United Irishman in Dublin.[115]

By February 1795, when Drennan commented that 'the lower people are in greater habits of connection with the higher than [he] at first imagined',[116] the 'habit' had no doubt been forged through the medium of the journeymen clubs. Before the end of 1794, moreover, the Dublin United Irishmen appear to have already been developing parallel structures.

About fifty members of the society, which was suppressed in May, met in Henry Jackson's house in Church Street in October. At this meeting John Sheares proposed reorganising into fifteen man 'sections', which would each delegate a representative to 'a council or central committee'. This plan prefigures the structure of the clandestine United Irish organisation which becomes discernible by 1796. But it is probable that a more shadowy organisation, on a smaller scale, was in place before then. In mid-1795, for instance, government intelligence identified a cell called '"the Strugglers" at the head of the Dublin United Irishmen'. Certainly, 'the mechanics, petty shopkeepers and farmers' in Ulster had initiated the underground phase of the United Irishmen there by late 1794.[117]

The most important lower-class association in Dublin was the Defenders. Whereas the interaction between the Defenders and the combinations remains largely conjecture, so many members of the Philanthropic and Telegraphic societies were recruited as Defenders that the distinction between them became blurred. Musgrave described those societies as so many 'ramifications of Defenderism'. Although Defenderism was essentially a sectarian movement, it tended to adapt its 'ideology' to local conditions. Sectarianism caused tensions in Dublin, yet there were protestant Defenders – Dry and Lawler were two. As well as drawing on its indigenous urban sources, the clubs and combinations, Defenderism was also a rural import. The metropolis attracted a steady flow of country workers throughout the eighteenth century. These migrants often settled at their point of entry which, as the Dublin Defenders had a strong connection with county Meath, would partly explain the concentration of Defenders in the markets/Stoneybatter area in the north of the city. Two of those tried for high treason in 1795, James Weldon and Patrick Hart, were originally Meathmen, and Meath Defenders allegedly attended a meeting in Dublin in the summer of 1795, to discuss plans to take the capital.[118] Migrants represented only one element of the rural presence. The militia was another. As one Defender observed, 'I never heard of any being in Dublin until the militia came here and I am sure that it was them and the Defenders that ran away from the country that first brought it to Dublin.' Defender-infiltrated militia regiments helped spread the system across the country, the capital not excepted.[119] Some members of the Philanthropic Society were sworn as Defenders by a Fermanagh militia man and by September, 1795, a rumoured 5,000 or 6,000 militia men stationed in Dublin had taken the oath.[120] The figure is almost certainly exaggerated, although serious disaffection in the ranks of the militia is not in doubt. As for those who 'ran away' from fear of arrest, the metropolis, with its possibilities of anonymity and employment, was the obvious destination.

Some rural Defenders were captured in the city: two Meathmen at a house in Smithfield in November, 1793, in connection with the assassination of a magistrate at Arbracken, and a Kildare man, on a similar charge, while working in a distillery in Irishtown in 1796. These are only the ones who were caught. In March, 1793, there were reports from Louth 'that upwards of 300 have fled their homes, from the perpetual dread they were in of being arrested, owing to the number of approvers that have come forward'. Even if only half this number were involved: where did they go to? Coincidentally, one of the first references to Defenders meeting in Dublin (near Ormond market), dates from March, 1793.[121] Of course the urban-rural relationship also worked the other way. The country Defenders may have got arms and powder from the city, while Lord Clonmell claimed that the outrages in the 'slaughter-house' of Meath had 'originated in nests of clubs in the city of Dublin'. 'Dublin', he said, 'is the mint for coining treason and circulating it'.[122]

By the beginning of 1795, then, a substantial section of Dublin's lower classes – there were an estimated 4,000 Defenders[123] – were politicised and organised, and the predictable accusation that the riot of 31 March was conducted by a 'hired mob', is plainly wrong.[124] This riot marks the last major excursion of the eighteenth-century Dublin crowd. However, the degree of planning and leadership evident on this occasion sets it apart from earlier episodes. The riot occurred on the night Lord Camden was sworn in as lord lieutenant and forms a coda to the tremendous political excitement aroused by the appointment and swift recall of his predecessor, Earl Fitzwilliam. Fitzwilliam had encouraged popular expectations of total catholic emancipation and had moved quickly to purge the Castle 'junto'. In consequence his dismissal provoked a great public outcry. This focused on the catholic question and large public meetings were held and petitions organised in Dublin. Popular feeling was running high when Grattan issued a forceful, and widely circulated, address to the catholics of the city. A government supporter was later able, wrongly but plausibly, to fix the blame for the disturbances on Grattan's emotive rhetoric, specifically the assertion that, 'THEY WILL EXTINGUISH IRELAND, OR IRELAND MUST REMOVE THEM'.[125] 'THEY' being Fitzgibbon, Foster, Beresford and so on; all targets of the crowd. The United Irishmen seem to have been the instigators. According to one report some of the rioters wore green cockades emblazoned with the motto, 'Liberty, Equality and no lord lieutenant'. Others were 'well dressed' and 'appeared to be above the common class'.[126] The riot itself was executed with military precision. The carriages of the primate and the lord chancellor were showered with stones as they returned from the swearing-in ceremony in Dublin Castle.

At Grafton Street the chancellor, Fitzgibbon, was struck above the eye, and a detachment of the crowd smashed the windows of his house in Ely Place. The houses of Speaker Foster and Alderman Warren were likewise stoned. At the Custom House Beresford's son, John Claudius, opened fire, killing one and wounding another rioter. By now the military were on the streets and the crowd dispersed. Nevertheless, when the dust had settled the following morning, as even Grattan's accuser conceded, 'little damage' had been inflicted on either 'persons or property'.[127]

This incident might be better interpreted as a more skilfully-organised version of a 1759-style riot-demonstration, than as a serious attempt to injure or intimidate government. The events of 31 March have more of a symbolic than a practical importance. They registered both a beginning and an end. In one sense this was the last outing of the crowd, although since it was by now 'composed of republican clubs',[128] the term 'crowd' scarcely seems applicable. 'Popular', 'revolutionary' or 'republican movement', might be more accurate. The timing of the riot is significant too. Occurring during Camden's first hours in office, it marks a decisive moment in the crisis of the 1790s. As lord lieutenant, Camden presided over (and was partly responsible for) an exponential escalation of violence which climaxed in a bloody rebellion. There is a grisly appropriateness then, to the fact that his Irish career was inaugurated by violence on the streets of the capital. But this was still the violence of gesture. Dublin's lower classes were no Hibernian *sans culottes* with the power to make or unmake governments. As the political situation became more critical, however, and the city's disparate 'underground' was absorbed by a nation-wide revolutionary coalition, the possibilities, as Carhampton knew, were incalculable.

III 'THE MARATS OF PILL LANE': UNITED IRISH ORGANISATION BEFORE THE REBELLION

By the spring of 1795, outside Ulster, Dublin was the best organised area in Ireland. As in Ulster the Defenders there were ready for an alliance with the United Irishmen. Indeed, they were too ready. The United Irish strategy of insurrection hinged on anticipated French military intervention, a strategy which the Defenders might jeopardise by staging their own, premature, 'insurrection', thus precipitating a government clamp-down. This was a real possibility. As early as February that year one Dublin Defender remarked, 'we will recover our estates, sweep clean the protestants, kill the lord lieutenant and leave none alive'. The jurors at the Jackson treason trial were likewise marked down for assassination. 'You said you were in constant expectation of something?', another Defender was asked in court, to which he replied: 'of a rebellion breaking out. Where? In Dublin. When did that commence? Last April. [1795]'.[129] At some point during the summer a delegation from the Meath Defenders reportedly met with their Dublin 'brothers' to lay plans for seizing the capital, and at the beginning of August residents of the city's northern suburbs were suddenly subjected to a co-ordinated spate of arms raids. This upsurge was swiftly denounced from every catholic pulpit in Dublin.[130]

Trouble next erupted in the metropolis itself. On 22 August, faced with the prospect of being redrafted for service in the West Indies, a number of soldiers in the (English) 104th and 111th regiments garrisoned in Dublin 'mutinied'. Troops from outlying camps were rushed in and several of the mutineers arrested. As the news spread a crowd quickly gathered outside the barracks at the old Custom House near Essex Bridge. Then, on the morning of the 24th, as rumours circulated that a mutineer had been flogged to death – twenty-three were, in fact, 'severely punished' – the crowd induced over fifty soldiers to desert. The deserters disappeared into the Liberty, where they received 'protection, food and employment . . . for above ten days'. They were also relieved of their equipment, which was sent to the country.[131] The Castle guard was stoned and crowds clashed with the army in Parliament Street and on Ormond Quay.[132] Among the Defenders arrested within the following week were Thomas Dry (also a United Irishman), Richard Turner, an 'active citizen' who had tried to snatch the regimental colours during the affray in Parliament Street, and the inevitable schoolmaster. Although the prisoners generally came from 'the lower order of people, their connections', commented the *Dublin Journal*, 'are by no means obscure, they are, generally speaking, well known characters – such as we have described under the term Jacobins'.[133]

The authorities seem to have been impressed by the extent of popular disaffection and Defenderism in the city, and by the degree of organisation which the events of August suggested. 'Many [were] thrown into Newgate'. The possibility of intoducing martial law was canvassed and, at a meeting called to consider 'the conspiracy said to be formed by the Defenders for attacking the metropolis', Lords Carhampton and Mountjoy and the chief magistrates proposed establishing armed associations.[134] Fearful that these might be used as a precedent for Volunteering under a different name, it was only with difficulty that the lord lieutenant dissuaded the 'friends of government' from arming.[135] The promptness and vigour of the authorities' response on this occasion notwithstanding, to date, from the government's standpoint, the activities of Dublin's political underground had proved manageable. Neither the Philanthropic Society's nor the Defenders' ambitions to capture the Castle were ever realistic. However, given a central leadership, better discipline and – as Carhampton noted – French assistance, the city's ramshackle network of clubs and Defenders might become truly formidable.

After an apparent lull which followed the arrests in late August – a 'lull' which may merely reflect a gap in the evidence – the 'Telegraphic societies' as the government informer, Francis Higgins, called them, began to revive in 1796. Higgins identified, among others, a 'Union club' which met in Dame Lane, a club in Poolbeg Street attended by Simon Maguire, sometime delegate to the Catholic Convention and 'treasurer for defraying the expenses of prosecution against the Defenders', and a group, including Watty Cox, gunsmith and future editor of the *Union Star*, which met under the guise of a masonic lodge.[136] Many of the thirty or so masonic lodges in Dublin at the time were suspected of radical sympathies, and on 1 November, 1798, the Grand Master suspended all the lodges in the city, pending an inquiry 'into the conduct of their members during the late rebellion'.[137]

Meanwhile, in the summer of 1796, two emissaries from Belfast, James Hope and James Metcalfe, arrived in Dublin 'to disseminate [United Irish] views among the operatives of the capital'. Hope first stayed in the outlying village of Balbriggan, where he posed as a silk weaver, and commuted to town each day before moving to the Liberty. After a short stay back in Belfast he returned to Dublin where he was assisted in his efforts by some of the Defenders who had been acquitted at the big treason trials the previous winter.[138] A veteran of the Philanthropic Society also travelled to Belfast with Metcalfe, 'in order to join the Defenders of Dublin with the United Irishmen of the north'. There he met two other former Philanthropic members, Thomas Dry and Edward Newell, was inducted into the United organisation and given two books of 'constitutions', with which to promote the coalition in the capital.[139] When Hope first arrived, carrying a bundle of *Northern Stars* and a letter of introduction from Neilson, he contacted Edward Dunn and Thomas Dry's brother, Richard – the two men who had been pilloried for using seditious expressions in 1793. Initially they were cautious of the northerner, but once he had established his *bona fides* they co-operated with him.[140] Other sources confirm Hope's claim that his mission was successful. In August the lord lieutenant informed London that 'clubs of Defenders have again begun meeting in Dublin'. Prominent northern Defenders, including Coigly, Coile and Magennis visited Dublin that month. In October Under-Secretary Cooke received intelligence of 'all

the little clubs in and about Dublin . . . again reviving', while the next
month, one of Henry Jackson's young employees, 'a violent republican',
boasted that there were more United Irishmen in the city than could be
imagined.[141]

As the new United Irish structure began to take shape, references to
Defenders and to the 'little clubs' became less frequent. Although an
internal handbill claimed that the organisation of the metropolis was
complete by July, 1796, Oliver Bond was probably more accurate when
he suggested early 1797.[142] The nucleus of the new organisation was based
not, as might be expected, in the Liberty, but in the Church Street-Pill
Lane area. According to Leonard McNally, 'the Dublin party (active
men) mostly live in Church Street and are employed at the foundry'.
Presumably Jackson's workforce were all United Irishmen because during
these years the foundry and the 'mills' in Clonskea functioned as virtual
munitions factories, manufacturing heavy shot, pike-heads and 'cats' –
metal-spiked traps for use against cavalry in street fighting.[143] Jackson, of
course, lived in Church Street, while that other city leader, his son-in-law,
Bond, formerly of Pill Lane, resided just over the Liffey at Bridge Street.
So prominent was the Pill Lane-Church Street axis that in Higgins' reports
'Pill Lane Society' (or, more colourfully, 'the Pill Lane King Killers')
became synonymous with United Irishmen. Giffard's *Dublin Journal* once
described the United Irishmen as the 'emissaries from Pill Lane'.[144]
Indicative of the political complexion of this group was its association,
through Bond – a presbyterian and Dublin agent for the *Northern Star* –
with the militant Belfast leadership.[145]

Pill Lane had been disproportionately represented in the original Society
of United Irishmen. Another example of continuity from the earlier,
legal, years, can be traced through the persistent involvement of the
'democratic' faction of the Catholic Committee in conspiratorial politics.
This at a time when, to judge by the near-silence of the literature, they
had retired from the fray. Richard McCormick remained an important
figure within the United Irishmen until the eve of the rebellion. More
surprisingly, John Keogh's name continues to appear in the archives,
if not in the historiography. Keogh opposed recruitment to the new
Yeomanry corps in 1796 and supported an election boycott in 1797.[146]
Simon Maguire of the Poolbeg Street club and his Catholic Committee
colleague, Richard Dillon (another Bridge Street resident) were also,
like the 'Teeling connection' in the north, among those who carried
the grievances and experience of the catholic agitations of 1791–3 into
the overtly revolutionary period.[147]

Although such continuities provide further evidence which conflicts with the notion of a sharp break between the 'reformist' and the 'revolutionary' phases, it was inevitable that, as the United Irishmen grew into a truly mass-movement, its character changed. The rank and file were now generally younger men (and women)[148] and lower down the social scale than their typical predecessors in the first society. The 'dregs of the people', of whom Carhampton was so wary, were being welded into an underground army.

The organisation of that army, or 'military department', as Miles Digenam, a Grafton Street grocer and active United Irishman, termed it,[149] had a pyramidal structure. At the base were twelve-man cells, or 'splits'. Secretaries from each group of ten splits then formed 'baronial committees', which in turn elected delegates to the 'district committee', on up in the country areas to county and provincial level. Dublin instead had four 'divisions': the Rotunda, Barrack, Stephen's Green and Workhouse, corresponding to the north east, north west, south east and south west quarters of the city. The principal organisers 'on the ground' were Dunn in the Church Street area and, south of the river, Dry and Digenam. On 25 April, 1797, the returns for the capital were 4,420; in May, 1798, 9,889.[150] Over that year the estimates varied wildly, but a figure of perhaps 6,000 probably approximates to the average paper membership. Recruitment on this scale often took place – in a manner reminiscent of the social anatomy of the urban crowd – in the workshop, or by vocation. 'All the journeymen of a distillery in the Liberty, [who were] sworn Defenders,' 'four clubs of servants . . . of a very dangerous tendency', Jackson's foundry workers and his 'clerks', Dunn, White in Clonskea, and John McCann (later, secretary of the Leinster provincial committee), all conform to the pattern.[151]

Unavoidably the success of the United Irishmen in building a mass-movement created its own problems. The quality of recruit was diluted by a 'bandwagon effect' which continued to gather momentum. Secret organisation of this scope posed obvious difficulties for security. This is illustrated by the practice of conducting seditious business in public houses, the 'White Cross' in Pill Lane, for example. Nor was there any shortage of venues. Dublin in the 1790s had over 500 licenced premises, 52 in Thomas Street alone.[152] One informer supplied the government with a list of twenty-three meeting places, eight of which were definitely pubs and a further six probably so. In February, 1798, the leadership explicitly warned against this habit,[153] but to no avail. Many of the arrests made between then and the outbreak of the rebellion resulted from police raids on public houses. If the United Irishmen's security was lax or their organisation never as formidable in reality as it was on paper, it was nevertheless more impressive than the hotchpotch of Defender lodges and republican clubs which it had assimilated.

The Dubliners decided to demonstrate their numerical strength and organisational capacity with two great funeral processions in April, 1797. The tactic had already been employed in Ulster, as well as huge, orchestrated, 'potato-diggings', when thousands marched with fife and drum to raise the potato crops of state prisoners' dependents. These exercises afforded the United organisation opportunities for 'dry runs' and, by virtue of their scale and operational precision, were thought to boost popular morale. The first Dublin funeral on 3 April was that of Edward Dunn (who had died, seemingly, of natural causes). His coffin was accompanied along the quays, over Essex bridge and up to James Street churchyard by about 5,000 well-drilled men, including Henry Jackson and one of his brothers, Keogh, Digenam, and the 'Marats of Pill Lane'.[154] The marchers wore green handkerchiefs and breast ribbons and, more ominously, some militia men were said to have joined the procession.[155] The next funeral, of an obscure millwright named Ryan, took place on 30 April and was even larger. The quality of a political demonstration was further emphasised on this occasion by the 'mourners' circuitous route: looping down from Pimlico into Dame Street and then up past the Castle gates before making their way to James Street. The procession was marshalled by 'certain notorious United Irishmen'[156] and this time the authorities reacted. The army and Yeomanry were called-out and an ugly situation was only narrowly averted as the cry went up from the crowd 'let us get arms!'[157] Besides their value as *agitprop* – the United Irishmen hoped to 'engage the common people by showing numbers' – the funerals were also used to collect funds and to recruit.[158] Yet in at least one respect these public displays were a tactical miscalculation.

'It was them damn funerals', complained one radical, 'which opened the government's eyes'.[159] And to the government's eyes these demonstrations must have appeared all the more menacing against a background of mass unemployment. United Irish handbills advocating a public meeting about the recession had been distributed at the end of March, and the Castle probably read the funerals as a sign that the radicals were better placed than ever to manipulate popular discontent.[160] Such displays were henceforward prohibited and the military were now instructed to disperse illegal assembles without first consulting the civil power. Already, before the second funeral, Dublin was likened to 'a besieged city',[161] and in May Drennan wrote that 'they are taking the lower kind of people up by the dozens . . . the Yeomanry mount a real guard of duty every night'. On the 24th May Miles Digenam was arrested, along with his clerk, an event which 'alarmed many [and] made all cautious'.[162] But though the metropolitan organisation was shaken it was still intact. Who, in the spring of 1797, who, in particular, among the men who had led those impressive funeral-demonstrations, could have foreseen that organisation's collapse?

7 The Politics of Disaffection, 1795–9

To many observers in the winter of 1792–3 Ireland appeared to be on the brink of rebellion. Little distinction was made, in the ascendancy mind, between the politics of catholic relief or parliamentary reform on the one hand, and Defenderism, disloyalty or outright subversion on the other. However exaggerated that view may have been in 1793 – and it is far from clear that the hard men of the ascendancy, like Fitzgibbon, had got it entirely wrong – by 1795 the iron rod of coercion had hammered the equation into reality. Moreover, with hindsight it is hard to disagree with the ubiquitous contemporary perception that after the recall of Fitzwilliam the last hope of a peaceful, 'political', resolution of the Irish crisis had passed. Revolution or complete submission, as the radicals (and many catholic activists) now saw it, were the only alternatives; repression, as the ascendancy saw it, the only reply.

I BUILDING THE REVOLUTIONARY MOVEMENT

The part allegedly played by 'emissaries' in stirring up trouble and poisoning the minds of the common people with subversive ideas, was a familiar refrain among conservatives, spies and magistrates in the 1790s. This variant of the conspiracy theory of social upheaval underestimates the levels of popular political awareness and the complexity of the processes through which that awareness was achieved. Several forces were at work pushing great numbers of people away from government and pulling them into the radical, then revolutionary, camp: the influence of the French revolution and a collapse of confidence in the 'rule of law', for example. Nevertheless the impact of revolutionary evangelism cannot be discounted.

United Irish emissaries attempted to politicise the common people in two ways: by popularising revolutionary doctrines and by extending their organisation. Certain United Irishmen had been on the move as early as 1792, but it was not until the northern militants resolved on an alliance with the Defenders that they began to implement a full scale missionary policy. During 1795 and 1796 the northerners concentrated on the area they knew best: Ulster. According to government intelligence Henry Joy McCracken toured the province in December 'to unite the Defenders with the United Irishmen'. In 1796 James Hope travelled through Armagh, Monaghan, Cavan and Leitrim, where he met delegates from 'the old Defenders and initiated them' and helped form 'county committees'. Each emissary carried certificates which empowered him to 'take tests and create new clubs'. They conveyed instructions from the Belfast leadership and 'so numerous [were] the societies that some missionary [was] always out'.[1] As the organisation matured and expanded the northerners moved further afield, some as far south as Tralee, county Kerry, some even, to Scotland.[2] By October 1796 emissaries had arrived in Connaught 'to organise the catholics who were drove [sic] out of the county of Armagh by the Orangemen'.[3] The following May 'twelve persons styled commissioners or agents', 'north country men' who had come 'by way of Dublin', were busy swearing in the people of Munster. The Dubliner, Richard Dry, was in Cork City at the time and in receipt of funds from one of the brothers Sheares'. Sheares meanwhile had made his way to Limerick 'to consult with the society there'. Munster was supposedly 'organised' by September 1797, and the next month Camden reported renewed activity in Wexford, Carlow and Queen's county.[4]

For two years, from the summer of 1796, Dublin acted as a kind of operational headquarters for much of southern Ireland. Indeed, during the course of 1797, as the northern organisation reeled from the blows of General Lake's 'pacification' campaign, Dublin overtook Belfast as the principal 'mint' and exporter of sedition. Emissaries – propagandists, recruiting sergeants, organisers and couriers rolled into one – travelled from the city to Longford, Meath, Kildare, Wicklow, Wexford and Carlow.[5] Richard Dry was arrested in Roscommon in February, 1797, on a mission to bail John O'Leary – one of the men acquitted at the Dublin Defender trials. After escaping Dry was rearrested in May for administering the United Irish oath in county Cork.[6] The capital also served as quartermaster and paymaster: pikes made in North King Street found their way to Meath. In 1798 Bond sent Arthur O'Connor's brother, Roger, £100, to set up the short-lived *Harp of Erin* newspaper in Cork.[7]

As the hub of Ireland's communications and trade network the capital was ideally placed to perform these functions. Many country people had relatives in, or business connections with, Dublin. Edward Kennedy, step-brother of the Wexford rebel Miles Byrne, lived in New Street and assisted refugees from the county after the rebellion. Antony Perry of Wexford was sworn a United Irishman in 1797, in the Dublin home of Matthew Dowling. Henry Jackson, a city leader of the first rank, had a brother and nephews in

Ballybay and vicinity on the Monaghan-Cavan-Meath borders and during the later nineties the family trades, iron mongery and linen bleaching, were supplemented by the manufacture of pikes and the organisation of the locals into the secret army.[8] A third Teeling brother, George, lived in Lurgan Street near the linen hall. A United Irishman, he once supplied O'Connor, who was travelling north, with a letter of introduction to his father.[9] An intricate web of family and commercial relationships bound town and country together. The business nexus also operated at an impersonal level. Wexford 'carmen' arrived in the metropolis every Sunday night for the markets the following morning. Along with pedlars, carmen were widely used to distribute radical literature. In January 1797 it was reported that 'not a carrier or country dealer has left Pill Lane for two days past without a supply' of the latest radical *Address*.[10]

Similar techniques were used elsewhere. A Belfast emissary named Gordon, a freemason and nephew of Neilson, travelled 'under the pretext of selling muslins'. A Mr Clark of Lisburn, who later fought at Ballinahinch, 'by frequently sending cottons to the province of Connaught . . . had unsuspected means of communicating with the Connaught men and making them United Irishmen'.[11] Other devices used to propagate the 'cause' were somewhat more exotic, not to say eccentric. A Belfast presbyterian minister operating in Tyrone posed as 'an itinerant astronomer'. His colleague, the Rev. James Porter, went 'through the country spreading revolutionary principles while he gave lectures on natural philosophy and performed experiments with his tiny electric battery and his little Montgolfier balloons'.[12] Freemasonry was also utilised. At the precise moment, the spring of 1795, when the missionary policy was adopted in a sytematic way, a number of key agents, McCracken, Bartholomew Teeling and Samuel Kennedy, foreman printer of the *Northern Star*, joined their local masonic lodges. That most energetic and successful of all emissaries, William Putnam McCabe, was a mason.[13] Presumably membership of the craft gave these men access to a host of masonic contacts, while their brothers' obligation to hospitality facilitated the longer journeys.

The emissary technique was elaborate, effective and resilient. Late in 1796 Charles Teeling, McCracken and Kennedy were imprisoned. In 1797 Bartholmew Teeling fled to France. Troops in Ulster were stationed 'with a view to interrupt the communication between those . . . suspect[ed] of evil designs'.[14] But still the emissaries came. From the United Irish and Defender strongholds of Ulster, north Connaught, Meath and Dublin, they extended the organisation into south Leinster and Munster. Tens of thousands were enrolled, though the United Irishmen themselves thought the paper membership an inflated and unreliable guide to their true strength.[15] Corps of agents were dispatched, although the United Irish success in building a nation-wide revolutionary movement owed a great deal to a few indefatigable individuals. After McCracken, Kennedy and Teeling were removed, the task of national co-ordination and organisation in large part fell to James Hope and Putnam McCabe. In his memoir Hope retraces his movements in the winter of 1796–7. He travelled from Roscommon to Belfast to Dublin, Kildare, Wexford, 'astray in the mountains of Wicklow', to Athlone and back to Belfast, 707 miles in all. Earlier he had visited Wicklow with McCabe, 'a person of great energy and character, and gifted with some talents as a speaker'.[16] McCabe's father, a Belfast watchmaker, had been a founder member of the United Irishmen. A young man in his twenties, 'one of the earliest promoters of republicanism', in the years before the rebellion he was extraordinarily mobile. It was said of him that he had 'covered the greatest part of Ireland' but never stayed 'more than one or two days in the same place'.[17] In Ulster McCabe would attract crowds by masquerading as a preacher then, half way into his 'sermon', switch to a discourse on politics. In March, 1796, he was observed in Longford in possession of 'a number of printed handbills'. In May, 1797, disguised as a woman, he attempted to visit Richard Dry in gaol in Cork.[18] By 1798, now 'styled a General' but posing alternately as 'a mendicant, a farmer and a pedlar', McCabe was organising in Kildare, Wexford, Tipperary, Carlow and Westmeath. In May that year he acted as one of Lord Edward Fitzgerald's armed bodyguard.[19]

William Putnam McCabe might be described as a 'professional' revolutionary. His achievement, and that of his comrades, was an impressive one: 279,896 men in Ulster, Munster and Leinster took the United Irish oath before the rebellion.[20] Swearing an oath, however, did not automatically turn a man or woman into a doctrinaire republican. Sectarian undercurrents continued to trouble the coalition. In some ways the integration of the Defenders into the United Irish command structure proved a superficial exercise.'Great fears of catholics and dissenters becoming separate parties', were expressed in county Down in 1797.[21] Defender lodges generally appear to have remained intact and, more importantly, to have retained a sense of distinct identity. Moreover, by raising the spectre of an 'Orange extermination oath', the United Irishmen must share responsibility for exacerbating sectarian tensions. It might be argued, too, that the emissaries simply gave some coherence to mass disaffection not of their, but of the government's, making. As Elliott put it, 'the significance of the events of the 1790s is not that they created a widespread support for independence but that they temporarily gave existing discontent a republican leadership'.[22] But United Irish emissaries were proselytists as well as organisers.

Along with the 'constitutions' and 'certificates' which they used to swear in new members and institute new societies or 'splits', they carried bundles of handbills, newspapers and pamphlets. They did not merely exploit, but articulated, directed and politicised popular discontents.

II 'LEVELLING PRINCIPLES': UNITED IRISH PROPAGANDA

It would be hard to overstate the sheer volume of printed paper dis-seminated in town and country at the time. Distribution on this scale was implemented by itinerant agents and facilitated by the comparative cheapness of production. An estimated 20,000 handbills could be printed 'for about a crown'. One Dublin United Irishman, Robert White, had a 'private printing press in his mother's house'.[23] In addition to emissaries the United Irishmen employed pedlars and carmen. 'Great numbers of printed papers on half sheets . . . dispersed over the hills' of Tipperary in 1797, 'were mostly distributed by persons appearing as pedlars, whose boxes had underdrawers to them'. A carman who carried goods between Dublin and Wexford, engaged in 'harangues at common ale houses against the king's government' and handed-out 'seditious papers'. At the village of Baltinglass, two men from Carlow would arrive after mass every Sunday and read 'what the[y] plase [sic] to the ignorant country peopel'. [sic][24] The speed and scope of distribution was impressive. 'The appeal of the people of Ulster', a handbill attacking government repression in the north, turned up at Kilkenny on 22 April, Balbriggan, north county Dublin, on the 24th, and Enniscorthy, county Wexford, on 1 May 1797. In June it was passed among mass-goers at Arklow, south Wicklow. In Wexford, 'The appeal' was disseminated by Charles Nowlan, the nephew of a Dublin pawnbroker, and by a northern schoolmaster named McGuire. The Balbriggan copy (now deposited in the Rebellion papers) arrived by post.[25] The postal service was widely used, and on one occasion a parcel of handbills *en route* from Dublin to a county Antrim village was intercepted at Belfast's post office.[26]

Ballads – 'liberty songs for an Irish climate' (some of which were composed in the Irish language)[27] – proved as effective as pamphlets or handbills. 'It was the observation of a very sensible statesman,' noted an harassed loyalist, 'that "let him make the popular songs, and he would tune the people to whatever measures he thought fit."' The songbook which prompted this quotation included the following toast: 'May the potato-beds of Ireland be manured with the blood of its tyrants'.[28] When Arthur O'Connor was arrested in February, 1797 – he was held for six months – 'several copies of the song *Erin go brah*' were found in his room. Depending on one's point of view, these ballads were either 'admirably calculated to rouse the national spirit', or a means of raising 'the passions of the multitude'.[29] A booklet entitled *Songs of the French revolution* had been issued at Belfast in 1792. In 1795 and '96 the United Irishmen produced another two collections, *Paddy's resource*, followed a year or two later by *The Irish harp new strung*.[30] Almost certainly there were many more, not to mention broadsheets containing four or eight ballads each. The two *Paddy's resource* volumes are compact, pocket-size booklets, containing over 100 political songs, 'set to traditional airs', as well as toasts and 'sentiments', carefully pitched, in style and content, at a lower-class audience. The songs and toasts celebrate the 'labours of the plow and the loom' and mount an assault upon places, pensions, bishops, taxes, tithes, high rents, slavery, monarchy, aristocracy and English influence. They advocate a union of Irishmen, catholic emancipation and emulation of the French.

By the variety of techniques adopted the revolutionaries exhibited energy, imagination and resourcefulness as emissaries and proselytes.[31] The United Irishmen pioneered new forms of 'active propaganda' by drawing people into set-piece political demonstrations. Like the Dublin funerals, the potato-diggings in Ulster – over 6,000 were once employed to dig a state prisoner's one and a half acres – were similarly devised to convince the people of their strength by illustrating 'the facility with which a number of them could be collected in a short time'.[32] Despite the fact that theirs was supposedly a secret society, the United Irishmen also resorted to public symbolism. Many openly displayed badges of disaffection: green ribbons or hair cropped short in the French style. But the printed word continued to be the chief medium through which radical ideas were popularised.

In 1796 activists in Cork discussed the possibility of producing an Irish language newspaper.[33] Meanwhile the mass-circulation of the *Northern Star* continued to feed loyalist anxieties. Lord Abercorn's correspondent was surely exaggerating, though not very much, when he complained in February, 1797, that 'the country [is] completely corrupted or dangerously infected so far as the delivery of the *Northern Star* extends and no further'. And it extended as far, it seems, as the coffee houses of Waterford. The next month General Lake thought the paper 'should be stop'd, the mischief that it does is beyond all imagination'.[34] In fact the *Star* had been under pressure for some time. The editor, Neilson, and the printer, Kennedy, were among the state prisoners taken-up in the swoops of September-October, 1796. But far from disrupting distribution the arrests, as the editor of the

Star's government-subsidised rival reported, had the reverse effect: 'The tide of popularity has taken so strong and unexpected a run in favour of that paper, as almost to overturn the *Belfast Newsletter*'.[35] 'Combinations of Orangemen' intimidated *Star* carriers in Armagh, and Lord Downshire ordered the people of Hillsborough not to subscribe to it 'on pain of his lordship's displeasure'.[36] Eventually in May, 1797, the Belfast offices were ransacked and the presses destroyed by a mob of Monaghan militia men. The lord lieutenant thought the soldiers action 'unwarrantable', but decided that since 'no engine of disaffection has been so prevalent and successful' as the *Northern Star*, he would neither order an inquiry nor permit a 'renewal of publication'.[37]

With the enforced demise of the *Star* in the north, and the suppression of the *Cork Gazette* in the south,[38] Ireland was for a time without a radical paper. It is a measure of the increasing importance of Dublin relative to Belfast in this period that the next United Irish paper, *The Press*, was written and printed in capital. It first appeared in October, edited by Arthur O'Connor and published three times weekly. It was an instant success. The circulation and sales – reflected by the volume of advertising – quickly exceeded even the *Northern Star's*. Drennan disdainfully labelled it 'vulgar for the vulgar'.[39] (So much the better for the purposes of popular politicisation.) The ideology of *The Press* is indistinguishable from that of its great predecessor, although the emphasis differed. Its prospectus announced that 'particular attention shall be paid to the detail of domestic occurrences, and faithful report given of the various conflagrations, transportations and executions, without the intervention of judge or jury'.[40] In March, 1798, the second issue of *The Harp of Erin* served notice that it would 'proclaim to the world the acts of violence, of robbery and inhumanity, which have been committed, and are still committing upon our miserable fellow countrymen in different parts of this island'. After Fitzwilliam, as the Irish crisis deepened, with terror and counter-terror the order of the day, the politics of reform and of catholic emancipation were overshadowed by the debate on 'law and order'. State repression became the principle theme of United Irish propaganda. 'At clubs and publick societies, in their conversation they harp[ed] eternally on the same string, the wickedness of government and the wrongs done to the people'.[41]

While the emphasis upon repression naturally increased, in other ways the radical message in the later nineties remained the same. The *Northern Star* kept up the attack on tithes: 'They establish one sect of religion, enslave another and trample upon a third and make the slaves pay for the proud and haughty clergy of the minority'. Nor was there any novelty about the Cork-produced 'manifesto' which demanded 'rents at 1770 levels, food at 1780 prices and a drastic reduction in the tithe'.[42] The Whiteboy objectives are familiar, though now the sponsors and the context had changed. At Coleraine a young man spoke to a French traveller about oppressive taxation, corrupt elections and the need for parliamentary reform. 'Ideas', thought the Frenchman, which 'have been instilled in the minds of the peasantry by men of another stamp'. Some material – Keogh's 1792 'Common Sense' for example – was even reprinted and redistributed.[43] But as the United Irishmen moved towards overt separatism, republicanism and a strategy of insurrection, the populist tone of their propaganda grew louder. Crucially, just as activists earlier in the decade had mobilised popular support for catholic relief or parliamentary reform by stressing the immediate, concrete, social changes which must follow, so, after 1795, the logic of popular revolution introduced an unmistakable note of egalitarianism into United Irish rhetoric.

Subsequent estimates of the social-radical tendencies of the United Irish movement conflict. Some left-wing writers have made large claims about the proto-socialist impulse of the movement, based on little more that a few scattered quotations from Tone or McCracken – 'the rich always betray the poor'.[44] The political tendentiousness of these writers, the thinness of their evidence and the absence of 'critical aparatus', undermines their case. Academic historians have generally taken a different view. McDowell argues that practically all late eighteenth-century radicals 'accepted the orthodoxies of political economy' and doubts that they ever 'contemplated making extensive changes to the economic system'. Elliott states that 'Tone and his friends . . . were uncomfortable with the concept of popular revolution'. This discomfiture, elsewhere characterised as 'instinctive fear of the people' and 'horror at social revolution', together with the movements lack of 'any major social programme', are recurrent themes in Elliott's already substantial body of work on early Irish republicanism. Even Curtin, an historian who emphasises the political extremism, militancy and lower-class dimensions of 1790s radicalism, minimises the social elements in United Irish thinking.[45] According to the conventional wisdom, then, the United Irishmen were politically radical but socially conservative. Moreover, and unlike the social-radical reading which it implicitly refutes, the conservative interpretation is based on an examination of the movement's publications and of the utterances of its spokesmen. For example, it is clear from W. J. MacNevin's own testimony that he had a 'horror of social revolution', and that he considered United Irish contacts with the Defenders as a way of controlling an unruly peasantry.[46] Similarly, the well-documented United Irish hostility to journeymen combinations underlines the bourgeois character of late eighteenth-century radicalism.

Strong though the social-conservative thesis may be, it is not unchallengeable; it is, on the contrary, open to question on at least three counts. Firstly, the underlying methodological dynamic has loaded the conclusion. The care taken to demonstrate what the United Irishmen were *not* (and, as Moody points out, they were 'emphatically not socialists')[47] suggests that the insistence upon social conservativism is a reaction against the wilfull anachronisms of left-wing polemicists and the misconceptions of popular 'myth'. The risk with this kind of historical revisionism is that it tends, as in this instance, to overcompensate. The original misreading or 'myth' is replaced by a new, inverted, misreading or anti-myth.[48] Secondly, it is logically flawed. Thomas Russell's social-radical inclinations are acknowledged, but this, presumably, is merely the exception which proves the rule. Yet it is unclear why Russell (or McCracken, or Hope, or Coigly)[49] is deemed unrepresentative, while it is somehow legitimate to base generalisations about the social outlook of the United Irish movement upon the attitudes of 'moderates' like MacNevin, or the intellectually patrican Drennan. It makes more sense, in fact, to view radical ideology, as it relates to the social question, as unformed and contradictory. MacNevin represents one tendency; Russell represents another. Finally, and substantively, only the most elastic and meaningless definition of 'conservativism' could, as we shall see, accomodate all the evidence of contemporary publication.

Thomas Russell has been singled out as the radical-populist voice of United Irish ideology. 'Property', he once remarked, 'must be altered in some measure – he who knew the recesses of the heart loved not the rich'. As seneschal of county Tyrone, Russell once championed the journeymen weavers in an industrial dispute with local linen merchants, an episode which earned him the reputation of 'a man with dangerous leanings towards the people, in fact a republican'. He also seems to have been the author of a series of anti-slavery poems published in the early issues of the *Northern Star*.[50] Shortly before he was arrested in September 1796 the *Northern Star* office printed his *Letter to the people of Ireland.* This pamphlet attributes the collapse of the reform movement and of catholic aspirations in the 1780s to betrayal by the Volunteer's gentry leadership. These, 'the first lordly and landed interests in Ireland', had 'shamefully and meanly deserted the people'. The oppressions of tax-gathers, tithe-proctors and landlords are condemned along with the war and the slave trade. The government and opposition, asserted Russell, would always close ranks against the 'common enemy' – the people. As with his friend, Henry Joy McCracken, strong religious convictions underpinned Russell's egalitarianism. He argues that since God endowed all men with 'the same passions and the same reason', all men are entitled to the same 'liberty, happiness and virtue'; that as 'the earth was given to men by he who alone had a right to give it, for his subsistence; let not those who raise the fruits of it among us be despised'.[51]

The social-radicalism of the United Irishmen had limits. It was ferociously anti-aristocratic, but essentially bourgeois in perspective. Russell made a distinction between commercial wealth which was non-parasitic, and landed wealth, which was.[52] This is hardly surprising: many of his close political associates in Belfast were merchants or businessmen. However, like the words themselves, the antithesis between *laissez-faire* 'liberalism' and collectivist social policies lacked sharp definition in the 1790s. It was possible, therefore, for radicals to subscribe to what would later be seen as opposed positions. This point has recently been made about Paine. *The Rights of Man* part I anticipates nineteenth-century liberalism, whereas part II prefigures the welfare state. It is thus 'a work at odds with itself'.[53] In its unresolved tensions between bourgeois liberalism and incipient social radicalism, as in so much else, United Irish ideology was Paineite.

Although it would be wrong to measure that ideology by the standards of nineteenth or twentieth-century socialism, the radical critique of aristocracy, combined with the imperatives of populist politics, did produce a crude diagnosis of the causes of social inequality. In 1796 Francis Higgins discovered a handbill, 'The cry of the poor for bread', stuck to a tree in north county Dublin:[54]

> Oh! lords of manors, and other men of landed property, as you have monopolised to yourselves the land, its vegetation and its game, the fish of the rivers and the fowls of heaven . . . in the present condition of things can the labourer, who cultivates your land with the sweat of his brow, the working manufacturer, or the mechanic, support himself, a wife and 5 or 6 children? How much comfort do you extort from their misery, by places, offices and pensions and consume in idleness, dissipation, riot and luxury?

'The torch; extracted from DeVolney's ruins', a broadsheet printed in Belfast and disseminated as far south, at least, as Carlow, extends the argument: 'The dialogue between the people and the idle classes is the analysis of all society. All the vices, all the political disorders are deducible from this source, men who do nothing and who devour the substance of others'. The language and analysis of these leaflets does not mark a departure or an advance on the anti-aristocratic tirades of the *Rights of Man* or the *Northern Star* earlier in the decade. Indeed the 'extract' from deVolney is reproduced from the French *philosophe*'s *Ruins of Empire*, published in 1791. This was a popular book with the English 'Jacobins' and in E. P. Thompson's opinion, 'by a curious effect of translation, Volney's views appeared more radical in English than in French'.[55] Yet by the second half of the decade the attack is more concentrated. A pamphlet in circulation some time later returns to the theme: 'The laborious class are the essential part of society, the rest are only accessary, some useful, some ornamental, and some a nuisance. The former could well subsist without the latter; the latter must perish, or change their mode of living without the former'.[56]

Like so much radical propaganda in this period, these handbills and pamphlets, including Russell's *Letter*, are more specific about what they are against – the abuse of power and wealth – than what they are for. All radicals sought to ameliorate the lives of the poor by lightening the financial burdens of church and state; beyond that their programme was more vague. The United Irishmen never produced a blueprint of for their new social order. Yet, particularly in the years before the rebellion, more sweeping proposals than reductions in taxes and tithes were advanced. The *Cork Gazette*, for example, advocated full employment and the abolition of the primogeniture laws.[57] After the revolution loyalist and church property would be confiscated and 'converted to the national benefit'.[58] Conversion to the national benefit is a characteristically nebulous concept, illustrating the theoretical underdevelopment of United Irish social policy, but the potentialities contained in this proposal are at least as interesting as its want of clarity.

The potentialities of the social-radical position emerge most strongly in a remarkable eleven page pamphlet, *The Union doctrine; or poor man's catechism*, published anonymously about the same time as Russell's *Letter*. The *catechism* probably drew on *The Rights of Man* part II, which called for the redistribution of income and the provision of child care benefits and old age pensions. Thus the pamphlet, which employed the popular pedagogic techniques of creed and catechism, proclaims:

I believe that old age, pregnant women and labour should be honoured . . . I believe applying the lands of the Church to relieve old age, to give education and protection to infancy, will be more acceptable to an United people, than maintaining lazy hypocrites and ravenous tythe proctors.[59]

In other respects the *catechism* is even more radical than Paine:

> I believe in a revolution founded on the rights of man, in the natural and
> imprescriptable right of *all* citizens to all the land. I believe the soil, nor
> any part of it, cannot be transferred without the consent of the people,
> or their representatives, convened and authorised, by the votes of every
> man having arrived at the age of twenty one years . . .
> *Q.* As an Irishman, what do you hope for?
> *A.* The emancipation of my country, an equality of rights, a fair division
> of land, an abolition of religious establishments, and a representative
> government.
> *Q.* What good could a fair division of land be to Ireland?
> *A.* As the land and its produce was intended for the use of man 'tis unfair
> for fifty or a hundred men to possess what is for the subsistence of near
> five millions . . . the almighty intended all mankind to lord the soil.[60]

However, the *catechism* is not quite the proto-socialist manifesto it might
at first appear. In the first place it rejects any form of 'agrarian law': 'an
equality of property' is 'too absurd to imagine'. In the second place, the
'fair division of land' shrewdly addressed the sense of historic grievance
felt by the catholic dispossessed. Explicitly, it advocated 'dividing the
ancient estates among the descendants of those Irish families, who were
pillaged by English invaders, giving every person without exception, a
compedent share to enable him or her to get a comfortable livelihood'.[61]
Finally, there is a latent contradiction between the pamphlet's espousal of
full public employment, for instance, and its commitment to such classic
bourgeois nostrums as unrestricted commerce and the career open to
talents.[62] Nevertheless, this is an extraordinary document in which the
social-radical elements of United Irish ideology are expressed with great
verve.

How effective were the pedagogues of the poor? It is important to
remember, in this respect, that United Irish 'social policy', such as it
was, was piecemeal and that social reform, as such, was never at the top
of their agenda. Issues of social injustice were always secondary in radical
propaganda to political reform and, especially in the period immediately
preceding the rebellion, law and order or coercion. According to David
Kelly, a labourer from Ardee, county Louth, who was arrested after the
rebellion, 'The purpose of the United Irishmen was to overthrow the
government, a parliamentary reform and destruction to the Orangemen –
to have the same laws as France, he heard them talk of having no king'.[63]
Ultimately the ruling elite had more to fear from republicanism, than from

'levelling principles'. Yet levelling doctrines, like those so forcefully articulated by the *Poor man's catechism*, gave that republicanism a popular edge. Pakenham uses the *catechism* as evidence that 'a new egalitarianism had begun to develop' among the rebels in Wexford town in 1798, although he cites a version reproduced by Musgrave as 'The Catechism of the United Irishmen', which, claimed Musgrave, was 'published and circulated since the rebellion for the purpose of keeping the flame of it alive'.[64] In any event the war against the ascendancy and the English connection would also be a war of the underprivileged (and the dispossessed) against the rich.

The radical-populist critique developed by these pre-socialist revolutionaries had mixed inspiration. At a practical level it helped to enlist popular support; but it also derived from genuine political, particularly anti-aristocratic, convictions. For others it represented the application of the true christian message to society. This complexity of motive also lay behind what might be described as a sub-*genre* of United Irish propaganda: the politicised prophecy.[65] The *Northern Star* editor, Samuel Neilson, once remarked in private that he had received 'a foolish old prophecy' from a correspondent, which nevertheless 'he said he must insert to please his country readers'. Thomas Russell, on the other hand, shared the eschatological vision of such prominent English radicals as Richard Price and Joseph Priestley.[66]

Thompson refers to 'a sudden emergence' in England in 1793–4, 'of millenarial fantasies, on a scale unknown since the seventeenth century'. In the wake of the cataclysmic-seeming French revolution 'prophetic' literature gained wide circulation, notably Richard Brothers *Revealed knowledge of the prophecies and times*, published in early 1794. Brothers had links with members of the London Corresponding Society, and in Thompson's opinion may even have been 'prompted' by them.[67] Irish radicals too, were quick to recognise the political potential of millenarian ideas:

> The vast number of emissaries constantly going through the country to seduce every person they can, and swear them [had] songs and prophecies, *just written*, stating all the late events and what is to happen, as if written several years ago in order to persuade people that, as a great part has already come to pass, so the remainder will certainly happen.[68]

Some of these prophecies were indeed obvious frauds. One which came to Lord Castlereagh's attention predicted a 'great land tax' and that 'the natives of Ireland would rise in rebellion', assisted by the Scots, the French and the Spanish.[69] However, most millenarian tracts were slightly more subtle. The 'Beast', the 'anti-Christ', 'Babylon' and 'Armageddon' were all invoked in such a way that they could be interpreted as England (or, depending upon the audience, the pope), the French revolution or the war. The apocalypse, which was evidently imminent, had clear social-revolutionary implications. The high and the mighty would be humbled, or as one prophecy, 'Christ triumphant coming to judgement!', put it, 'the poor will be held in equal (or perhaps superior) estimation with the rich'. On that day the 'cobbler and caesar' would be made level.[70] Radicals turned popular credulity to political advantage. The *Northern Star*, for example, advertised a pamphlet, James Bicheno's *The signs of the times*, 'wherein is most clearly and concisely shown that the late transactions in Europe are the accomplishment of scripture prophecies, and a prelude to still greater events shortly to be expected'. This publication, which was offered 'at reduced price' and available 'from all the booksellers in the north', was 'recommended to the friends of liberty'. This was strange advice from an organisation, another of whose publications asserted, 'superstition [can no] longer hold man in chains than it can hold him in darkness'.[71]

The activities of United Irish emissaries, the movement's alignment with the Defenders, its contacts with the French and the populist and millenarian elements in its propaganda, all signalled a serious revolutionary challenge to the ascendancy. The ascendancy, however, was not prepared passively to await the radical millennium. As with the catholic and reform crisis in 1791–3, so during the years 1795–8 the ascendancy responded to the extremism of its opponents in kind. It met the challenge head-on.

III   REACTION

Government repression began in earnest with the arrival of Camden in 1795; not that the young lord lieutenant was a notably tough or determined politician – rather the opposite. Camden quickly became a creature of his strong-minded Anglo-Irish 'cabinet', and John Fitzgibbon, the newly enobled Lord Clare, and his associates were certainly both tough and determined.[72] The mass transportations conducted by General Carhampton in Connaught that summer provide the first spectacular examples of the application of coercion untrammelled by legal niceties. These and other legally dubious procedures were regularised during 1796 by the insurrection act, the suspension of habeas corpus and the indemnification of magistrates who had acted outside the law. But it was not until 1797 that full-scale repression was exerted. The critical psychological moment for the ascendancy seems to have been reached in Christmas week, 1796, when a French fleet arrived at Bantry Bay, west Cork.

The fleet, the product of Wolfe Tone's diplomatic efforts in Paris, idled helplessly off shore for some days before being scattered by a 'protestant wind'. Anglo-Ireland had had a lucky, or as Beresford preferred, a 'providential', escape. While the French were in the bay the southern 'peasantry' remained quiescent – a fact which, according to both Lecky and McDowell, the ascendancy found 'reassuring'. Here was evidence, in Lecky's view, that 'treason, although zealously propagated [was] yet very superficial'.[73] Recent interpretations of this episode are less conclusive. 'As the loyalists realised only too well', observes Elliott, 'the proof of silence was no proof at all'. Dickson makes the same point when he writes, 'the sight of French squadrons did not lead to any sympathetic action on land, although what would have happened if the wind had changed is another matter'.[74] At the time several leading ascendancy figures were equally unsure about the significance of what had (and had not) happened. As Lord Clare put it 'the lower order of people in the south also manifested a general good disposition in assisting the march of the army and in giving every accommodation within their reach . . . if the enemy had landed and obtained any decisive advantage, I will not flatter myself that the same good disposition would have continued'. Beresford and Cooke concurred.[75] Beyond Cork city and its immediate hinterland there is little evidence of United Irish penetration of the province of Munster before 1797. *If* Lecky referred to this region only, then perhaps he got it right. However, the wind did not change so we cannot know. In practice this brush with disaster seems to have spurred the ascendancy into a race to disarm and neutralise the domestic rebel army before a professional French army had a second chance.

Miles Byrne recalled how in the months following Bantry Bay recruitment to the Yeomanry was stepped up in Wexford, Wicklow and Carlow.[76] Already in January 1797 'ten thousand of the best troops' were stationed in east and mid-Ulster to keep down the 'rebellion there'.[77] On 13 March General Lake issued a proclamation placing the province under martial law. The countryside was scoured for weapons and hundreds of suspects were arrested. In June Lord Cavan, operating in Derry, warned that the county gaols and guard houses were overflowing.[78] It was a brutal 'pacification' campaign, with scant respect paid to the rule of law. General Knox, the army commander in Tyrone, looked upon Ulster as another Vendée, and advocated the same tactics as Paris had used to suppress that uprising, 'namely spreading devastation through the most disaffected parts'. But, he thought, 'nothing effectual [could be] done unless the trial by jury in all cases of sedition and treason is completely done away'.[79] Down south, in county Cork, General Coote felt 'obliged to take steps further than the law will admit' – conduct swifly condoned by his political masters in Dublin Castle.[80] During the summer and autumn and into 1798, as the theatre of operations extended across the midlands into south Leinster, the reign of officially-sanctioned lawlessness intensified. Reports of half-hangings, floggings and house-burning multiplied. According to *The Press* in the six months to late November three hundred houses were burned in Westmeath alone.[81] This was the period too when 'pitch-capping' was invented. This consisted of tarring the heads of 'croppies' (men who wore their hair short, or 'cropp'd', in the French style) and then setting them alight. The commander-in-chief, General Sir Ralph Abercromby, observed that the 'irregularities' and 'abuses' of his own troops 'could scarcely be believed'.[82]

One of the more irresponsible aspects of the strategy of coercion was the use made by the authorites of the Orange Order. In Tyrone Knox even carried out arms searches, 'not so much with a hope to succeed to any extent, as to increase the animosity between the Orangemen and the United Irishmen or Liberty men as they also call themselves. Upon that animosity depends the safety of the centre counties of the north'.[83] Mullingar, the base from which the repression of Westmeath was organised, was alleged to be a nest of Orange lodges, 'sanctioned and attended by some of the leading gentry of that county'. In Dublin and Carlow, regular troops, Yeomanry and militia men sported orange ribbons and played 'croppies lie down'.[84] The behaviour of the United Irishmen was equally irresponsible. In the *Northern Star* and *The Press*, in handbills, and by word of mouth, they industriously promoted the story of an Orange 'extermination oath'.[85] These were Enlightenment rationalists who pedalled millenarian fantasies; apostles of a union of Irishmen of all creeds who stoked the fires of sectarian hatred.

It is not always possible to disentangle cause from effect when analysing the upsurge of violence which swept the Irish countryside in 1797 and 1798, but clearly the United Irishmen must share the blame. Watty Cox's *Union Star* openly advocated assassination.[86] Terror and intimidation were systematically applied in an attempt to paralyse law-enforcement, and in Lake's opinion these methods did in fact 'completely destroy all idea of exertion in most of the magistrates through the country'. In 1798 the beleagured loyalist gentry of Kildare 'went about completely armed' and 'boarded or bricked up' their windows 'with mere holes left to fire or look through'.[87] Terror and the prospect of French invasion helps to account for, but not to excuse, the excesses of official counter-terror. However in the eyes of his majesty's rapidly shrinking loyal opposition, nothing could justify such flagrantly extra-legal coercion. Not surprisingly, law and order, or more accurately lawlessness and disorder, became the pre-emminent issue in Irish politics in the eighteen months before the rebellion. In parliament Grattan condemned martial law on 16 and 20 March, 1797, and eventually resigned from the Yeomanry in protest at the repressive measures adopted by the administration. Sir Lawrence Parsons and the liberal duke of Leinster likewise resigned their commissions in the King's county and Kildare militias.[88] Another liberal peer, Lord Moira, condemned 'torture' in both the English and Irish lords in 1797 and 1798, while Parsons tried to raise the question of coercion in the Irish commons. Both men found themselves in risible minorities.[89] The United Irishmen, many of whose leaders were lawyers, extracted as much political capital as they could from goverment brutalities. Early in 1798, under the chairmanship of a barrister, William Sampson, they established a 'Committee for collecting proofs of the enormities lately committed against the rights of the people'. The committee quickly gathered over 300 affidavits, detailing house-burnings and other acts of gross misconduct by the military – information which was then placed at the disposal of Moira and Parsons.[90] Meanwhile the United Irishmen hammered relentlessly on the theme in handbills, in pamphlets and in the pages of *The Press*.

What were the consequences of the ascendancy's military clamp-down? Grattan had no doubt. 'The more you hang, the more you transport,' he warned parliament, 'the more you inflame, disturb, and disaffect'. Even before repression had reached the heights of 1797 and 1798, Tone reasoned that the administration 'by openly trampling on law and decency', succeeded merely in spreading 'the affiliation of the United Irishmen more rapidly than could have been done by all the efforts of the patriotic leaders'.[91] In short, the mail-fisted security policy pursued from 1795 (or 1793) sharpened and extended popular animosity towards the government, raised tensions and acted as a recruiting sergeant for the United Irishmen. The polarisation of Irish politics so characteristic of the 1790s was pushed to new extremes. The frenetic pace of events, the undisguised revolutionary designs of the United Irish leadership and the ruthless punitive reaction of magistrate, Yeoman and soldier, all seemed to point ineluctably to a bloody climactic.

IV REBELLION AND DEFEAT

Several of the participants in the rebellion, which commenced on 23 May,

1798, later took Tone's and Grattan's argument a step further. Thomas Cloney of Wexford explained the outbreak of rebellion as 'a necessary consequence of the lawless excesses which had been committed on the people'. The Wicklow rebel, Joesph Holt, excused his and his fellow rebels actions as part of the popular response to house-burnings and persecution.[92] This version of events was accepted at face value by certain politicans and historians. In 1807 the United Irish leader, W. J. MacNevin, alleged that the government had applied repressive measures in a deliberate attempt to provoke a rebellion (before the insurgents were fully prepared and before the arrival of the French.) This view was then repeated by Watty Cox the following year, by Daniel O'Connell and by R. R. Madden in the 1840s and by Charles Dickson in the 1950s.[93] But it is an allegation which appears to rest on a single remark by Castlereagh about the means taken to secure a premature explosion.[94] On the other hand, the case against the MacNevin/Madden/Dickson thesis is strong. The evidence of witnesses such as Holt and Cloney is too self-interested to be reliable. As the (unrepentant) rebel, James Hope, afterwards pointed out, 'it is hard for a man who did not live at the time to believe or comprehend the extent to which misrepresentations were carried at the close of our struggle . . . the men who flinched and fell away from our cause, grasped at any apology for their own delinquency'.[95] The 'reluctant insurgent' school of apologia absolved the insurgents of responsibility and placed the blame for the rebellion squarely with government misdeeds. Nor, more recently, has the credibility of this 'school' survived the close scrutiny and analysis of modern scholarship.[96]

The spontaneous combustion explanation of the Wexford rebellion raises more questions than it answers. If repression did, in fact, provoke the uprising in Wexford and south Wicklow, why, then, did it not have a similar effect in Tipperary? Why did repression not spark off a revolt in Westmeath during 1797? Why did repression 'succeed' in Dublin city? This last question is particularly important. The failure of the United Irishmen to seize the capital – the locus of power and administration – has been cited as a key reason for the defeat of the rebellion generally.[97] Certainly the break-down of leadership and co-ordination at the centre contributed to the piecemeal and unsynchronized character of the insurrection nationally. What happened (and what did *not* happen) in Dublin in May–June 1798 thus demands attention.

Dublin, of course, had presented the authorities with major public order problems throughout the century; problems which became critical by the late 1790s. The police were – to say the least – inadequate, the mainly catholic militia politically unreliable. In these circumstances the ascendancy elected to arm itself. The government, as we have seen, prevented independent associations from arming in the city and county in September, 1795, but the following year it established the Yeomanry. By February 1797 in Dublin and its environs an estimated 3,000 men had enrolled in fourteen infantry and five cavalry companies,[98] and henceforward Yeomanry guards and patrols became a familiar sight on the streets of the capital.

In the months preceding the rebellion, however, the Castle relied to an extraordinary degree upon the energies and abilities of one man: the town major, Henry Sirr. 'From the want of any efficient system of police in this city,' wrote Castlereagh, 'he has been constantly employed confidentially by government . . . during the most trying period of public danger, the metropolis was particularly indebted for its tranquility to the unceasing activity of Major Sirr'.[99] This vigour and his close working relationship with the Castle account for Sirr's effectiveness. Indeed, before his appointment in 1796 the office of town major appears to have been merely a sinecure. In contrast Sirr had ready access to up-to-date intellegence garnered from the governments' extensive spy network, and could call on the resources of the garrison and the Yeomanry. During 1797 he used these resourses to keep the pressure on the United Irishmen, yet if anything, from the governments standpoint, the situation in the capital was dangerously deteriorating.

In the winter of 1797–8 the national leadership of the United Irish movement, based in Dublin, split. One faction, represented by Arthur O'Connor, Lord Edward Fitzgerald, Oliver Bond and Henry Jackson, advocated insurrection, with or without French assistance. The other faction, represented by Thomas Emmet, Richard McCormick and William MacNevin, counselled delay.[100] Significantly, the O'Connor-Fitzgerald group were stronger in the city. If Emmet deprecated the extreme rhetoric of O'Connor's *The Press*, Watty Cox remarked that 'it is not conceivable with what avidity the lower classes read it'.[101] Cox's own *Union Star* was even more extreme. The leadership publicly distanced themselves from this allegedly 'freelance' broadsheet, yet Cox joined the United Irishmen and his paper circulated at meetings in Dublin.[102] Some of the moderates even suspected that O'Connor himself was behind the *Union Star* 'it being known to several of them that his political associates among the lower orders are those who disperse it'.[103] Cox surrendered himself to the authorities in December, 1797, and *The Press* was shut down in March, 1798. A few weeks earlier O'Connor had been arrested *en route* to France. The vice tightened.

The decisive blow against the Dublin organisation came on 12 March.

Acting on information from Thomas Reynolds, a party of soldiers led by the indefatigable Sirr surrounded Oliver Bond's home and warehouse in Bridge Street. Inside county delegates of the 'Leinster Directory' were meeting. Bond himself and the Directory's secretary (and Henry Jackson's bookkeeper) John McCann were captured together with delegates from Carlow, Kildare, county Dublin, Queen's county and Meath. A simultaneous swoop netted Jackson, MacNevin, Emmet and John Sweetman. McCormick and Lord Edward went into hiding. Leadership of the metropolitan organisation now devolved on Lord Edward, John and Henry Sheares and, recently released from prison, Samuel Neilson. All, including a fatally wounded Lord Edward, were in custody by the eve of the rebellion. Indeed the list of those arrested shortly before or during the rebellion reads like a roll-call of Dublin radicalism in the 1790s: John Stockdale (printer of *The Press*), Patrick Byrne (printer of Wolfe Tone's *Argument on behalf of the Catholics*), Matthew Dowling, Jackson's son, Hugh, Ignatius Weldon, Richard Dillon . . .

From March onwards hardly a day passed during which Sirr did not make arrests or uncover concealed arms. As William Sampson recalled 'I remained in Dublin until the 16th April, when the terror became so atrocious that humanity could no longer bear it . . . men were taken at random without process or accusation'. On the 10 May Giffard's *Dublin Journal* crowed 'the leaders of the organised bands of rebels are either in custody, or have marked their guilt by flight – the subordinate agents feel themselves weak and deserted'.[104] Up to 20,000 pikes were seized by 20 May, when the city was placed under martial law and the Yeomen commenced a house-to-house search.[105]

These measures inflicted immense damage on the capital's revolutionary underground, although the Castle, acutely aware of 'the too great disposition of the inhabitants of this city to insurrection', never felt secure enough to relax its grip. It felt too insecure, in fact, to release badly-needed troops from the garrison at the very height of the rebellion in Wexford, for fear that upon their return they would find Dublin in the hands of a rebel army.[106] And even if the United Irishmen had weathered Sirr's spring-time offensive, they would have found little room to manoeuvre in a city saturated by Yeomen and ringed by regular troops and militia.

Shortly before his capture Lord Edward, the United Irishmen's principal 'military' strategist, committed some of his rather amateurish reflections on urban warfare to paper. In his view the narrow city streets would give the insurgents, 'acting in concert with the adjoining counties', an advantage over regular soldiers, unable to advance in large formations, and pelted from the roof tops with stones and slates.[107] This scenario was not to be. On the night of 23 May there were reports – nothing more – of pikemen assembling in the alleyways off Church Street and, further north, in a field near Eccles Street. According to another account some years later, a number of middle- ranking leaders met in a house in Abbey Street but dispersed without instructions when Neilson was arrested outside Newgate prison.[108] The militia did not desert *en masse* to the rebel side. The only fighting which Dublin did witness, some skirmishes on the western outskirts at Rathfarnham and Clondalkin, was over by day-break.

In the event, for all its size and density, the urban environment favoured the authorities. Though a sprawling metropolis in contemporary perception, for military purposes Dublin between the Grand and Royal canals was compact and defensible. The canal bridges leading into the city were closely guarded and quickly reinforced by makeshift gates and palisades.[109] An enforceable 9 pm to 5 am curfew came into operation on 24 May and, as General Lake observed 'the military posts are so judiciously arranged that no great bodies can be assembled within the city without the notice of the centinals [sic] or patrols'.[110] Alongside the facts of urban geography the capital's social structure weighted the scales against the disaffected. In addition to its 4,000-strong garrison Dublin boasted three or more thousand Yeomen, staunchly loyalist men of property, or as Sir Jonah Barrington put it 'barristers, attorneys, merchants, bankers, revenue officers, shopkeepers, students of the university, doctors, apothecarys, and corporators, of an immense metropolis, in red coats, with a sprinkling of parsons'[111] arrayed in arms to defend the constitution, the social order and their fortunes. The attorney's corps in particular were active throughout the rebellion period, patrolling the streets, searching for arms and guarding public buildings and bridges.

It is difficult now to imagine the atmosphere which must have prevaded the city in those long tense summer days of 1798, as rumours spread about the piking to death of protestant infants in Wexford, or of insurgents massing in the nearby Wicklow mountains. A kind of collective paranoid psychosis gripped the loyalist mind. Lamplighters were arrested for deliberately leaving the streets in darkness; a master sweep named Horish was accused of a plot to burn down the homes of prominent citizens; an apothecary and his apprentice in Grafton Street 'confessed' to selling over 1,000 ounces of arsenic to domestic servants – United Irishmen conspiring to poison their employers.[112] These fears help to explain the behaviour of the Yeomen and the authorities. For example, on 27 May a suspect, 'in consequence', as the *Freeman's Journal* so elegantly phrased it, 'of a little flagellation', directed the Yeomen to a cache of pikes hidden in a house in Carter's Ally off Townsend Street. After the pikes were recovered the house was set ablaze. 'This mode of punishment persevered in wherever concealed arms are found' continued the *Freemans Journal*:

> will be attended with the best effects, as it will make not only the *guilty* deliver up their instruments of massacre and treason, but it will also induce the innocent, but *inactive,* to take some interest in the public peace . . . no punishment can be too severe.[113]

Three corpses publicly displayed in Barrack Street had 'the pikes which the[y] carried affixed to them, as dreadful examples to that rebellious spirit'. Others, summarily convicted of treason, were strung up and left for days on gallows erected on the main bridges across the Liffey.[114] If this was street theatre designed to terrorise the disaffected, it worked. Dublin, noted Castlereagh with satisfaction, remained 'tranquil'.

The sequence of events outside Dublin underlines the achievement of the authorities in keeping the lid on so potentially explosive a situation within the city. The 1798 rising has been described as 'probably the most concentrated episode of violence in Irish history' and, along with the Vendée, as 'the last rural civil war in western Europe north of the Pyrenees'.[115] Between 20–30,000 people died, the great majority of them within the span of a month, and on the rebel side. In terms of casualties, if not balladry, the French assisted Connaught rising was an epilogue. Afterwards claims for damages to property, over half coming from Wexford, Wicklow and Kildare, topped one million pounds.[116] The unique scale and horror of these events are not in doubt, and were indelibly etched on the popular imagination for years to come. The dynamics of the insurrection – the motivations driving pikemen to charge cannon – are more problematic. The risings in Carlow, Kildare and Meath in Leinster, and even more clearly, in Antrim and Down in Ulster, were 'United Irish' in character – the outcome of previous revolutionary organisation and preparation. After some initial successes the numerically superior insurgents were quickly beaten by the better armed and disciplined loyalist forces. The intense repression of the preceding year must also have taken its toll. But the fiercest fighting occurred in an unexpected quarter: county Wexford.

What happened in Wexford bewildered contemporaries and, until quite recently,[117] subsequent interpretations treated the rebellion there as an ultimately unfathomable eruption of popular fury. As we have seen, the 'cause' of the eruption was sought in the local reaction to floggings, house-burnings and executions. The sparks which lit the conflagration were the executions of twenty-eight prisoners at Dunlavin and a further twenty-eight at Carnew in south Wicklow on 25 May.[118] The savage fighting which followed has been depicted either as a huge peasant *jacquerie*, 'a rural riot on an enormous scale',[119] or as a prolonged sectarian pogrom. In either case the Wexford experience appears strangely unrelated to the immediate pre-history of politicisation and United Irish organisation discussed by this study.

In fact these explanations are inadequate and patronising. The 'peasant' *jacquerie* interpretation underestimates both the complex stratification of rural society and the political dimension of the insurrection. The charge of sectarianism is harder to dismiss. The massacres at Scullabogue and on Wexford bridge were sectarian atrocities. However, accounts which focus exclusively on this aspect of events are reductionist. The sectarian interpretation, as Kevin Whelan points out, was 'essentially a propagandist creation' designed to alienate northern presbyterian (and it might be added liberal protestant and British) opinion from the rebels. This process can be detected in operation at the time. On 7 June the *Freeman's Journal* printed the text of a rebel oath, allegedly circulating in Wexford:

> I, A.B. do solemnly swear by our Lord Jesus Christ, who suffered on the cross, and by the blessed Virgin Mary, that I will burn, destroy, and murder all heretics, up to my knees in blood. So help me God.

Sectarian animosity was never the whole story. Wexford, it is now becoming clear, was an exceptionally politicised county and in the north, where the fighting began, an organised one.

In some ways mass politicisation in Wexford conformed to national patterns. 20,000 signatures were collected for the catholic declaration in 1792 and another 22,251 at the time of Fitzwilliam's brief tenure in 1795.[120] This is evidence of the mobilisation of public opinion. The county's politics were particularly devisive, however. Significantly, George Ogle, the outspoken champion of 'Protestant Ascendancy' during the 1792 debates on catholic relief, was one of the members for Wexford. The hardline ascendancy faction, headed by Ogle and Lord Ely, were opposed by an 'independent' interest, 'liberal' on the catholic issue and represented in the first Dublin Society of United Irishmen.[121] These rivalries were fought out at the bitterly contested 1797 election, when victory went, as in 1790, to the Ely faction. On the vexed question of United Irish military organisation, Dublin and northern emmisaries, including the ubiquitous Putnam McCabe, had visited the county in 1797–8. Moreover, Cullen has recently demolished 'the argument that the rebels were mere frightened crowds of peasants'[122] by uncovering the extent to which revolutionary structures were in place in north Wexford by the spring of 1798. It is here, at the intersection between national patterns and specifically local tensions, that the explanation for the scale of the rebellion in this region lies.

The old image of a blind sectarian frenzy is breaking down. The 'clarity of intention, tenacity of memory and grimness of purpose' of the rebels left local Quakers unmolested.[123] The signs of politicisation, the stock slogans and symbols of the period ('The Rights of Man', 'Erin go Bragh', green cockades and liberty trees) made their appearance. In the 'republic' of Wexford town occupied, and largely administered by 'ordinary working men', for the first three weeks of June, one of the catechisms used by the rebels concisely expressed the radical and anglophobic thrust of popular ideology:

> What have you got in your hand?
> A green bough.
> Where did it first grow?
> In America.
> Where did it bud?
> In France.
> Where are you going to plant it?
> In the crown of Great Britain.[124]

Like the Defender catechisms it so closely resembles, this document conveys the distinct revolutionary inflexion of popular politics in the 1790s.

The rebellion – or the act of union (1800–1) – provides the political historian with a tidy cut-off date. However, like most cut-off dates, it is somewhat arbitrary and artificial. The processes of politicisation did not simply stop with the defeat of the rebels and the collapse of the United Irish organisation. Indeed one of those processes, the alienating effect of repression, was intensified by the experience of rebellion and of the 'White Terror' which followed. At least sixty-nine catholic churches were burnt-out, damaged, or destroyed, mainly in south Leinster, between 1798 and 1800.[125] The mood of reaction which set in after the rebellion is illustrated by the victimisation of Henry Grattan. Grattan, the doyen of conciliation, lost his place on the Irish privy council and along (with more reason) with Henry Jackson and Richard Dillon, was expelled from the merchants guild in Dublin. Grattan Street in Cork was renamed and his portrait was removed from Trinity College.[126] Bitterness and recrimination were double-edged.

The popular movements examined in this study continued after the rebellion. Defenders were active in county Antrim in 1799,[127] and the story of Dublin's political underground can clearly be followed through to the Emmet rising in 1803. But in another sense 1798 did mark a turning-point. The 'propagandist creation' of the sectarian bloodbath in Wexford, for the manufacture of which there was so much material, struck its target. In his speech from the dock on 10 November, Wolfe Tone remarked 'for a fair and open war I was prepared; if that degenerated into a system of assassination, massacre and plunder I do again most sincerly lament it'. Tone also spoke of 'very great atrocities . . . committed on both sides',[128] but the disclaimer stands. The rebellion represented not only a defeat for the United Irish organisation but for the republican ideal.

Conclusion

The historians' first task is to try to understand the past in its own terms. It is a notorious whig fallacy which evaluates insitutions, ideas, events or whatever, by reference to later or present-day criteria. Nevertheless, while it is incumbent upon the historian to 'get behind hindsight' as best he can, it is also perfectly legitimate to explore the ways in which the past shaped its own future or our present. Thus Marianne Elliott has argued that 'the history of Irish republicanism has always suffered from an excessive concentration on its later phases. But much light can be thrown on its essential characteristics by a closer examination of its origins'.[1] The legend of the United Irish movement, of Wolfe Tone, and of the 1798 rebellion, became the foundation myths of the republican tradition, although the vitality of that tradition was not soon apparent.

By contrast the years following the rebellion (and Robert Emmet's coda) and before the O'Connellite mobilisation of the 1820s appear politically inert. The high levels of mass politicisation which obtained during the 1790s were not sustained, were in fact probably unsustainable. There are tides in the affairs of men, and there is nothing surprising or unusual about a political movement, particularly a revolutionary one, running out of energy. However, the early 1800s did not witness a sudden 'depoliticisation'. What survived from the period in the short term was not a coherent popular ideology, but 'a sense of grievance and a set of symbols of opposition to the political and social establishment'.[2] In the longer term, several features of Defenderism – its secrecy, nationalism and geography, for example – were reproduced by the Ribbonmen of pre-famine Ireland. In this respect Ribbonism, it has been argued, acted as the link between the militant separatism of the 1790s and the 'physical force' republicans of the Young Ireland movement in the 1840s and the post-famine Fenian Botherhood.[3] Ribbonmen, Young Irelanders and Fenians were all inspired by the martyrology and powerful romantic myth of '98. And that heroic idea, reiterated in ballads, reaffirmed by Madden's *Lives* and publicly commemorated in 1898, carried into the twentieth century in the shape of the cult of Wolfe Tone.

While militant republicanism was undoubtedly tenacious, its adherents were always a minority in nineteenth-century Ireland. The other legacy of the 1790s, popular sectarianism, proved more pervasive. The tenacity of orangism should not be underestimated either. The United Irishmen set out to bury ancient animosities and to unite catholic, protestant and dissenter. Certain Defenders had less ecumenical ideas. And, as Thomas Reynolds put it, since 'the Defenders . . . formed the great majority, instead of becoming United Irishmen, they induced the mass of the United Irishmen to become Defenders in principle, in practice, in short, in everything except name'.[4] Reynolds undoubtedly overstated his case – influence worked in both directions – yet a tension did exist between Defender sectarianism and the urbane secular republicanism of the United Irish leadership. The United Irishmen never resolved this problem. Indeed the journalist and critic, Anthony Cronin, suggests that the persistence of what he calls the 'Defender pyschology' – or gut catholic nationalism – remains the central dilemma of modern Irish republicanism.[5] Viewed from that perspective, the United Irish-Defender alliance (or more broadly, the relationship between Irish radicals and popular politics) emerges as the most significant development of the 1790s.

Notes

A NOTE ON THE TITLE

1. W. T. W. Tone, *The life of Wolfe Tone* (Washington, 1826), ii, 46.
2. Marianne Elliott, *Wolfe Tone, prophet of Irish independence* (New Haven and London, 1989), 414–18, P. H. Pearse, *Political writings and speeches* (Dublin, 1952), 283–4, C. D. Greaves, *Liam Mellows and the Irish revolution* (London, 1971), 365.
3. T. A. Jackson, *Ireland her own* (London, 1946), 132, P. Berrisford Ellis, *A history of the Irish working class* (London, 1972), 74, J. Bennett, S. Cronin and R. Roche, *Freedom the Wolfe Tone way* (Tralee, 1973), 73.
4. Elliott, *Wolfe Tone,* 418.
5. Tom Dunne, *Wolfe Tone, colonial outsider* (Cork, 1982), 31–2, Elliott, *Tone,* 418.
6. 'We were the children of unimportant people – the men of no property of whom Wolfe Tone spoke': C. S. Andrews, *Man of no property* (Dublin and Cork, 1982), 28. See also pp. 3 and 321.

INTRODUCTION

1. R. R. Palmer, *The age of the democratic revolution, 1760–1800* (Princeton, 1959–64), 2 vols.
2. Johnston, *Ireland in the eighteenth century* (Dublin, 1974), preface.
3. T. Bartlett, 'A new history of Ireland', *Past and Present* no. 116 (1987), 210, T. W. Moody and W. E. Vaughan, eds, *A new history of Ireland, iv, eighteenth-century Ireland, 1692–1800* (Oxford, 1986). Related chapters dealing with the period 1714–1760 outline political, social and ecclesiastical *structures*. Interestingly, Jonathan Clark has complained about an analogous neglect in English historiography: J. C. D. Clark, *Revolution and Rebellion, state and society in the seventeenth and eighteenth centuries* (Cambridge, 1987), 115–16.
4. Lecky, iii, 111, McDowell, *Irish public opinion, 1750–1800* (London, 1944), 5–6.
5. Among the essays written from a popular perspective are Elliott, 'The origins and transformation of early Irish republicanism', *International Review of Social History*, xxiii, pt. 3 (1978), 405–28, J. S. Donnelly jnr. 'Propagating the cause of the United Irishmen', *Studies*, lxix (1980), 5–23, T. Bartlett, 'An end to moral economy: the Irish

militia disturbances of 1793', *Past and Present*, no. 99 (1983), 41–64, N. J. Curtin, 'The transformation of the society of United Irishmen into a mass-based revolutionary organization', *I.H.S.*, xxix, no. 96 (1985), 463–92, J. Smyth, 'Dublin's political underground in the 1790s' in G. O'Brien (ed.), *Parliament, politics and people, essays in eighteenth-century Irish history* (Dublin, 1989), 129–48, and several contributions to D. Dickson and H. Gough, eds, *Ireland and the French revolution* (Dublin, 1990).

6.   An exception to this rule is Peter Gibbon, 'The origins of the Orange Order and the United Irishmen', *Economy and Society*, i (1972), 136–63.

7.   McDowell, *Age*, 462, 473, Elliott, *Partners in revolution, the United Irishmen and France* (New Haven, 1982), 40–2.

8.   M. R. Beames, *Peasants and power, the Whiteboy movements and their control in pre-famine Ireland* (Brighton, 1983), 17.

9.   D. Dickson, *New foundations: Ireland 1660–1800* (Dublin, 1987), 153, L. M. Cullen, *The emergence of modern Ireland* (London, 1981), 14.

10.   *A candid and impartial account of the disturbances in Meath in the years 1792, 1793, 1794, by a County Meath Freeholder* (Dublin, 1794), 8.

11.   Peter Burke, *Popular culture in early modern Europe* (London, 1978), 259.

12.   George Rudé, *Ideology and popular protest* (London, 1980), 9, 27–30.

13.   Samuel McSkimmin (E. J. McCrum, ed.), *Annals of Ulster, 1790–1800* (Belfast, 1906 edn), 31. McSkimmin's book is a primary source in the sense that he was witness to some of the events which he describes.

14.   John O'Neill, M.P., *Proceedings of the parliament of Ireland,* (1793), i, 29–30.

15.   Tone, *Life*, i, 278.

16.   *N.S.*, 11–14 April, 1792 & 28 September–2 October, 1793.

17.   S. J. Connolly in W. E. Vaughan (ed.), *A new history of Ireland, v, Ireland under the union I, 1801–70* (Oxford, 1989), 78–9.

18.   *Dub. Soc.*, 129.

19.   Olivia Smith, *The politics of language, 1791–1819* (Oxford, 1986), 43, John Brewer, *Party ideology and popular politics at the accession of George III* (Cambridge, 1976), 238.

20.   Enclosure, Rev. Edward Hudson to Lord Charlemont, July, 1794, *H.M.C.*, 13th report, app. pt. viii, *Charlemont Mss* (1894), ii, 245–6.

21.   Thomas Russell, *A letter to the people of Ireland on the present situation of the country* (Belfast, 1796), 23.

22.   W. J. MacNevin, *Pieces of Irish history* (New York, 1807), 77.

23.   Hudson to Charlemont, 3 August, 1794, *Charl. Mss.*, 246.

24.   Connolly in Vaughan (ed.), *New history of Ireland, v*, 98–99.

25.   Elliott, 'Ireland and the French revolution' in H. T. Dickinson (ed.), *Britain and the French revolution, 1789–1815* (London, 1989), 92.

26. Information of 'JW' (McNally) 11 September, 1795, I.S.P.O. Reb. papers, 620/10/121/28.
27. S. J. Connolly, *Priests and people in pre-famine Ireland, 1780–1845* (Dublin, 1982), 239–55, at 255.
28. *F.D.J.*, 5 January, 1795.
29. The Orange Order was also, at least at the outset in 1795–6, another manifestation of popular politicisation during this decade. If the movement's political *raison d'etre*, the defence of the protestant constitution, was reactionary, Orangism was nevertheless both popular and political. However, non-radical popular politics of this kind fall outside the scope of this study.
30. Bearing the complexity of the class structure and the diversity of the language of class in mind, hereafter the terms middle- and lower-class will generally be used as a matter of convenience.
31. *Letter to the people of Ireland*, 17.
32. Westmorland to Dundas, 17 November, 1792, P.R.O. H.O. 100/38/78–82.

CHAPTER 1: EIGHTEENTH-CENTURY IRELAND: POLITICS, ECONOMY, SOCIETY

1. J. C. Beckett, *The Anglo-Irish Tradition* (London, 1976), ch. vi. 'The Anglo-Irish achievement', 63–83.
2. Dickson, *New foundations*, vii.
3. See Bartlett's and Elliott's comments on Moody and Vaughan, eds, *New history of Ireland, iv*: 'A new history of Ireland', *Past and Present*, no. 116 (1987), and *I.H.S.* xxv (1987), 427–30.
4. Ian R. Christie, *Stress and stability, Britain's avoidance of revolution* (Oxford, 1986).
5. The best and most detailed consideration of the history and effects of the penal code can be found in the essays collected in T. P. Power and K. Whelan, eds, *Endurance and emergence, catholics in Ireland in the eighteenth century* (Dublin, 1990).
6. The religious aspects of penal legislation is most fully dealt with by Maureen Wall, *The penal laws, 1690–1760* (Dundalk, 1961): reprinted in G. O'Brien (ed.), *Catholic Ireland in the eighteenth century, collected essays of Maureen Wall* (Dublin, 1989), 1–60.
7. Lecky, ii, 181, 208–9, Patrick Rogers, *The Volunteers and catholic emancipation* (Belfast, 1938), 1, 41. Cullen associates this view in particular with Beckett and McDowell: 'Catholics under the penal laws', *Eigtheenth-Century Ireland,* i (1986).
8. Elliott, *Wolfe Tone*, 35, 113, 26–8.
9. Cullen, *The emergence of modern Ireland*, 37.
10. Aidan Clarke, 'Ireland, 1534–1660' in J. Lee (ed.), *Irish historiography, 1970–79* (Cork, 1981), 34.

11. S. J. Connolly, 'Religion and history', *Irish Economic and Social History* x (1983), 66–80, L. M. Cullen, 'Catholics under the penal laws', *Eighteenth-Century Ireland* i (1986), 23–36, J. Hill, 'The meaning and significance of Protestant Ascendancy, 1787–1840' in *Ireland after the union* (Oxford, 1989), 1–22.

12. Dickson, *New foundations*, 85.

13. J. C. D. Clark, *English society, 1688–1832* (Cambridge, 1986).

14. Connolly, *Priests and people*, 25–7, Cullen, 'Catholics and the penal laws'. Particular stress is laid on the political influence of converts by T. P. Power in his essay, 'Converts' in Power and Whelan, eds, *Endurance and emergence*, 101–27.

15. Johnston, *Ireland in the eighteenth century*, 26.

16. Lecky, ii, 182.

17. G. O'Brien, 'Francophobia in later eighteenth-century Irish history' in Dickson and Gough, eds, *Ireland and the French revolution*, 40–51.

18. A. P. W. Malcomson, *John Foster, the politics of the Anglo- Irish Ascendancy* (Oxford, 1978), xx.

19. O'Flaherty, 'Irish Catholics and the French revolution' in Dickson and Gough, eds, *Ireland and the French revolution*, 52–3.

20. Malcomson, *John Foster,* xviii–xix.

21. See the essays by Hayton, O'Donovan and Bartlett in T. Bartlett and D. Hayton, eds, *Penal age and golden era, essays in Irish history, 1690–1800* (Belfast, 1979) and the chapter 'The structure of politics' in R. F. Foster, *Modern Ireland, 1600– 1972* (Harmondsworth, 1988).

22. Christie, *Stress and stability*, ch. vi, 156–82, H. T. Dickenson, *Liberty and property, political ideology in eighteenth-century Britain*, (London, 1978), 272.

23. Malcomson provides a pithy summary of the eighteenth-century parliament in 'The parliamentary traffic of this country', in Bartlett and Hayton, eds, *Penal age*, 137–69.

24. F. G. James, *Ireland in the old empire, 1690–1770* (Cambridge, Mass., 1973), 95n. Catholic peers could not take their seats.

25. See Isolde Victory, 'The making of the 1720 declaratory act' in G. O'Brien (ed.), *Parliament, politics and people*, 9–29.

26. A. P. W. Malcomson, 'A lost natural leader: John James Hamilton, first marquess of Abercorn (1756–1818)' *Proceedings of the Royal Irish Academy*, vol. 88, c, no. 4 (1988), 62.

27. Wall, 'The quest for Catholic equality, 1745–1778' in *Collected essays of Maureen Wall*, 120–22, *Morning Post,* 24 March, 1792.

28. E. M. Johnston, *Great Britian and Ireland 1760–1800, a study in political administration* (Edinburgh, 1963), 257 & app. B., 321–30.

29. Clark, *English society*, 277, J.Cannon, *The aristocratic century, the peerage in eighteenth-century England* (Cambridge, 1987), 152.

30. J. Kelly, 'The genesis of "Protestant Ascendancy": the Rightboy disturbances of the 1780s and their impact upon protestant opinion' in O'Brien (ed.), *Parliament, politics and people*, 91–127. The historical

significance of the concept and articulation of Protestant Ascendancy had been previously identified and elaborated by W. J. McCormack: *Ascendancy and tradition in Anglo-Irish literary history from 1789 to 1939* (Oxford, 1985), 61–96, *The battle of the books* (Mullingar, 1986), 73–6, 'Vision and revision in the study of eighteenth-century Irish parliamentary rhetoric' in *Eighteenth-Century Ireland* ii (1987), 15–18.

31. Hill, 'The meaning and significance of "Protestant Ascendancy"', 15, Lecky, iii, 64.

32. Cullen, 'The 1798 rebellion in its eighteenth-century context' in P. Corish (ed.), *Radicals, rebels and establishments* (Belfast, 1985), 105–6.

33. H. T. Dickinson, 'Popular conservativism and militant loyalism, 1789–1815' in Dickinson (ed.), *Britain and the French revolution*, 103–25.

34. See Bartlett's suggestive comments on this episode in 'The origins and progress of the Catholic Question in Ireland', Power and Whelan, eds, *Endurance and emergence*, 6–7.

35. Daniel Corkery, *The hidden Ireland, a study of Gaelic Munster in the eighteenth century* (Dublin, 1925), Peter Brooke, *Ulster presbyterianism, the historical perspective*, 1618–1970 (Dublin, 1987).

36. Edward Wakefield, *An account of Ireland, stastical and political* 2 vols (Dublin, 1812), ii, 759.

37. P. Lynch and J. Vaizey, *Guinness's brewery in the Irish economy, 1759–1876* (Cambridge, 1960), 9–17, J. Lee, 'The dual economy in Ireland, 1800–50' in *Historical Studies,* viii (Dublin, 1971), 191–201, J. H. Johnson, 'The two "Irelands" at the beginning of the nineteenth century' in N. Staples and R. E. Glassock, eds, *Irish Geographical Studies* (Belfast, 1970), 224–43.

38. Dickson, *New foundations*, 97.

39. J. H. Andrews in Moody and Vaughan, eds, *New history of Ireland,* iv, 259.

40. Arthur Young, *A tour in Ireland, 1776–1779* (4th edition, London, 1892, Shannon, 1970), i, 19.

41. Cullen in Moody and Vaughan, eds, *New history,* iv, 181.

42. S. Clark and J. S. Donnelly, eds, *Irish peasants and political unrest, 1780–1900* (Wisconsin, 1984), 26.

43. Young, *Tour,* i, 217, 247–9, 299.

44. Cullen in Moody and Vaughan, eds, *New history,* 180.

45. Young, *Tour,* ii, 77, Andrews in Moody and Vaughan, eds, *New history,* 254–5. See Andrews Map, p. 256.

46. N. J. Curtin, 'Symbols and rituals of United Irish mobilisation' in Dickson and Gough, eds, *Ireland and the French revolution,* 68–82.

47. R. A. Houstan, *Literacy and the Scottish identity, literacy and illiteracy in Scotland and northern England, 1600–1900* (Cambridge, 1986), 136.

48. Burke, *Popular Culture*, 37–8, 251, Rude, *Ideology and popular protest*, 34.
49. McDowell, *Age*, 473, Musgrave, 155.
50. Houstan, 153.
51. Lawrence Stone, 'Literacy and Education in England, 1600–1900', *Past and Present* (1969), 78–81.
52. *Enquiry*, 23, Brooke, *Ulster presbyterianism*, 112.
53. Peter Gibbon, 'Origins of the Orange Order and United Irishmen', 147.
54. Adams, *The printed word and the common man, popular culture in Ulster, 1700–1900* (Belfast, 1987), 39–40, 'Reading societies in Ulster', *Ulster Folklife* xxvi, no.26 (1980), 55–64.
55. *N.S.* journeybook, I.S.P.O. Reb. papers, 620/1/55, Adams, *The printed word*, 36.
56. Musgrave, 153, *N.S.*, 28–31 December, 1795.
57. Musgrave, 153.
58. The account of the provincial press is based on McDowell, 'The Irish government and the provincial press', *Hermathena* liii (1939), 138–47, and Madden, *The history of Irish periodical literature* (London, 1867), ii, 164–252.
59. Young, *Tour*, i, 446.
60. Madden, *Lives of the United Irishmen*, 3rd ser. vol. i, 225–6.
61. Connolly, *Priests and people*, 28, 77.
62. *Hib. Jrnl.* 7 September, 1792, *Morning Post*, 15 June, 1793.
63. T.C.D. Sirr papers, 869/10,18.
64. B. O'Cuiv in Moody and Vaughan, eds, *New history*, 381.
65. J[ohn] Byrne, *An impartial account of the late disturbances in the county of Armagh*, reproduced in D. W. Miller (ed.), *Peep O'Day Boys and Defenders, selected documents on the Armagh disturbances, 1784–96* (Belfast, 1990), 105.
66. Cullen, *Emergence*, 108, *An enquiry into the causes of popular discontents . . . , 6.*

CHAPTER 2:   AGRARIAN REBELS, SECRET SOCIETIES AND DEFENDERS, 1761–91

1. Bishop of Cloyne to Westmorland, 12 January, 1795, I.S.P.O. Westmorland Corr.
2. Cited, S. H. Palmer, *Police and protest in England and Ireland, 1780–1850* (Cambridge, 1988), xix.
3. See the chapter 'Landscape with bandits', in A. T. Q. Stewart, *The narrow ground, aspects of Ulster, 1609–1969* (London, 1977), and S. J. Connolly, 'Law, order and popular protest in early eighteenth-century Ireland', in P. J. Corish (ed.), *Radicals, rebels and establishments* (Belfast, 1985), 51–68, 'The Houghers: agrarian

protest in early eighteenth-century Connaught', in C. H. E. Philpin (ed.), *Nationalism and popular protest in Ireland* (Cambridge, 1987), 139–162.

4. Lewis, *On local disturbances in Ireland* (London, 1836), Beames, *Peasants and power*.

5. Beames, 'The Ribbon societies: lower-class nationalism in pre-famine Ireland', *Past and Present*, no. 97 (1982), 128–43, T. Garvin, 'Defenders, Ribbonmen and others: underground political networks in pre-famine Ireland', *Past and Present*, no. 96 (1982), 133–55. Both articles are reprinted in Philipin (ed.), *Nationalism and popular protest*.

6. T. C. Croker, *Researches in the south of Ireland* (Dublin, 1824), 14.

7. A detailed, and long overdue, examination of the tithe question is offered by M. J. Bric, 'The tithe system in eighteenth-century Ireland', *Proceedings of the Royal Irish Academy*, vol. 86, c, (1986), 271–88.

8. For discussions of the first Whiteboy movement see M. Wall, 'The Whiteboys', in T. D. Williams (ed.), *Secret societies in Ireland* (Dublin, 1973), 122–40, and J. S. Donnelly, 'The Whiteboy movement, 1761–5', *I.H.S.,* xxi, no. 81 (1978), 20–54.

9. Lecky, ii, 32.

10. Lecky, ii, 41–4.

11. The most detailed treatments of these Ulster secret societies are by J. S. Donnelly, 'Hearts of Oak, Hearts of Steel', *Studia Hibernica*, no. 21 (1981), 7–73, and W. A. Maguire, 'Lord Donegall and the Hearts of Steel', *I.H.S.*, xxi, no. 84 (1979), 351–76.

12. See Donnolly, 'Irish agrarian rebellions: the Whiteboys of 1769–76', *Proceedings of the Royal Irish Academy,* 83, c. no. 12 (1983), 293–332.

13. Donnolly, 'The Rightboy movement', *Studia Hibernica*, nos 17–18 (1977–8), 120–202, M. J. Bric, 'Priests, parsons and politics: the Rightboy protest in County Cork, 1785–1788', *Past and Present*, no. 100 (1983), 100–23. Reprinted in Philipin (ed.), *Nationalism and popular protest*.

14. Fitzgibbon to Eden, 25 August, 1787, P.R.O.N.I. Sneyd papers T 3229/1/5.

15. *Cork Gazette*, 20 August, 9, 16 & 30 November, 1791.

16. *Hib. Jrnl.*, 16 December, 1791, R.D.Edwards (ed.), 'The minute-book of the Catholic Committee, 1772–1792', *Archivium Hiberinicum*, ix (1941), 140–1.

17. Connolly, 'Violence and order in the eighteenth century' in P. Ferguson, P. O'Flanagan and K. Whelan, eds, *Rural Ireland, modernisation and change, 1600–1900* (Cork, 1987), 42–61.

18. C. Winslow 'Sussex smugglers' in D. Hay *et al.*, *Albion's fatal tree, crime and society in eighteenth-century England* (London, 1975),

119–66, E. P. Thompson, *Whigs and hunters, the origins of the Black Act* (London, 1975).

19. Lecky, i, 356–7, n.
20. Wakefield, *Account of Ireland*, ii, 568.
21. John Gillingham, 'Images of Ireland, 1170–1600: The origins of English imperialism', *History Today*, vol. 37 (1987), 16–22, L. P. Curtis, *Anglo-Saxons and Celts, a study in anti-Irish prejudice in Victorian England* (New York, 1968), S. Deane, 'Irish National Character 1790–1900' in T. Dunne (ed.), *The writer as witness: literature as historical evidence* (Cork, 1987), 90–113.
22. Stewart, *Narrow ground*, 113.
23. Clare to Camden, 28 August, 1796, P.R.O.N.I. Camden papers (photocopies) T 2627/4/199. Young, *Tour*, ii, 429.
24. Pelham to [Portland?], 27 September, 1797, P.R.O., H.O. 100/70/148.
25. Wakefield, ii, 568, Lecky, i, 36.
26. T. M. Devine, 'Unrest and stability in rural Ireland and Scotland, 1780–1840' in R. Mitchison and P. Roebuck, eds, *Economy and society in Scotland and Ireland* (Edinburgh, 1988), 126–39.
27. Cullen, *Emergence*, 57.
28. Clark and Donnelly, *Irish peasants*, 15.
29. Devine, 'Unrest and stablity', 129–30.
30. Connolly, 'Violence and order in the eighteenth century', 53.
31. Stewart, *The narrow ground*, 115–16.
32. E. J. Hobsbawn, *Bandits* (London, 1969), 13–14, 35, Burke, *Popular culture*, 165–66. Michael Davitt described the celebrated Tory, Redmond O'Hanlon, as 'this Irish Robin Hood', *The fall of feudalism in Ireland* (London & New York, 1904, Shannon, 1970), 12, Connolly, 'Violence and order in the eighteenth century', 42–6.
33. John Cosgrove, *Genuine history* (Dublin, 12th edn c.1760), 7, 10.
34. Cullen, *Emergence*, 206, Lecky, i, 355.
35. Davitt, *Fall of feudalism*, 14.
36. Robert Bell, *A description of the condition and manners, as well as the moral and political character, education, etc, of the peasantry of Ireland . . . between the years 1780 and 1790 . . .* (London, 1804), 41, K. Boyle, 'Police in Ireland before the union', *Irish Jurist*, new ser. vii, part 1 (1972), 129.
37. Information of Thomas Kennedy, 9 March, 1796, I.S.P.O. Reb. papers 620/23/59.
38. Clark, *English society*, 119–98, 374, *Revolution and rebellion*, 111–16 and app. B, 174–77, for a summary of the historiography. P. K. Monod, *Jacobitism and the English people, 1688–1788* (Cambridge, 1989).[Monod is an American scholar].
39. Clark, *Revolution and rebellion*, 175.
40. Cullen, 'The hidden Ireland: re-assessment of a concept', *Studia Hibernica*, no. 9 (1969), 17–18.
41. Cullen, *Emergence*, 19, Johnston, 'The two "Irelands"', 231–2.

42.   K. H. Connell, *Irish peasant society* (Oxford, 1968), 36.
43.   Wakefield, i, 730. The Scottish Highlands presented a similar picture at this time, but it is an interesting commentary on contemporary perceptions that the authorities there were worried that the practice of illicit distillation threatened to turn the region into 'the lawless and disorganised state existing in Ireland': T. M. Devine, 'The rise and fall of illicit whiskey-making in northern Scotland, c.1780–1840', *Scottish Historical Review*, liv, 2, no. 158 (1975), 155–77.
44.   Connell, 10, Bell, 29.
45.   Bell, 29.
46.   *F.D.J.*, 28 April, 1795, G. Holdcroft to J. Lees, 13 April 1797, I.S.P.O. Reb. papers, 620/29/246. Thomas J. Barran, 'A poitin affray near Ballybay in 1797', *Clogher Record*, viii, no. 2 (1974), 182–93.
47.   *Morning Post*, 12 January, 1796.
48.   T. Bartlett, 'The Irish militia disturbances of 1793', 43.
49.   Wall, 'Whiteboys', 15.
50.   R. McHugh (ed.), *Carlow in '98, the autobiography of William Farrell* (Dublin, 1949), 41, R. R. Madden, *Lives of the United Irishmen* (Dublin, 1843–6), 3rd ser. vol, i, 229.
51.   *The autobiography of William Carleton* (London, 1968), 76–80.
52.   E. P. Thompson, 'The "moral economy" of the English crowd in the eighteenth century', *Past and Present*, no. 50 (1971), 76–136, K. J. Logue, *Popular disturbances in Scotland, 1780–1815* (Edinburgh, 1979), *passim*.
53.   Henry Collins (ed.), Thomas Paine, *The Rights of Man* (Harmonsworth, 1976), 80.
54.   Alborough to Cooke, 9 August, 1796, I.S.P.O. Reb. papers, 620/24/97.
55.   Donnolly, 'Hearts of Oak, Hearts of Steel', 59 (for the Steelboy captains), 'Whiteboys', *I.H.S.*, 40 (for 'Fearnot'), and vol. xxvii, T. B. and T. J. Howell, *A complete collection of State trials* (London, 1811–26), 34 vols, (for the trial of 'Captain Fearnought').
56.   'JC' to Rev. F. Archer, 3 June, 1798, I.S.P.O. Reb. papers, 620/38/36.
57.   *Report of the committee of secrecy . . . (commons), 1798*, 67, A. T. Q. Stewart, '"A stable unseen power": Dr William Drennan and the origins of the United Irishmen', in John Bossy and Peter Jupp, eds, *Essays presented to Michael Roberts* (Belfast, 1976), 80–92.
58.   John Pollock of Newry refers to a 'Free Mason lodge of a low order', of which one of his servants was a member: Pollock to Pelham, 28 February, 1798, I.S.P.O. Reb. papers, 620/35/152. Clashes between masons and others are reported by the Maghera (south Derry) magistrate, Clotworthy Soden, 26 May, 1796, 620/23/124, and in *S.N.L.*, 20 July, 1796, and P. Robinson, 'Hanging ropes and buried secrets', *Ulster Folklife*, no. 32 (1986), 8.

59. Charles Downes, *Downes list of Irish masonic lodges in 1804* (Comber, 1908), H. J. Lepper and P.Crossle, *A history of the Grand Lodge of free and accepted masons of Ireland* (Dublin, 1925).

60. Lepper and Crossle, 247–8, Rogers, *The Irish Volunteers and catholic emancipation*, 61–2, W. Geoghan, *The history and antiquities of the first Volunteer lodge of Ireland* (Dublin, 1921).

61. T. G. F. Paterson, 'The County Armagh Volunteers of 1778–1793', *Ulster Journal of Archeology*, v (1942), 38.

62. Cooke to Pelham, 4 December, 1795, P.R.O.N.I. Pelham transcripts, T 755/2, f.253–5.

63. J[ohn] Byrne, *An impartial account of the late disturbances in the county of Armagh . . . since the year 1784, down to the year 1791* (Dublin, 1792), 15. This rare pamphlet is reproduced and annotated, along with other documents, in D. W. Miller (ed.), *Peep O'Day Boys and Defenders, selected documents on the County Armagh disturbances, 1784–96*. Cullen speculates that Byrne may have been a pseudonym for the Defender-United Irishman, Rev. James Quigley [Coigly]: 'Political structures of the Defenders' in Dickson and Gough, eds, *Ireland and the French revolution*, 120. In A. T. Q. Stewart's opinion he may have been the John Byrne who represented Armagh at the Catholic Convention in 1792: *Narrow ground*, 132.

64. Young, *Tour*, ii, 55.

65. Byrne, 31, *D.E.P.*, 17 May, 1794.

66. Hereward Senior, *Orangism in Ireland and Britain, 1795–1836* (London, 1966). The debate about the relative importance of land competition is summarised by D. W. Miller, 'The Armagh troubles, 1785–95', in Clark and Donnelly, eds, *Irish peasants*, 163. For protestant resentment about catholics obtaining long leases see Byrne, 9, and Dr Richardson to Lord Abercorn, 14 February, 1797, P.R.O.N.I. Abercorn papers, T 2541/IB3/6/4. The reference to the Steelboys is from J. A. Froude, *The English in Ireland in the eighteenth century* (London, 1882), ii, 132–3.

67. Miller, 157–8.

68. Byrne, 21.

69. Byrne, 5.

70. Young, *Tour*, i, 129, Byrne, 27.

71. P.R.O.N.I. Abercorn papers, T 2541/1B3/6/4.

72. Byrne, 20–22.

73. Byrne, 25.

74. Byrne, 31–7, Hudson to Charlemont, *Charlemont Ms, H.M.C., 13th. report, app. part 8*, ii (London, 1894), 78–83.

75. Byrne, 26.

76. Petition of Norman Steele, JP, 27 December, 1795, I.S.P.O. Reb. papers, 620/22/58, Musgrave, 57–8, *Charlemont Ms*, ii, 102–3.

77. Hudson to Charlemont, 11 July, 1789, *Charlemont Ms*, ii, 102–3, Byrne, 7.

78. Musgrave, 59–61, Miller, 'Armagh troubles', 177–80.
79. Byrne, 52–3.
80. Anonymous memo, 1796, I.S.P.O. Reb. papers, 620/26/51, Thomas Reynolds, jnr., *Life of Thomas Reynolds* (London, 1839), i, 43, *Hib. Jrnl.*, 20 April, 1791.
81. Drennan described the catholics as 'savages' and thought the events at Forkhill would 'put off the day of general freedom'. That is that it would delay catholic emancipation. D. A. Chart (ed.), *Drennan letters* (Belfast, 1931), 53.
82. Rev. B. McEvoy, 'Peep of Day Boys and Defenders in the County Armagh', *Seanchas ArdMhacha* (1986), 157, *Cork Gazette*, 30 November, 1791.
83. Tone, *Life*, i, 174.
84. Cooke to Nepean, 26 February, P.R.O. HO 100/43/15–16.
85. Westmorland to Dundas, 17 November, 1792, P.R.O. HO 100/38/78–82.
86. Francis Plowden, *An historical review of the state of Ireland, from the invasion of that country . . . to its union with Great Britain* (London, 1803), i, 395.
87. Cullen, *Emergence*, 57, 202, 249, Wakefield, ii, 616, *A candid and impartial account of the disturbances in the county Meath*, 2.
88. Rev. J. Gordon, *History of the rebellion in Ireland* (Dublin, 1801), 70.

CHAPTER 3:   'RUMOURS OF WAR': THE CATHOLIC AGITATION, 1791–3

1. W. J. MacNevin, *Pieces of Irish history*, 47.
2. Lecky, iii, 22–176, McDowell, *Age*, ch. 11., T. D. H. Mahoney, *Edmund Burke and Ireland* (London, 1960), E. O'Flaherty, 'The catholic question in Ireland, 1774–1793', unpublished MA thesis, NUI (1981), 'The catholic question and Anglo-Irish politics, 1791–3', *Archivium Hibernicum*, xl (1985), 14–34.
3. Lecky, ii, 211, 364, 380, 399.
4. J. Lawless, *The Belfast politics enlarged; being a compendium of the political history of Ireland, for the last forty years* (Belfast, 1818), 187–9.
5. Elliott, *Wolfe Tone*, 114.
6. Both Richard Price and Chistopher Wyvell argued that under Irish conditions the franchise could only safely be extended to propertied catholics: J. Kelly, 'The parliamentary reform movement of the 1780s and the catholic question', *Archivium Hibernicum*, xlii (1988), 98. For John Jebb's views on the matter see Elliott, 'Ireland and the French revolution, 1789–1815' in Dickinson (ed.), *Britain and the French Revolution*, 86.

7. M. Wall, 'The United Irish movement', *Historical Studies*, v (1965), 124.

8. J. Kelly, Select documents xliii: A secret return of the Volunteers of Ireland in 1784', *I.H.S.* xxvi, no. 103 (1989), 268–92.

9. Kelly, 272.

10. Rutland to Sydney, 24 May and 20 September, 1784, P.R.O. H.O. 100/13/18–20, H.O. 100/14/102–5.

11. Edwards (ed.), 'The minutebook of the Catholic Committee, 1772–1792', 116.

12. Henry Grattan (jnr.) *Memoirs of the life and times of the Rt. Hon. Henry Grattan* (London, 1839–46), iv, 40.

13. Minutebook, 116, O'Flaherty, 'Catholic question', 115, D. Dickson, *New foundations*, 174.

14. Minutebook, 117–20, R. B. McDowell, 'The personnel of the Dublin Society of United Irishmen, 1791–4', *I.H.S.*, ii (1940–1), 12–53.

15. Minutebook, 123–4.

16. *Hib. Jrnl*, 11 July, 1792, Hobart to Nepean, 8 October, 1792, P.R.O. H.O. 100/38/11–18, Westmorland to Dundas, 11 July, 1791, H.O. 100/35/81–2.

17. Minutebook, 136, Grattan, iv, 40–1, Westmorland to Grenville, *The manuscripts of J. B. Fortesque esq, preserved at Dropmore, HMC, 13th report, app. part 3 & 14th report, app. part 5* (London, 1892–4), ii, 39–40.

18. Grenville to Westmorland, 20 October, 1791, *Dropmore Ms*, ii, 213–4.

19. Cooke to Nepean, 30 October, 1784, P.R.O. H.O. 100/14/209–10. *Parl. reg.* (1792), 84. The latter part of Boyle's remark refers to Dryden's couplet:

> God's pamper'd People, whom, debauch'd with ease,
> No King could govern nor no God could please
> (Absalom and Achitophel, ll. 47–8).

20. *N.S.*, 22–26 September, 1792.

21. Westmorland to Grenville, 7 March, 1791, *Dropmore Ms*, ii, 39–40.

22. Tone, *Life*, i, 140.

23. Tone, *Life*, i, 52–3. The *Argument* was suggested, apparently, by Tone's friend Thomas Russell, and may have drawn on notes which Russell prepared on the catholic question. John Gray, 'Millennial vision . . . Thomas Russell re-assessed', *Linen Hall Review*, vol. 6, no. 1. (1989), 6.

24. *Drennan letters*, 59–60.

25. J. O'Donovan, *The O'Connors of Connaught* (Dublin, 1891), 298.

26. In his diary entry of 27 August, 1792, Tone expressed doubts about catholic good faith but remarked, 'however I will go on – their cause is just, independent of reform': *Life*, i, 179. On the catholic side leading

committee-men, such as McCormick and MacNevin, remained active United Irishmen long after the catholic issue had been – temporarily – subsumed under the revolutionary separatist struggle.

27. *Drennan letters*, 70–1.
28. Westmorland to —— 21 November, 1791, P.R.O. H.O. 100/33/116, *Drennan letters*, 61.
29. *Tracts on Catholic affairs* (Dublin, 1792), 163–4.
30. Tone, *Life*, i, 141.
31. Mahoney, *Edmund Burke and Ireland*, 59–60, MacNevin *Pieces of Irish history*, 19.
32. Mahoney, 165.
33. Malcomson, *John Foster*, 410, J. D. Mackie, *A history of Scotland* (London, 1969 edition), 284.
34. Dundas to Westmorland, 26 December, 1791, P.R.O. H.O. 100/33/207.
35. Dundas to Westmorland, 29 January, 1792, P.R.O. H.O. 100/36/180–2.
36. Dundas to Westmorland, 26 December, 1791, N.L.I. Ms 54, 47.
37. Westmorland to Dundas, 21 January, 1792, P.R.O. H.O. 100/36/126–5. Dundas to Westmorland, H.O. 100/36/169–74.
38. Minutebook, 136–40.
39. Westmorland to Nepean, 8 October, 1792, I.S.P.O. Official papers, 510/30/3/23.
40. *Hib. Jrnl*, 9 December, 1791.
41. Minutebook, 141.
42. Reynolds, *Life*, i, 35.
43. 'The rise of a catholic middle class', *Collected essays of Maureen Wall*, 81, McDowell, 'Personnel . . . '.
44. O'Donovan, 300.
45. *N.E.S.*, 10 January, 1792.
46. *N.E.S.*, 5 & 7 January, 1792.
47. *Drennan letters*, 64. From clear internal evidence this letter has been wrongly dated by the editor.
48. M. Duggan, 'County Carlow, 1791–1801, a study in an era of revolution', unpublished MA thesis, NUI (1969), 50–2.
49. *N.E.S.*, 14 January, 1792, *Hib. Jrnl*, 4 January, 1792.
50. MacNevin, *Pieces of history*, 21.
51. Lecky, iii, 54.
52. *Morning Post, F.D.J.*, 14 January, 1792.
53. *Drennan letters*, 75.
54. *Parliamentary proceedings, i* (Dublin, 1793), 141.
55. Westmorland to Dundas, January, 1792, I.S.P.O. Westmorland corr. *Parl. reg.* (1792), 24.
56. *Parl. reg.* (1792), 37.
57. The petition was drawn up at the instigation of the local United Irishmen in the teeth of opposition which advocated a slower rate of change. For an account of this episode in Belfast politics, see Lawless, 284–310.

58. *F.D.J.*, 14 Feburary, 1792.
59. O'Donovan, 313.
60. Minutebook, 157–9, *Drennan letters*, 62, Byrne to Kelburne, *N.S.*, 4 April, 1792.
61. The English Catholic Committee had issued a similar document in 1789, and as early as the 1750s some Irish bishops and clergy had drawn up a public statement which denied the deposing power of the pope and 'other odious tenets': P. J. Corish, *The Catholic community in the seventeenth and eighteenth centuries* (Dublin, 1981), 119.
62. Minutebook, 157–8.
63. Musgrave, app. xi, p. 24.
64. Lawless, 318–9.
65. *Morning Post*, 13 September, 1792.
66. J. G. O. Kerrane, 'The background to the 1798 rebellion in County Meath', unpublished MA thesis, NUI (1971), 35.
67. T.C.D. Sirr papers, 869/10, 18–35, *Morning Post*, 15 June, 1793.
68. Minutebook, 156.
69. R. B. McDowell, 'Proceedings of the Dublin Society of United Irishmen', *Analecta Hibernia*, 17 (1949), 19–20.
70. W. P. Cary, *An appeal to the people of Ireland* (Dublin, 1794), 4.
71. Enclosure, Westmorland to Hobart, 7 July, 1792, P.R.O. H.O. 100/37/142–9.
72. O'Flaherty, 145.
73. I.S.P.O. Braughall papers, Reb. papers, 620/34/50, Tone, *Life*, i, 161–2, 171–4.
74. 'Report of the committee of accounts', P.R.O. H.O. 100/46/61–2.
75. Hobart to Nepean, 29 December, 1792, P.R.O. H.O. 100/42/9–11. Cooke to Westmorland, 11 March, 1795, I.S.P.O. Westmorland corr, letterbook iii. It is almost 100 years since W.J. Fitzpatrick observed that Keogh was a man 'of rare sagacity – whose life has still to be written'. *The secret service under Pitt* (London, 1892), 166. Unfortunately the latter part of this statement is still true.
76. Tone, *Life*, i, 162.
77. Copy of a letter, Keogh to [Hussy?], 2 October, 1792, P.R.O. H.O. 100/38/275–8. Ironically, when Keogh was himself an 'old man', the boot was on the other foot. By 1807–8, when he was sixty-seven, and chastened perhaps by the experience of living through rebellion and repression, Keogh was aligned in catholic politics with the 'nobles and squires' against the emerging, more forward O'Connellites. This faction, like Keogh in 1792, had 'no taste for patrician restraint' when dealing with the authorities: Oliver MacDonagh, *'The hereditary bondsman', Daniel O,Connell, 1775–1829* (London, 1988), 97–99.
78. Westmorland to Nepean, 8 October, 1792, I.S.P.O. Official papers, 510/30/3/23. Keogh may have in this instance deliberately played on recent memories of the Rightboys organized refusal to pay Church dues. I am grateful to Mr. Peter Tesch for this suggestion.

79. Foster to Westmorland, 17 June, 1792, P.R.O. H.O. 100/37/156–7. Westmorland to —— 13 August, 1792, H.O. 100/37/210–3, copy of a letter from Keogh, 2 October, 1792, H.O. 100/38/275–8, Tone, *Life*, i, 205.
80. Westmorland to Pitt, 3 November, 1792, I.S.P.O. Westmorland Corr.
81. *An impartial account of the disturbances in Meath, 1792–4*, 7.
82. 'JW', 27 July, 1796, I.S.P.O. Reb. papers 620/36/227.
83. Hobart memo. P.R.O. H.O. 100/42/13–14, Musgrave, 63, Westmorland to Dundas, 9 January, 1792, H.O. 100/38/70–82.
84. *Drennan letters*, 52–3.
85. Tone, *Life*, i, 185. *Hib. Jrnl*, 1 November, 1792.
86. Westmorland to Dundas, 17 November, 1792, P.R.O. H.O. 100/38/70–82.
87. *Cork Gazette*, 8 May, 1793.
88. William Coyningham to Abercorn, 13 July, 1792, P.R.O.N.I. Abercorn papers, T2541/1B3/3/48.
89. *An impartial account of the disturbances in Meath, 1792–4*, 8.
90. Elliott, 'Origins of early Irish republicanism', 420.
91. *Drennan letters*, 81.
92. *Morning Post*, 5 July, 1792, Westmorland to Nepean, 8 October, 1792, I.S.P.O. Official papers, 510/30/3/23.
93. Foster to Westmorland, 17 June, 1792, P.R.O. H.O. 100/37/156–7.
94. 'Extract of a letter from Ireland', 26 July, 1792, P.R.O. H.O. 100/38/266–8.
95. *Hib. Jrnl*, 5 November, 1792.
96. *Morning Post*, 7 July, 1792.
97. *N.S.*, 12–16 May, 1792, W.D. Bailie, 'The Reverend Samuel Barber, 1738–1811, national Volunteer, and United Irishman', in J. L. M. Haire (ed.), *Challenge and conflict, essays in Irish presbyterian history and doctrine* (Antrim, 1981), 83.
98. Downshire to Westmorland, 18 May, 1792, P.R.O.N.I. Downshire papers, D 607/B/361.
99. *N.E.S.*, 15 May, 1792, Westmorland to Hillsborough, 25 June, 1792, P.R.O.N.I. Downshire papers, D 607/B/369.
100. Annesley to Downshire, 1 June, 1792, P.R.O.N.I. Downshire papers, D 607/B/364.
101. *N.S.*, 27–30 June, 1792.
102. 'Extract of a letter from Ireland', 26 July, 1792, P.R.O. H.O. 100/38/266–8, *Drennan letters*, 190, McDowell, 'Proceedings . . . ', 31–4. The political head of the Beresford family, John, was first commissioner of the revenue. One of the most enduring and important members of the Dublin Castle 'junto' which came to dominate Irish politics and administration in the last two decades of the century, Beresford was also known as the 'king of Ireland' – a reference to his extensive connections (one brother was a bishop) and to the vast amounts of patronage which he controlled.

103. Grattan, *Life*, iv, 75. See also pp. 158–9.
104. Tone, *Life*, i, 162.
105. Tone, *Life*, i, 162–3, 167, 176, *N.S.*, 25–29, August, 1792.
106. Madden, *United Irishmen* 2nd ser. vol. i, 97. McNally, a barrister, is chiefly remembered as an informer, although he does not appear to have been in the pay of the Castle until late 1794. See Lecky, iii, 374–80.
107. Tone, *Life*, i, 171, 174.
108. Westmorland to Nepean, 8 October, 1792, I.S.P.O. Official papers, 510/30/3/23, Musgrave, 90.
109. Madden, *United Irishmen*, 3rd ser, vol. ii, 2. R.J. Coughlan, *Napper Tandy* (1976), 98, *The life of the Rev. James Coigly* (London, 1798).
110. McSkimmin, *Annals of Ulster*, 24.
111. *F.D.J.*, 23 October, 1792, *Drennan letters*, 91, Tone, *Life*, i, 204.
112. McDowell, 'Proceedings . . . ', 67.
113. See P.R.O. H.O. 100/37/156–7, 210–13, 214–5.
114. Westmorland to Dundas, 17 November, 1792, P.R.O. H.O. 100/38/70–82.
115. Tone, *Life*, i, 65, Westmorland to Hobart, 7 June, 1792, P.R.O. H.O. 100/37/145–9, 26 November, 1792, H.O. 100/38/148–9.
116. Tone, *Life*, i, 208.
117. Tone, *Life*, i, 185–6, G. Knox to Abercorn, 13 December, 1792, P.R.O.N.I. Abercorn papers, T 2541/1B1/3/35.
118. Malcomson, *Foster*, 404–7, *Drennan letters*, 88, Dickson, *New foundations*, 179, T. Knox to Abercorn, 23 May, 1792, P.R.O.N.I. Abercorn papers, T 2541/1B1/1/10. More recently Malcomson has given the possibilities of an Abercorn lord lieutenancy extended treatment in his paper, 'A lost natural leader: John James Hamilton, first marquess of Abercorn (1756–1818)', *Proceedings of the Royal Irish Academy*, vol. 88, c, no. 4. (1988), 61–86.
119. Abercorn to T. Knox 5 January, 1792, P.R.O.N.I. Abercorn papers, T2541/1B2/1/10.
120. Abercorn to Hobart, 26 October, 1792, P.R.O.N.I. T 2541/1K/12/64.
121. Westmorland to Pitt, 16 October, 1792, I.S.P.O. Westmorland corr. letterbook iv.
122. Hobart to Nepean, 17 November, 1792, P.R.O. H.O. 100/38/87–9.
123. *Hib. Jrnl*, 1 October, 1792.
124. Westmorland to Pitt, 20 October, 1792, I.S.P.O. Westmorland corr. letterbook iv.
125. E. Cormac to R. Cormac, 6 October, 1792. T.C.D. Sirr papers 869/9, ff 27–8.
126. Grattan, *Life*, iv, 73.
127. Tone, *Life*, i, 204, MacDermot, *Theobald Wolfe Tone* (Tralee, 1969), 104.
128. Westmorland to Dundas, 17 November, 1792, P.R.O. H.O. 100/38/70–82, Westmorland to Pitt, 7 December, 1792, N.L.I. Ms 886, 33–41.

129. Cooke to Nepean, 24 October, 1792, P.R.O. H.O. 100/38/46–7.
130. Hobart to Nepean, 20 December, 1792, P.R.O. H.O. 100/38/180–1, Westmorland to Dundas, 5 December, 1792, H.O. 100/38/115–7.
131. *Hib. Jrnl*, 3 and 12 December, 1792. G. Knox to Abercorn, 13 December, 1792, P.R.O.N.I. Abercorn papers, T 2541/1B1/3/35, *A narrative of the confinement and exile of William Steele Dickson* (Dublin, 1812), 66, 'Report of the committee of privy council on the merchants memorial, 8 May, 1793.' *JHC*, xv, part 2 (1792–4).
132. John Stevenson, 'Popular radicalism and popular protest, 1789–1815' in Dickinson, ed., *Britain and the French revolution*, 69–70, John Ehrman, *The Younger Pitt, ii, the reluctant transition* (London, 1983), chaps iv and v, '1792: the dimensions of unrest', 91–171.
133. Tone, *Life*, i, 229.
134. Grenville, 16 October, 1792. *Dropmore Ms*, ii, 232.
135. Tone, *Life*, i, 78.
136. McDowell, 'Personnel . . . '.
137. N.L.I. Ms 886, *F.D.J.*, 22 December, 1792.
138. *Drennan letters*, 97–8.
139. McDowell, 'Personnel . . . '.
140. P.R.O. H.O. 100/46/61–2, Tone, *Life*, i, 220–22, 226–27.
141. Tone, *Life*, i, 80–82, 207.
142. Lecky, iii, 117, 139.
143. Knox to Abercorn, 10 December, 1792, P.R.O.N.I. Abercorn papers, T 2541/1B1/3/34.
144. *Hib. Jrnl*, 12 & 17 December, 1792, *Morning Post*, 20 December, 1792. *Dub. Soc.*, 43.
145. Lecky, iii, 117, 142, Westmorland to Dundas, 2 November, 1792, N.L.I. Ms 88, 17–31.
146. Westmorland to Dundas, 30 December, 1792, I.S.P.O. Westmorland corr. letterbook iv.
147. *S.N.L.*, 3 January, 1793. *Morning Post*, 5 January, 1793.
148. Grattan, *Life*, iv, 77.
149. *Parliamentary proceedings* (1793), i, 125.
150. Cooke to Nepean, 26 February, 1792, P.R.O. H.O. 100/43/15–16.
151. For a summary of a virulent anti-catholic speech, delivered on this occasion by Fitzgibbon (and afterwards published), see Lecky, iii, 169–76.
152. *Drennan letters*, 158.
153. Hobart. Memorial on the sate of the north, 29, December, 1792 P.R.O. H.O. 100/42/194–7, Tone, *Life*, i, 206, *F.D.J.*, 5, January, 1793.
154. Enclosure, Geo. Holdcroft to Hobart, 24 January, 1793, P.R.O. H.O. 100/42/194–7, *The Times*, 30 January, 1793, S. O'Loinsigh, 'The rebellion of 1798 in Meath', *Riocht Na Midhe*, iii, no. 4 (1966), 342–4.
155. *An impartial account of the disturbances in Meath, 1792–4*, 3.

156. Musgrave, 65.
157. O'Loinsigh, 340.
158. Bartlett, 'Militia disturbances . . . ', 48, Lecky, iii, 152, J. Kelly, The origins of the act of union: an examination of unionist opinion, 1650–1800', *I.H.S.*, xxv, no. 99 (1987), 260.

CHAPTER 4:   RADICAL IDEOLOGY, POPULAR POLITICS AND
             PARLIAMENTARY REFORM

1. For accounts which stress the essential constitutionality of the United Irishmen, 1791–94, see Elliott, *Partners*, 26–9, and Rosamond Jacob, *The rise of the United Irishmen* (London, 1937), *passim*. A new perspective which emphasises the internal sources of radicalisation has recently been offered by N.J.Curtin, 'The transformation of the Society of United Irishmen into a mass-based revolutionary organisation, 1794–6', *I.H.S.*, xxiv (1985), 463–92.
2. Cooke to Nepean, P.R.O. H.O. 100/43/101–2.
3. Sean Cronin, *Irish nationalism, a history of its roots and ideology* (Dublin, 1980), 46, *Dub. Soc.*, 7.
4. Elliott, *Partners*, especially pp. 252–58 and ch. 9, 'Early Irish republicanism in England, the first phase, 1797–9', in Bartlett and Hayton, eds, *Penal age and golden era*, 204–21, Roger Wells, *Insurrection, the British experience, 1795–1803* (Gloucester, 1983).
5. *D.E.P.*, 17 May 1794.
6. Musgrave, 332.
7. *Dub. Soc.*, 3–4, Carey, *An appeal to the people of Ireland*, 2. See also Tom Dunne, *Wolfe Tone, colonial outsider*, 19–21, 29.
8. Of course the nature and legacy of 1688 and of Locke's writings is ambivalent and, as J. C. D. Clark reminds us, a matter of some historiographical controversy: *English society*, 45–50. Unfortunately, although Caroline Robbins included a chapter on 'The case of Ireland' in her seminal study, *The eighteenth-century Commonwealthman* (Harvard, 1959), the history of whig ideas in eighteenth-century Ireland has yet to be written. On the evidence of United Irish publications it seems to me that they were untroubled either by the complexities or by the conservative interpretation of the Glorious Revolution. Apparently their use of Locke is also unproblematic. For example, the *Northern Star* (11–14 July, 1792) tacitly justified its politics by publishing what it ironically entitled 'Seditious Extracts from Locke's *Essay on Human Understanding*'.
9. The phrase is taken from the title of a book by J. T. Boulton (1966).
10. Robbins, 8–9.
11. Dickinson, *Liberty and property*, 196–7.
12. Isaac Kramnick (ed.), Thomas Paine, *Common Sense* (Harmondsworth, 1982), 76.

13. Staughton Lynd, *Intellectual origins of American radicalism* (Harvard, 1982), 46–48.
14 *Cork Gazette*, 6 August, 1796, *N.S.*, 17–20 June, 1796.
15. J. G. Simms, *Colonial nationalism* (Cork, 1976), 35, *William Molyneux of Dublin* (Dublin, 1982), 106.
16. Simms, *Molyneux*, 106, *Colonial nationalism*, 51–2, *Dub. Soc.*, 59.
17. *Dub. Soc.*, 3.
18. The term 'colonial nationalism' is unlikely to survive current revision. See, for example, Bartlett, 'A new history of Ireland', and Kelly, 'The origins of the act of union', in which he employs the term 'Anglo-Irish nationalism'.
19. Tone, *Life*, i, 143, 32.
20. McDowell, 'Proceedings . . . ', 69, *F.D.J.*, 2 April, 1793.
21. See, for example, McDowell, 'The personnel of the Dublin Society of United Irishmen, 1791–4', *I.H.S.*, ii (I94I), 12–53.
22. *N.S.*, 2–5 March, 1795, A. T. Q. Stewart, '"The Harp New Strung": nationalism, culture and the United Irishmen', in O. MacDonagh and W. F. Mandle, eds, *Ireland and Irish Australia, studies in cultural history* (London, 1986), 258–69. Norman Vance, 'Celts, Cathaginians and constitutions: Anglo-Irish literary relations, 1780–1820', *I.H.S.*, xxii, no. 87 (1981), 216–36. Thomas Russell took lessons in Irish when he was librarian of Belfast's Linen Hall library: John Gray, 'Millennial vision . . . Thomas Russell re-assessed', *Linen Hall Review*, vol. 6, no. 1.(1989), 7.
23. Burke, *Popular culture*, 11–12.
24. Elliott, 'Origins of early Irish republicanism', 405, *Partners*, xvi.
25. Tone, *Life*, i, 52, Clare to Camden, 28 August, 1796, P.R.O.N.I. Camden papers (photocopies), T 2627/4/199. T. A. Emmet likewise assumed the Irish catholic's 'hereditary hatred' of England: MacNevin, *Pieces of history*, 11.
26 *Dub. Soc.*, 6.
27. F. MacDermot, 'Arthur O'Connor', *I.H.S.*, xv, no. 57 (1966), 49.
28. W. D. Bailie, 'The Reverend Samuel Barber, 1738–1811, national Volunteer and United Irishman', in Haire (ed.), *Challenge and conflict*, 82.
29. *A narrative of the confinement and exile of the Reverend William Steele Dickson* (Dublin, 1812), 7, Lecky, iii, 191.
30. B. Neville to Cooke, enclosure, 'To the Men of Landed Property in County Down', 10 December, 1797, I.S.P.O. Reb. papers, 620/33/139.
31. Paine, *Common Sense*, 63, R. J. Dickson, *Ulster emigration to colonial America, 1718–1775* (London, 1966).
32. Palmer, *Age of the democratic revolution*, i, 240.
33. Lecky, iii, 194, *N.S.*, 19–23 May, 1792, McDowell, 'Proceedings . . . ', 32–4.
34. The Irish-American relationship is discussed in D. N. Doyle, *Ireland,*

Irishmen and Revolutionary America, 1760–1820 (Dublin & Cork, 1981).

35. J. H. Billington *Fire in the minds of men, origins of the revolutionary faith* (London, 1980), 92.

36. For an account of the conspiracy theory phenomenon see J. M. Roberts, *The mythology of the secret societies* (London, 1972).

37. Pelham to Donaghmore, 24 October, 1797, I.S.P.O. Reb. papers, 620/32/184.

38. A good example of the embarrassment of later masons at the politics of some of their revolutionary forebears can be found in Samuel Leighton, *A history of freemasonry in the province of Antrim, Northern Ireland* (Belfast, 1938). In the section of the book which purports to deal with the 1790s (25–28) Leighton only refers to – and commends – those lodges which publicly expressed their loyalty to the government.

39. Rogers, *The Irish Volunteers and catholic emancipation*, 61–2. One masonic toast declared 'May the gallant Volunteers of Ireland invariably unite in Brotherly ties, and be as faithful to each other as Free-Masons have ever been found to be'. Laurence Dermot, *Ahiman Rezon: or, a help to a Brother . . .* (Belfast, 1783), xviv.

40. T. DeVere White, 'The Freemasons', in Williams (ed.), *Secret societies*, 49, 'Petition of the Protestant Associations forming the Loyal Union of Orange.' P.R.O.N.I. Pelham transcripts, T 755/2.

41. Jacob, *The rise of the United Irishmen*, 54.

42. Free Masons Hall, Dublin, 'Grand Lodge of Ireland, Members Register, 1st. ser.' (microfilm), (for the Tandy's, MacNevin, McCabe, McAllister, Kennedy and Haslett), *Ahiman Rezon*, xxv (Tennant and McCleary) Rogers, 61–2, (Jones and Reynolds), Geoghan, *First Volunteer Lodge* (Rowan), Robison, 'Buried secrets and hanging ropes' (Orr), and I.S.P.O. Reb. papers, Information of Higgins, 20 January, 1797, 620/18/14 (Cooney and Dowling), 'JW', 12 December, 1796, 620/36/227 (Stockdale).

43. Abercorn to G. Knox, 27 September, 1795, P.R.O.N.I. Abercorn papers, T 2441/Ik/1 5124.

44. *B.N.L.*, 18–22 January, 1793, *N.S.*, 5–9, 9–12, January, 1793.

45. Crossle and Lepper, 297–8. The Armagh masons also condemned the Tyrone meeting.

46. *B.N.L.*, 18–22 January, 1793.

47. Stewart, *The narrow ground*, 102, see also, Elliott, *Watchmen in Sion, the protestant idea of liberty* (*Field Day* pamphlet, 1985).

48. This orthodoxy has recently been vigorously contested by Clark: *English society*, ch. 5. Again the Irish may be exempt. Whether or not English dissenters were primarily exercised by theological issues, as Clark suggests, in Ireland the history, size and cohesion of the presbyterian community in Ulster ensured that the quarrel with episcopalianism was politicised.

49. Peter Brooke, *Ulster presbyterianism*, ix–x, 113.

50. Stewart, *Narrow ground*, 106–7. Italics added.
51. MacNevin, *Pieces of Irish history*, 9.
52. *B.N.L.*, 13–17, February, 1795.
53. For a provocative discussion of the influence and implications of covenanting see D. W. Miller, *Queen's rebels, Ulster loyalism in historical perspective* (Dublin, 1978), ch. 1, 7–42.
54. Elliott, *Watchmen in Sion*, 11. Representative of the advanced political ideas circulating in Glasgow was the Ulster presbyterian and professor of moral philosophy in the 1730s and 1740s, Francis Hutcheson. For an account of Hutcheson's career and influence see Caroline Robbins, '"When is it that colonies may turn independent": an analysis of the environment and politics of Francis Hutcheson (1694–1746)', *William and Mary Quarterly*, 3rd ser. xi (1954), 214–51.
55. *N.S.*, 22–26 September, 1792.
56. J. M. Barkley, 'The presbyterian minister in eighteenth-century Ireland', in Haire (ed.), *Challenge and conflict*, 65, Elliott, *Watchmen*, 8–9, Brooke, *Ulster presbyterianism*, 128–9, D.W.Miller, 'Presbyterianism and "modernization" in Ulster', *Past and Present*, no. 80 (1978), reproduced in Philipin, (ed.), *Nationalism and popular protest*, 92–5.
57. McDowell, *Age*, 352. This author offers a knowledgeable survey of the public reception of the revolution in ch. viii of *Irish public opinion*, 'Ireland and the French revolution', 141–78. Predictably, however, the impact of the revolution upon the 'outlook of the masses' is left unexamined.
58. For a detailed analysis of the revolutionary implications and consummate skill of Paine's prose style see Olivia Smith, *The politics of language*, ch. 2.
59. Thomas Paine, *Rights of Man*, 102–3. In relation to the game laws, James Burgh's 'Cessareans' would all be free in their radical utopia to hunt wild animals, birds or fish: Lynd, *American radicalism*, 47–8.
60. Paine, 168.
61. Paine, 126, Thomas Russell, *A letter to the people of Ireland*, 16.
62. Tone, *Life*, i, 42–3. The term 'aristocrat', as this passage indicates, was used in the 1790s not merely to describe those who inherited wealth or title, but was applied generally to supporters of the *status quo*.
63. *N.S.*, 22–26, September, 1792.
64. McSkimmen, 8–9, *Morning Post*, 10 & 22 May, 1792, *N.S.*, 6–9 June, 1792.
65. McDowell, *Age*, 353, *Hib. Jrnl*, 8 April, 1791, Johnston, *Ireland in the eighteenth century*, 168, J. R. R. Adams, *The printed word and the common man*, 86, Spenser to Auckland, 26 November, 1792, *Auckland corr.* ii, 468–9.
66. Westmorland to —— 29 October, 1792, I.S.P.O. Westmorland corr.
67. *N.S.*, 3–7, 7–10, 10–14 November, 1792, Musgrave, 111–13.
68. *N.S.*, 18–21 July, 1792.
69. Plowden, *Historical review of the state of Ireland*, 386.

70. *B.N.L.*, 17 January, 1792.
71. For example, Elliott, *Partners*, 35.
72. McDowell, *Age*, 389, Tone, *Life*, i, 176–7, McSkimmin, 5, *N.S.*, 31 March-3 April, 2–5 May, 15–19 September, 1792, 'JW', undated, P.R.O.N.I. Downshire papers, D207/C/56.
73. *Dub. Soc.*, 5.
74. MacNevin, *Pieces of Irish history*, 222.
75. *Dub. Soc.*, 192.
76. Paine, 147, McDowell, 'Proceedings . . . ', 32–4.
77. *N.S.*, 14–17 March, 1792, *Dub. Soc.*, 192, Paine, 96–7.
78. McDowell, 'Proceedings . . . ', 112.
79. *N.S.*, 9–12 May, 1792.
80. Plowden, 452.
81. See T. M. Parssinen, 'Association, convention and anti-parliament in British radical politics, 1771–1848', *English Historical Review*, lxxxviii, no. 348 (1973), 504–33.
82. Westmorland to Dundas, 5 December, 1792, I.S.P.O. Westmorland corr.
83. McSkimmin, 15.
84. G. Knox to Abercorn, 14 February, 1793, P.R.O.N.I. Abercorn papers, T 2541/1B1/4/12, Tone wrote of 'Volunteer companies springing up like mushrooms, nobody knows why'. *Life*, i, 173.
85. Hobart to Nepean, 20 December, 1792, P.R.O. H.O./100/38/180–1, same to same, 18 January, 1793, H.O. I00/42/120, Westmorland to Dundas, 5 December, 1792, I.S.P.O. Westmorland corr.
86. Westmorland to Dundas, Hobart to Nepean, 29 December, 1792. P.R.O. H.O. 100/42/1–4, 9–11, same to same, 9 February, 1793, H.O. 100/42/269.
87. Tone, *Life*, i, 224–5.
88. Malcomson raises this point in a slightly different way when he inquires: 'if a parliamentary reform of the sort that would have found favour with the Irish parliamentary opposition (which was the utmost which could conceivably have been granted) would really have prevented the United Irishmen from advancing to revolutionary politics?' *John Foster*, xx.

CHAPTER 5:   THE RISE OF THE DEFENDERS, 1793–5

1. Lecky, iii, 225, McDowell, *Age*, 438, 444, 463. Elliott, 'The origins . . . of early Irish republicanism', 423.
2 *D.E.P.*, 17 May, 28 August, 1794.
3. Dickson and Gough, eds, *Ireland and the French Revolution*, 48–9, 109–38, 145–7, 152, Elliott, 'The origins . . . of early Irish republicanism', Clark and Donnelly, eds, *Irish peasants*, 11, Bartlett, 'Select document xxxviii: Defenders and Defenderism in 1795' *I.H.S.*, xxiv, no. 90 (1985), 373–94.

4. Lecky, iii, 221.
5. Memorial, anon, 1796, I.S.P.O. Reb. papers, 620/26/51, *Proceedings of the parliament of Ireland* i (1793), 125.
6. Froude, iii, 127, Bartlett, 'Militia disturbances', 54.
7. Bartlett, 49–58.
8. Bartlett, 59–64.
9. *F.D.J.*, 1 June, 1793.
10. Hobart to Nepean, 17 June, 1793, P.R.O. H0 100/44/147–50, 'Extracts of various letters relative to the late disturbances,' Denis Browne, 6 June, 1793, P.R.O. H.O. 100/44/115–18.
11. *Dub. Soc.*, 63, *D.E.P.*, 25 July, 1793, Knox to Abercorn, 16 May 1793, P.R.O.N.I. T 2541/IBI/4/20. For the militia as a source patronage see T.Knox to Abercorn, 30 April & 11 June, 1793, T 2541/IBI/5/25 & 31. Several officers appointed in Tyrone were members of Abercorn's 'Household in England and [would] be absent for most of the year'.
12. 'Abstract of information with regard to the militia', P.R.O. H.O. 100/43/323–9, 'Extracts of various letters of information relative to the late disturbances', H.O. 100/44/115–18, Bartlett, 54, 57.
13. *Morning Post*, 27 June 1793, *F.D.J.*, 27 July, 1793.
14. *Cork Gazette*, 18 May, 1793, *F.D.J.*, 1 June, 1793, *D.E.P.*, 25 May 1793, *Morning Post*, 15 June, 1793.
15. *Parl. reg.*, xv (1795), 289. McNally claimed that Troy's ritual denunciations of Defenderism were 'scoffed at' by his flock: Lecky, iii, 381–2.
16. *D.E.P.*, 1 September, 1795.
17. McAnally, *The Irish militia, 1793–1818* (Dublin & London, 1949), 36.
18. Bartlett, 'Militia disturbances', 44, Charles Dickson, *The rebellion in Wexford* (Dublin, 1956), 10.
19. *A view of the present state of Ireland, with an account of the origins and progress of the disturbances in that country; and a narrative of facts addressed to the people of England, by an observer* (London, 1797), 11.
20. S. O'Loinsigh, 'The rebellion of 1798 in Meath,' *Riocht Na Midhe*, iii, no. 4 (1966), 338, Cullen, *Emergence*, 208, *An inquiry into the causes of popular discontents in Ireland*, 6, Kerrane, 17–19, *D.E.P.*, 8 April, 1794.
21. *The Irish Magazine and monthly asylum of negelected biography* (hereater *Irish Magazine*) December, 1814, 557.
22. O'Loinsigh, iii, no. 4 (1966), 388–40.
23. O'Loinsigh, iv, no. 4 (1967), 34, Cullen, *Emergence*, 208, *The Times*, 20 February, 1793.
24. *Morning Post*, 14 November, 1793, *An impartial account of the late disturbances in Meath, 1792–4*, 22.
25. Kerrane, 20–1, *F.D.J.*, 2, 12, 26 November, 1793, *N.S.*, 25–28 November, 1793.

26. *Impartial account*, 28, 33, *D.E.P.*, 25 February, 1794.
27. *Impartial account*, 17–18, Plowden, *An historical disquisition into the origins of the Orange Society* (London, 1812), 13–14, Keogh to Nepean, 15 April, 1794, P.R.O. H.O. 100/46/154–6. Foster's biographer is silent on this matter.
28. *N.S.*, 7–10 April, 1794, *D.E.P.*, 2 September, 1794.
29. In 1796 Thomas Russell wrote that 'it was to be expected that the bulk of the catholics would feel the vengeance of every petty county aristocracy *irritated* by their late defeat, every man must easily see that this was the case. Witness the prosecutions of Fay, Bird, Delahoyd, Byrne, etc,' *Letter to the people of Ireland*, 11.
30. *State trials*, xxv, 752–67, *N.S.*, 24–28 April, 1794, *Parl. reg.*, xvii (1796–7), 31.
31. *Irish Magazine*, March, 1810, 108, July, 1810, 299.
32. *The Times*,29 July, 20 August, 1795, I.S.P.O. Reb. papers, 620/22/32. *State trials*, xxvii (1820), 1127–32.
33. Musgrave, 164, *F.D.J.*, 5 & 7 January, 1796.
34. The politics of Fitzwilliam's appointment, tenure and recall are recounted in McDowell, 'The Fitzwilliam episode', *I.H.S.*, xvi, no. 58 (1966), 115–30, and Ehrman, *The younger Pitt*, 414–40.
35. *Morning Post*, 3 & 29 January, 1795.
36. *F.D.J.*, 24 May 1794, *A view of the present state of Ireland . . . by an observer*, 9–10.
37 *F.D.J.*, 26 July, 12 & 14 August, 1794, Cooke to Broderick, 16 August, 1794, P.R.O. H.O. 100/46/184.
38. 'Extract of a letter from Fitzwilliam to Portland,' 10 January, 1795, P.R.O. H.O. 100/46/263. Lecky, iii, 265–6.
39. C.H.Teeling, *History of the Irish rebellion of 1798: a personal narrative and sequel of the Irish rebellion of 1798* (Glasgow, 1876, Shannon, 1972), 5–6, E.Hay, *History of the insurrection in Wexford*, vi., 33.
40 *F.D.J.*, 3 March, 1795, *N.S.*, 18–21 May, 1795.
41. 'Instructions to Lord Camden', 16 March, 1795, P.R.O. H.O. I00/46/301–8, Camden to Portland, 6 April, 1795, H.O. 100/57/68–71. See also Pelham to Portland 6 April, Camden to Portland, 7 April, 1795 H.O. 100/57/76–7, 95–9. The underlining is Camden's. On 4 April, 1795, the duke of York wrote to the chief secretary, Thomas Pelham, 'you have no fears concerning the catholic question if the country can be kept quiet which I thoroughly agree with you can only be done by a strong military force'. P.R.O.N.I. Pelham transcripts, T 755/2 ff 111–12.
42. Malcomson, *Foster*, 409, Dickson, *New foundations*, 181–2. Other factors which might be considered are that the king, influenced by Fitzgibbon, had become convinced that more concessions to the catholics would violate his coronation oath, by which he was bound to uphold the protestant establishment in church and state. This view was then communicated to Pitt. Moreover, Dundas, the principal architect

of catholic relief in 1791–3, was no longer minister responsible for Ireland.

43. Camden to Portland, 28 May, 1795, I.S.P.O. Reb. papers, 620/22/8. Another copy of this letter is deposited at P.R.O. H.O. 10/57/336–41.

44. *N.S.*,18–21 May, 1795, *The Times*, 11 September, 1795, I.S.P.O. Reb. papers, 620/22/8.

45. Camden to Portland, 5 May, 1795, P.R.O. H.O. 100/57/257–9, Portland to Camden, 11 May, 1795, H.O. 100/57/265–6.

46. *D.E.P.*,25 June, 1795, MacNevin, *Pieces of Irish history*, 112, Musgrave, 145, *N.S.*,22–26 October, 1795, Lecky, iii, 420.

47. Camden to Pelham, 12 October, 1795. (This appears in the transcript as '1794', but that is clearly a mistake.) P.R.O.N.I. Pelham Transcripts, T 755/2 f 98, Cooke to ——— , 12 September, 1795, T 755/2 f 198. A 'catholic leader' wrote to Tone on 3 September, 1795, that 'our unfortunate and misguided peasantry have become more outrageous, neither the gaol or the gibbet deter them, they even meet death with firmness'.: Tone, *Life*, i, 291–3.

48. See P. Tohall, 'The Diamond fight of 1795 and the resultant expulsions', *Seanchas Ardmhacda* (1958–9), 17–50, Rev. B.McEvoy, 'The Peep of Day Boys and Defenders in the County Armagh', *Seanchas Ardmhacda* (1987), 60–127.

49. Bishop of Dromore to Hudson, 22 December, 1794, *H.M.C., Charl. Ms, ii*, 256–7. Memo, anon, 1796, I.S.P.O. Reb. papers, 620/26/51, *N.S.*, 16–20 July, 1795.

50. Musgrave, 67, Tohall, 21.

51. *Administration convicted of high treason* (1796), 16.

52. *D.E.P.*, 6 October, 1795, *N.S.*, 21–25 December, 1795, Lecky, iii, 429, 432, Teeling, *Personal narrative*, 9.

53. Dalrymple to Pelham, 25 September, 1795, P.R.O.N.I. Pelham transcripts, T 755/2 f 208.

54. Teeling, 9–10, Richardson to Abercorn, 22 February, 1797. P.R.O.N.I. Abercorn papers, T 2541/IB3/6/5.

55. Tohall, 28–9, Lord Altamount to Dublin Castle, 27 November, 1796. I.S.P.O. Reb. papers, 620/26/82. One family of refugees from county Derry moved as far south as Tralee, county Kerry. See 620/26/98. For reports of refugees and Defenders in Scotland: John Dalrymple Hay to the earl of Galloway, 10 June, 1797, P.R.O. H.O. 100/72/451.

56. Camden to Portland, 6 August, 1796, I.S.P.O. Reb. papers, 620/18/11/1, R. M. Young, *Ulster in '98, episodes and anecdotes* (Belfast, 1893), 2.

57. Beames, *Peasants and power*, 32, Camden to Portland, 28 May, 1795, I.S.P.O. Reb. papers, 620/22/8. *The Times*, 11 September, 1795.

58. See Bartlett, 'Defenders and Defenderism in 1795'.

59. *F.D.J.*, 2 April, 1796, *D.E.P.*, 14 April, 1796.

60. *Ahiman Rezon*, xxiv.

61. Bartlett, 'Defenders', 389–90. for further examples see Beames, 'Peasant movements in Ireland, 1785–1795', *Journal of Peasant Studies*, vol. 2, no. 4 (1975) 504; and I.S.P.O. Reb. papers, 620/22/36a, 51, 620/23/30.

62. MacNevin, *Pieces of Irish history*, 119.

63   *The Times*, 5 September, 1795, I.S.P.O. Reb. papers, 620/22/36A, Edward Newenham to Dublin Castle, 1795, 620/23/30.

64. Bartlett, 'Indiscipline and disaffection in the armed forces in Ireland in the 1790s', in Corish (ed.), *Radicals, rebels and establishments*, 115–34, Pelham to Loftus, 27 May, 1797, P.R.O.N.I. Pelham transcripts, T 755/5 f 94.

65. Cited, Bartlett, 'Defenders', 392.

66. Beames, *Peasants and power*, 32.

67. Geo. Devinish to ——— , 6 August, 1796, I.S.P.O. Reb. papers, 620/22/27, Information of Thomas Boyle, July, 1796, 620/18/3, *Morning Post*, 17 September, 1795.

68. Bartlett, 'Defenders', 394, Information of Bryan Egan, 8 November, 1796, I.S.P.O. Reb. papers, 620/26/42.

69. Information of Owen Murphy, October, 1796, I.S.P.O. Reb. papers, 620/25/185.

70. Camden to Portland, 28 May, 1795, P.R.O. H.O. 100/57/336–41, G. Devenish to ——— 6 August, 1795, I.S.P.O. Reb. papers, 620/22/27.

71. Cullen, *Emergence*, 236, P. J. Dowling, *The hedge schools of Ireland* (Dublin, 1935), 108, *Morning Post*, 10 September, 1795.

72. For examples of the distrust of schoolmasters in the nineteenth century see Wakefield: 'Their pupils imbibe from them enmity to England [and] hatred to the government': *Account . . . statistical and political*, ii, 398. Croker is more colourful. The schoolmasters' principles, he wrote, 'verge very closely indeed on the broadest republicanism . . . he denies the legality of the criminal code; deprecates and disclaims the union; dwells with enthusiasm on the memories of Curran, Grattan, "Lord Edward" and young Emmet; insists on catholic emancipation; attacks the *Peelers*, horse and foot; protests against tithes, and threatens a separation of the United kingdoms! . . . before congenial spirits he talks downright treason . . . he is frequently the promoter of insurrectional tumults; he plans the nocturnal operations of the disaffected; writes their threatening proclamations . . . nor are his effusions confined merely to manuscript, but pass into print, and, in the shape of penny ballads, obtain considerable and important circulation'.: *Researches in the south of Ireland*, 238–9.

73. 'JW', 13 September, 1795, I.S.P.O. Reb. papers, 620/10/121/38.

74. J. Brady, 'Lawrence O'Connor – a Meath schoolmaster', *Irish Ecclesiastical Record*, 5th ser. xlix (1937), 281–7, *Morning Post*, 8 & 10 September, 1795.

75. Lecky, iii, 223, O'Connor's speech is reproduced in Beames, 'Peasant movements in Ireland, 1785–1795', 502–6.

76. *D.E.P.*, 7 November, 1795,*The Times*, 12 January, 1796, *F.D.J.*, 31 May, 16 June, 1796, McEvoy 'Defenders and Peep O'Day Boys' *Seanchas Ardmhacha* (1987), 93, Miller, (ed.), *Defenders and Peep O'Day Boys*, 120, information of Thomas Boyle, undated, I.S.P.O. Reb. papers, 620/18/3, Clotworthy Soden to Dublin Castle, 21, 23, 25 May, 1796, 620/23/117, 120, 124.

77. *State trials*, xxvii, 1129.

78. MacNevin, *Pieces of Irish history*, 119.

79. ibid, 117–18. The term 'union' was used as shorthand for United Irishmen.

80. Elliott, *Partners*, 44, Madden, *Lives* 3rd ser. vol. ii, 2, *The life of the Rev. James Coigly . . . as written by himself* (London, 1798), 7. Coigly sometimes appears as Quigley, Fivy or O'Coigly, I have chosen Coigly because, as his autobiographical fragment shows, this was the form he himself used.

81. Madden, *Lives*, 3rd ser. vol. ii, 180, Curtin, 'Transformation of the society of United Irishmen . . . ', 469, 'J[ames] M[organ]' 'Sketch of the life of Thomas Russell', in *Ulster Magazine* (1830), (copy in N.L.I.) C. J. Woods rejects Curtin's account of Russell's political activities in these years as 'ill founded and, all considered, implausible'. Yet surely it is equally implausible to view these 'rambles' on which, as Woods himself points out, Russell 'got to know members of the lower classes in the countryside he traversed – predominantly catholic in south Ulster and north Leinster and inclined from the early 1790s to Defenderism', as politically innocent botanical expeditions. In the end, however, it must be conceded that Curtin (with whom I agree on this point) is thrown back on speculation. Woods, 'The place of Thomas Russell in the United Irish movement' in Dickson and Gough, eds, *Ireland and the French revolution*, 87, 92, 98n.

82. *N.S.*, 20–24 February, 1794.

83. MacNevin, *Pieces of Irish history*, 74–6.

84. Hobart to Nepean, 20 December, 1792, P.R.O. HO 100/38/180–1.

85. *N.S.*, 11–14 November, 1793.

86. MacNevin, *Pieces of Irish history*,77, 101–3. For an account of this process see Curtin, 'The transformation of the society of United Irishmen into a mass-based organization, 1794–6'.

87. Charles Teeling's journeybook, I.S.P.O. Reb. papers, 620/54/138, *Northern Star* journey/account book, 1796, 620/15/8/11, 'Draft memorial of Bartholomew Teeling by his nephew', T.C.D. Madden Ms 873.

88. Tone, *Life*,i, 128, 283–4.

89. C. H. Teeling, *Observations on the history and consequences of the battle of the Diamond* (Belfast, 1838), 12, Camden to Portland, 29 July, 1795, P.R.O. H.O. 100/58/186, MacNevin, *Pieces of Irish history*, 120, Tone, *Life*, i, 190, 'Memorial of Bartholomew Teeling,' T.C.D. Madden Ms 873.

90. *Northern Star* journey/account book, 1793, I.S.P.O. Reb. papers, 620/15/8/6.

91. *D.E.P.*, 7 April, 1795, Cooke to Pelham, 4 December, 1795, P.R.O.N.I. Pelham transcripts, T 755/2 f 253–5, Braughall papers, I.S.P.O. Reb. papers, 620/34/50.

92. Cullen, 'Catholics under the penal laws', 33–4. For the comparative backwardness of Ulster catholicism, see K.Whelan, 'The regional impact of Irish catholicism, 1700–1850', in W. J. Smyth and Whelan, eds, *Common ground, essays on the historical geography of Ireland* (Cork, 1988), 253–77.

93. *Northern Star* journey account book, 1793, I.S.P.0. 620/15/8/6, 'JW', 1795, 620/10/121/26, Further information of Byran Egan, 29 November, 1796, 620/26/109. Egan refers to 'Barney Kiles' from Lurgan and describes him as 'very rich' and a 'leading man among the Defenders'. Samuel Simms, *Rev. James O'Coigly, United Irishman* (Belfast, 1937). Simms calls him 'Barney Coyle'!

94. T.C.D. Hope Ms. 7256/ f 23, E. FitzHenry, *Henry Joy McCracken* (Dublin, 1936), 73–4, Teeling, *Personal narrative*, 114–5.

95. Coigly, *Life*, 11, Information of Boyle, undated, I.S.P.O. Reb. papers, 620/18/3, McEvoy, 'Father James Quigley', *Seanchas Ardmhacha*, v (1970), 248. Coigly's mother's maiden name was Donnelly and that side of his family were from Tyrone. Simms, 3, *Life*, 2, Cullen, 'The political structures of the Defenders' in Dickson and Gough, eds, *Ireland and the French Revolution*, 127.

96. Henry Clements to Dublin Castle, 27 January, 1797, I.S.P.O. Reb. papers, 620/28/136.

97. Cooke to Pelham, 4 December, 1795, P.R.O.N.I. Pelham transcripts, T 755/2 f 253–5, Information of Boyle, undated, I.S.P.O. Reb. papers, 620/18/3.

CHAPTER 6: FROM PRE-INDUSTRIAL CROWD TO REVOLUTIONARY UNDERGROUND: DUBLIN'S STREET POLITICS, 1759–97

1. George Rudé, *London and Paris in the eighteenth century, studies in popular protest* (London, 1974), *The crowd in history, a study in popular disturbances in France and England, 1730–1848* (New York, 1964).

2. *Parl. reg.*, (1786), vi, 350. (Alexander Knox) *Essays on the political circumstances of Ireland, by a gentleman of the north of Ireland* (Dublin, 1798), 3–4.

3. M. R. O'Connell, 'Class conflict in a pre-industrial society: Dublin in 1780', *Irish Ecclesiastical Record*, ciii (1965), 266.

4. O'Connell, *Irish politics and social conflict in the age of the American revolution* (Philadelphia, 1965), 184, 187.

5. D. Dickson, 'The place of Dublin in the eighteenth-century Irish economy', in D. Dickson and T. M. Devine, eds, *Ireland and Scotland, 1600–1850* (Edinburgh, 1983), 177–92, Cullen, *An economic history of Ireland since 1660* (London, 1976), 85.

6. Rev. J. Whitelaw, *An essay on the population of Dublin . . . in 1798* (Dublin, 1805), 15.

7. *F.D.J.*, 5 January, 24 March, 1792.

8. Whitelaw, 43.

9. J. S. Price, 'Dublin, 1750–1850: a study in spatial distribution and organization of economic activity', unpublished Msc dissertation, T.C.D. (1981), 36, 'Report of the grand committee of trade', *J.H.C.*, x (part 1), app. cxi–cxviii, p. cxv.

10. For definitions of 'artisan' and 'journeyman' as they would have been understood in the eighteenth century, see John Rule, *The experience of labour in eighteenth-century industry* (London, 1981), 21–2, 32–3.

11. C. R. Dobson, *Masters and journeymen, a prehistory of industrial relations, 1917–1800* (London, 1780), 154–70. *J.H.C.*, x (1), cxii.

12. Rudé, *London and Paris*, Thompson, 'The "moral economy" of the English crowd in the eighteenth century', *Past and Present*, no. 50 (1971), 76–136.

13. E. J. Hobsbawm, *Primitive rebels* (Manchester, 1959), 111–22.

14. For a cogent account of this affair see Sean Murphy, 'Charles Lucas and the Dublin election of 1748–1749', *Parliamentary History*, 2 (1983), 93–111, also, Dickson, *New foundations*, 48–9.

15. J. D. LaTouche, *A short but true history of the rise, progress and happy suppression of several late insurrections, commonly called rebellions in Ireland* (Dublin, 1760), 16.

16. M. Bodkin, 'Notes on the Irish parliament in 1773', *Proceedings of the Royal Irish Academy*, xlviii, c, (1942–3), 190–1.

17. Dickson, *New foundations*, 90–1.

18. Rigby to Sir Robert Wilmot, P.R.O.N.I. Wilmot papers, T 3019/3971.

19. *A dialogue between a protestant and a papist; concerning the late strange reports of an union, and the seditious consequences of them* (Dublin, c.1759), 7. I am grateful to Dr Jacqueline Hill for drawing my attention to this pamphlet. *Heads of a Bill, for better regulating the elections of the Lord Mayor, Aldermen, Sheriffs, Commons and other Officers of the City of Dublin, and for preserving Peace, Order and good Government in the said city* (Dublin, 1759), 3.

20. James, *Ireland in the empire*, 259, Rigby to Wilmot, 10 December, 1759, P.R.O.N.I. Wilmot papers, T 3019/3962. Rigby used almost exactly the same language in other letters in 1758–9 (McDowell, *Age*,209–10).

21. Rudé, *London and Paris*, 47, 339, Palmer, *Police and protest in England and Ireland*, 13.

22. *The clothier's letter to the inhabitants of the Liberties* (Dublin, 1759), 5–8.

23. Grattan, *Life*, i, 73, McDowell, *Age*, 210. For a recent account of the riot and its political aftermath, see Sean Murphy, 'The Dublin anti-union riot of 3 December, 1759', in O'Brien (ed.), *Parliament, politics and people*, 49–68.

24. Cullen, *Economic history*, 59, Lord John Russell (ed.), *Correspondence of John, fourth duke of Bedford* (London, 1842–6), ii, 373–7, LaTouche, *Short but true history*, 39.

25. Froude, i, 698, *A letter to the inhabitants of Dublin and the Liberty, by T. B. Journeyman Weaver* (Dublin, 1759), *F.D.J.*, 20–24 November, 1759, *B.N.L.*, 27 November, 1759, Kelly, 'The origins of the act of union', 247.

26. *F.D.J.*, 4–8, December, 1759, Grattan, *Life*, i, 75, *Clothier's letter*, 3, Examination of Robert Taylor, 29 January, 1760, enclosure, Bedford to Pitt, 29 January, 1760, P.R.O.N.I. State Papers (Ireland), transcripts, T 1060/6/3437, *Dialogue between a protestant and a papist*, 1–2.

27. See Bedford to Primate Stone, 22 May, and Bedford to Pitt, 1 November, 1759, *Bedford corr*, ii, 373–7, 386–91, Wall, 'Government policy towards catholics during the Viceroyalty of the Duke of Bedford', *Collected essays*, 104.

28. James, *Ireland in the empire*, 260.

29. *Clothier's Letter*, 9, *Dialogue between a protestant and a papist*, 7, *F.D.J.*, 4–8 December, 1759. It is worth noting perhaps, that following the act of union in 1801 these predictions were partly borne out. Many of the gentry and nobility did in fact leave Dublin. All of the city's great townhouses were built (or begun), during the Irish parliament's heyday. None were built after the union, and over the next fifty years the existing houses ceased to be private dwellings. For example, the biggest of these houses, the duke of Leinster's, was purchased by the Royal Dublin Society.

30. *Clothier's letter*, 14–15. Rigby to Wilmot, 10 December, 1759, P.R.O.N.I. Wilmot papers, T 3019/3962.

31. LaTouche, 31.

32. The personalised pattern of the 1759 riot was repeated. The attorney general, John Scott, was singled out in 1779, John Foster in 1784, and on a number of occasions during the 1790s, John Fitzgibbon, the *bete noire* of Irish radicals, received the special attention of the disorderly classes. The thriving political lampoon business provides further illustration of the personalised quality of urban politics. In the 1790s, for example, printed ballads entitled 'The dog in office', which satirised the editor of *Faulkners Dublin Journal* and that all-purpose government hack, John Giffard, were hawked around the streets of the capital.

33. Bedford to Pitt, 19 January, 1759, *Bedford corr*, ii, 401–4, Rigby to Wilmot, 23 December, 1759, P.R.O.N.I. Wilmot papers, T 3019/3969. *J.H.C.*, vi, 157–8.

34. Grattan, *Life*, i, 77–8.

35. James, *Ireland in the empire*, 261.

36. Information of Paul Flemming, 24 January, 1760. P.R.O.N.I. T 1060/6/3437. John Fisher to Lord Rawdon, 4 December, 1759, *H.M.C., Rep. Hastings Ms*, (1934), iii, 139.

37. Information of Robert Taylor, Matthew Cullinan and Paul Flemming, P.R.O.N.I. T 1060/6/3437.

38. E. J. Hobsbawm and J. W. Scott, 'Political shoemakers', *Past and Present*, no. 89 (1980), 86–114, Burke, *Popular Culture*, 38–9.

39. *F.D.J.*, 4–8 December, 1759. The most explicit accusation of catholic and clerical involvement is contained in *A dialogue between a protestant and a papist*.

40. Pitt to Bedford, 5 January, Bedford to Pitt, 19 January, 1760, *Bedford corr, ii*, 399–404, Grattan, *Life*, i, 75–6, Murphy, 'Anti-Union riot', 57–63.

41. Dickson, 'The place of Dublin . . . ', 188, James, *Ireland in the empire*, 229.

42. Corish, *The Catholic community in Ireland*, 129, Cooke to Auckland, 14 May, 1784, P.R.O.N.I. Sneyd papers, T 3229/2/3.

43. LaTouche, *Short but true history*, 17, 31, Kelly, 247.

44. *A dialogue between a protestant and a papist'*, 6.

45. O'Connell, *Irish politics . . . in the age of the American revolution*, 163. Short money bills were a traditional patriot procedural device calculated to put pressure on the executive by reducing the time limit on parliamentary supplies.

46. O'Connell, *Irish politics . . . '*, 61.

47. The parallels with the tactics so recently pursued by the rebellious American colonists can scarcely have been missed by Lord North and his ministers.

48. O'Connell, 'Class conflict . . . ', 101–2.

49. O'Connell, *Irish politics*, 138–9, Buckinghamshire to Lord George Germain, 2 June, 1779, *H.M.C., Mrs Stopford-Sackville Ms*, i (1904), 256.

50. *Freemans Journal*, 30 October–2 November, 1779.

51. *Freemans Journal*, 4–6 November, 1779, Froude, ii, 261.

52. *Freemans Journal*, 20–23 November, 1779, Beresford to Robinson, 18 November, 1779, in W. Beresford (ed.), *Correspondence of the rt. hon. John Beresford* (London, 1854), i, 78. *D.E.P.*, 18 November, 1779.

53. For accounts of the riot see *D.E.P.*, 16 November, *Freemans Journal*, 13–16 November, 1779.

54. Waite to Germain, 24 November, 1779, *H.M.C., Stopford-Sackville Ms*, i, 261, Beresford to Robinson, 2 December, 1779, *Beresford corr*, i, 101.

55. Andrew Boyd, *The rise of the Irish trade unions, 1729–1970* (Tralee, 1972), 7–18.

56. Cited, Boyd, 31.

57. Report of the grand committee on trade, *J.H.C.*, x (part 1), (1780), cxiii.

58. O'Connell, *Irish politics*, 264.
59. Yet, as Rule notes '"continuous association" need not imply permanent organization. Members of a trade regularly brought together in work-place or community, could acknowledge regular leaders, develop customs of work regulation and systematic trade practices and produced disciplined observance of the latter without necessarily embedding these procedures in any formal record. Such a collective presence could readily submerge but not necessarily disappear in times of trouble': *Experience of labour*, 150.
60. This episode is discussed by O'Connell, 'Class conflict . . . .'.
61. *Drennan letters*, 62.
62. Palmer, *Police and protest*, 129, *Drennan letters*, 51.
63. See R. J. Coughlan's short biography, *Napper Tandy* (1976).
64. Rutland to Pitt, 15 August, 1784, *Correspondence between the rt.Hon. William Pitt and Charles, duke of Rutland, 1781–1787* (Edinburgh, 1890), 37, Reynolds to Rutland, 24 September, 1784, *H.M.C., Rutland Ms, iii, 14th report, app. i*, (1894), 138–9.
65. Lecky, ii, 382, Rutland to Sidney, 27 February, 1784, P.R.O. H.O. 100/12/125–9. *Parl. reg.* (1783–4), ii, 359, Froude, ii, 444.
66. *Freemans Journal*, 19–21 February, 1784, Lecky, ii, 383, Rutland to Sydney, 27 February, 1784, P.R.O. H.O. 100/12/125–9.
67. *Freemans Journal*, 13–15, 15–17, January, 1784.
68. *Freemans Journal*, 6–8 January, 1784, Rutland to Sydney, 26 February, 1784, P.R.O. H.O. 100/12/118–9, *Parl. reg.* ii, 419, Froude, ii, 448.
69. *Parl. reg.* iii, 152.
70. Brian Inglis, *Freedom of the press in Ireland, 1784–1841* (London, 1954), 23. Orde to Nepean, 7 April, 1784, P.R.O. H.O. 100/12/268–9.
71. Beresford to Robison, 11 April, 1784, *Beresford Corr*, i, 255.
72. Orde to Nepean, 7 April, Rutland to Sydney, 12 April, 1784, P.R.O. H.O. 100/12/268–9, 300–8, *Freemans Journal*, 15–17 April, 1784.
73. *Freemans Journal*, 26–29 June, 15–17 July, 12–14 August, 1784, Froude, ii, 445, Fitzgibbon to Eden, 29 August, 1784, P.R.O.N.I. Sneyd papers, T 3229/1/2.
74. *Freemans Journal*, 22–25 May, 20–22 June, 1784, P.D.H. Smyth, 'The Volunteers and parliament, 1779–84', in Bartlett and Hayton, eds, *Penal age,* 134, Cooke to —— 14 May 1784, P.R.O.N.I. Sneyd papers, T 3223/2/3.
75. *Freemans Journal*, 8–10 June, 1784, Rutland to Sydney, 20 September, 1784, P.R.O. H.O. 100/11/102–5.
76. P.R.O. H.O. 100/14/123–4.
77. Orde to Rutland, *H.M.C., Rutland Ms*, iii, 113–14.
78. Rutland to Sydney, 12 & 24 April, 1784, P.R.O. H.O. 100/12/300–8, 372–3, Dickson, *New foundations*, 166–7.
79. Palmer, 8–11.

80. Palmer, xviii, 113, K. Boyle, 'Police in Ireland before the union, ii', *Irish Jurist*, 8 (1973), 95.
81. Palmer, 128–30, *Parl. reg.* (1786), vi, 340, Boyle, 'Police in Ireland before the union, iii' (1973), 329–33.
82. I.S.P.O. Reb. papers, 620/52/185, Information of Thomas Reynolds, 620/52/159, J. T. Gilbert, *Documents relating to Ireland, 1795–1804* (Dublin, 1893, Shannon, 970), 91.
83. It took an English historian, Roger Wells, to point out that 'the failure of Dublin to rise is one key cause of the insurrection's course and collapse'. *Insurrection: the British experience, 1795–1803*, 134.
84. See for example, *The Dublin Society of United Irishmen* (Dublin, 1794), R. Jacob, *The rise of the United Irishmen* (London, 1937), McDowell, 'The personnel of the Dublin Society of United Irishmen, 1791–4', *I.H.S.*, ii (1940–1), 12–53, 'The proceedings of the Dublin Society of United Irishmen', *Analecta Hibernia*, no. 17 (1949), 1–143, *Age*, ch. 10 & 12, and Elliott, *Partners*, part 1.
85. Cary, *An appeal to the people of Ireland* (1794), preface, 1st edn, p. x, McDowell 'Personnel . . . ', 15.
86. *J.H.C.*, x (part 1), cxv., Reynolds, *Life*, i, 201. (Bond's warehouse, according to Reynolds, 'went back for at least two hundred yards'). Petition of Henry Jackson, 13 April, 1799, I.S.P.O. S.P.P., carton 21. *Hib. Jrnl*, 9 January, 1792. See also, 'John Chambers, printer and United Irishman', *The Irish Book*, i (1964), 1–22.
87 *Drennan letters*, 63, *Dub. Soc.*, 87, *F.D.J.*, 2 April, 1793.
88. McDowell, 'Personnel . . . ', 18.
89. *Dub. Soc.*, 8, 55, 103.
90. Examples of this left-wing *genre* include S. Cronin and R. Roche, *Freedom the Wolfe Tone way* (Tralee, 1973) and P. Yeates, *Let the nation stand* (Repsol pamphlet no. 15, Dublin, 1974).
91. Elliott, *Partners*, 27–8, 369, 'Origins of early Irish republicanism', 422, Moody, 'The political ideas of the United Irishmen', *passim*.
92. McDowell, 'Proceedings . . . ', 62.
93. McDowell, 'Personnel . . . ', 15.
94. McDowell, 'Proceedings . . . ', 74, 67, Richard McCormick appears here as 'Henry' but this is almost certainly a mistake. (By the informer, Thomas Collins, not McDowell!) Information of Francis Higgins, 2 March, 1798, I.S.P.O. Reb. papers, 620/18/14.
95. *D.E.P.*, 8 August, 22 October, 1793, *F.D.J.*, 22 October, 1793, *Hib. Jrnl*, 14 August, 1793.
96. Cary, xi, 3, 7, Inglis, *Freedom of the press*, 64–5, 84, 87.
97. Price, 56, 61, 63, *J.H.C.*, xv, part 1 (1792–4), 209, *Hib. Jrnl*, 13 May, 1793, *F.D.J.*, 5 March, 1796.
98. *Hib. Jrnl*, 3 May, 24 June, 1793, *D.E.P.*, 4 April, 1793, *J.H.C.*, xv (part 1), 209, 291.
99. *Drennan letters*, 162, *Morning Post*, 9 May, 6 June, 1793, *D.E.P.*, 9 & 28 May, 4 June, 1793.

100. McDowell, 'Personnel . . . ', Pill Lane no longer exists. In the eighteenth century it ran from Church Street, behind the present site of the Four Courts.
101. *To the Manufacturers of Dublin*, Tone, *Life*, i, 369–72, enclosure, Cooke to Nepean, 29 May 1793, P.R.O. H.O. 100/44/15–17.
102. *The Times*, 23 April, 1793, *Morning Post*, 11 May, 1793.
103. *J.H.C.,* xi, part 1 (1792), 90, *J.H.L.*, (1792), 58, 63, *Hib. Jrnl*, 21 March, 1792.
104. *Morning Post*, 24 March, 1792.
105. *N.E.S.*, 20 & 22 March, 14 April, 1792.
106. *J.H.C.*, x (1), cxii, *N.S.*, 2–6 June, 1792, Boyd, *Irish trade unions*, 25–6, Petition of Richard Dry, I.S.P.O. S.P.P. Carton 19.
107. *N.E.S.*, 10 May, 1792, *Hib. Jrnl.*, 15 June, 1792, *F.D.J.*, 13 September, 1792.
108. *D.E.P.*, 20 September, 1794.
109. *Hib. Jrnl*, 25 July, 1794, *The Times*, 29 December, 1794, Gilbert, (ed.), *Documents relating to Ireland, 94.*
110. *The Times*, 25 August, 1795.
111. *State trials, xxvi* (1819), 336, 308, 310, 346, *F.D.J.*, 12 & 15 April, 1794.
112 *F.D.J.*, 6 December, 1792, 1 July, 1794, Musgrave, 113.
113 *State trials*, xxvi, 331, 303, *F.D.J.*, 8 March, 1796.
114 *State trials*, xxvi, 336, 314, 395, 303–4, information of Thomas Kennedy, 1796, I.S.P.O. Reb. papers, 620/23/59, Musgrave, 113–4.
115 *State trials*, xxvi, 251, 366.
116 *Drennan letters*, 223.
117 *Drennan letters*, 214–15, 'Digest of Information on the United Irishmen,' 29 July, 1795, P.R.O. H.O. 100/58/187, MacNevin, *Pieces of Irish history*, 77.
118 *State trials*, xxvi, 238, 413, information of Thomas Kennedy, 1796, I.S.P.O. Reb. papers, 620/23/59.
119. I.S.P.O. Reb. papers, 620/52/185. Bartlett, 'Defenders and Defenderism', 375.
120 *State trials*, xxvi, 366, Tone, *Life*, i, 209–10.
121 *Morning Post*, 14 November, 1793, 13 February, 1796, *S.N.L.*, 29 March, 1793, McDowell, 'Proceedings . . . ', 67.
122. Musgrave, 119, *State trials*, xxvi, 460.
123 *State trials*, xxvi, 394, *F.D.J.*, 1 September, 1795.
124. John Lees to Townsend, 1 April, 1795, N.L.I. Ms, 394, 18, *The Times*, 9 April, 1795.
125. Knox, *Essays on the political circumstances of Ireland*, 6. Grattan's speech is reproduced in C.H.Teeling, *Personal narrative*, 6–8. The upper case is Grattan's.
126. Information of Francis Higgins, 2 March, 1798, I.S.P.O. 620/18/14, *F.D.J.*, 2 April, 1795, Camden to Portland, Pelham to John King, 1 April, 1795, P.R.O. H.O. 100/57/41–5.

127. Knox, *Essays*, 2.
128. Information of Higgins, 27 December, 1797, I.S.P.O. Reb. papers, 620/18/14.
129. *State trials*, xxvi, 295, 359, 447.
130. Information of Thomas Kennedy, I.S.P.O. Reb. papers, 620/23/59, Camden to Portland, 7 August, 1795, P.R.O. H.O. 100/58/233–6, *Morning Post*, 6 August, *F.D.J.*, 6 & 11 August, *D.E.P.*, 11 August, 1795.
131. Camden to Pelham, 24 August, Cooke to (Pelham?) 31 August, 1795, P.R.O.N.I. Pelham transcripts, T 755/2, ff 162, 177, 'Second digest of intelligence . . . respecting Defenderism', 25 September, 1795, P.R.O. H.O. 100/58/347, *The Times*, 31 December, 1795. In the eighteenth century a tour of duty in the plague-infested tropics was often perceived as tantamount to a death sentence.
132. For accounts of the riot see *F.D.J. & D.E.P.*, 25 August, 1795.
133. *F.D.J.*, 1 September, 1795, *State trials*, xxvi, 259, examination of William Lawlor, 27 August, 1795 I.S.P.O. Reb. papers, 620/23/35, information of Richard Turner, 18 July, 1798, 620/39/38.
134. Letter to Tone, 3 September, 1795, *Life*, i, 291–3, *D.E.P.*,8 September, *S.N.L.*, 24 September, 1795.
135. Camden to Pelham, 3 October, Cooke to Pelham, 23 October, 1795, P.R.O.N.I. Pelham transcripts, T 755/2.
136. Information of Higgins, 1 & 19 August, 1796, I.S.P.O. Reb. papers, 620/18/14. The evidence relating to Dublin's revolutionary underground in the later nineties comes mainly from the reports of two men: Leonard McNally – 'JW' – and Francis Higgins. Both were alarmists, although the insider's knowledge to which McNally had access as a United Irishman makes him the more reliable source. Higgins' sometimes overblown and usually anti-catholic reports are more erratic. If we are always to take him at his word, virtually every catholic priest and doctor in Dublin was implicated in conspiratorial politics, and the city organisation grew to 25,000 strong (25 May, 8 July & 15 October, 1797, 620/18/14). However, such quickly recognisable distortions aside, Higgins remains a credible witness. Editor of the *Freemans Journal*, he had a 'knowledge of Dublin life', numerous contacts 'in many quarters' and a talent for 'hunting out obscure information': Lecky, iii, 468. This information was often corroborated by other sources and, in at least one spectacular instance, by events. Higgins accurately predicted the riot of 31 March, 1795 (29 December, 1797, 2 March, 1798, 620/18/14).
137. Higgins, undated (probably January, 1797), I.S.P.O. Reb. papers, 620/18/14, *Downes list of Masonic lodges in Ireland in 1804*, Geogheghan, *The first Volunteer lodge*, 23.
138. Madden, *Lives of the United Irishmen*, 3rd ser, vol. i, 238–49, Information of Richard Turner, 9 July, 1798, I.S.P.O. Reb. papers, 620/39/38.

139. Edward John Newell, *The apostasy of Newell* (London, 1798), 18–19.
140. Information of 'JW', 7 June, 11 July, 1796, I.S.P.O. Reb. papers, 620/36/227, 620/10/121/31.
141. Camden to Portland, 6 August, 1796, I.S.P.O. Reb. papers, 620/18/11, same to same, 8 August, 620/18/11/1, 'memorandum as to delegates' 3 August 620/24/77, E. Boyle to Cooke, 9 August, 620/24/93A, same to same, 22 October, 620/25/183, E. Nicholson to Cooke, 23 November, 1796, 620/26/73.
142. Enclosure, 25 July, 1796, P.R.O. H.O. 100/62/145–6, *Report of the committee of secrecy of the house of lords (1798)*, 49.
143. 'JW', 2 January, 1797, I.S.P.O. Reb. papers, 620/10/121/44, Higgins, 18 May, 620/18/14, Information of 'Left Hand', 620/30/60 & 211, 620/51/96. 'Narrative of Smith' (Bird), P.R.O.I. Frazer Ms. 1A 40 111a/18.
144. For example Higgins, 27 September, 1796, 14 & 31 March, 1797, I.S.P.O. Reb. papers, 620/18/14, *F.D.J.*, 13 October, 1796. See also the comments in the *Freemans Journal*, 2 June, 1798.
145. *Drennan letters*, 115, *N.S.*, 28–31 December, 1795, 'Left Hand', 27 May, 1797, I.S.P.O. Reb. papers, 620/30/211. Interestingly, Henry Jackson's bookkeeper, or clerk, John McCann of Church street, executed for treason in 1798, was a native of county Antrim and, apparently, a school fellow of the United Irish 'martyr', William Orr: Cox, *Irish Magazine*, September, 1808, 417.
146. Higgins, 11 & 13 October, 1796, 14 March, 1797, I.S.P.O. Reb. papers, 620/18/14. For United Irish opposition to the Yeomanry see, *F.D.J.*, 13 October, 1796, and Lecky, iv, 16. Wolfe Tone claimed that before he left Ireland in 1795, Keogh endorsed his plans to secure French military aid (*Life*, i, 126–7.) McDowell notes Keogh's opposition to the Yeomanry, but also his signature to a declaration, issued by leading catholics at the outbreak of the rebellion, calling upon their co-religionists to defend the constitution and social order (*Age*, 559, 611). Keogh's position in this instance was pragmatic and says more, perhaps, about his political astuteness (or unscrupulousness) than his convictions.
147. Higgins, 29 January, 1797, I.S.P.O. Reb. papers, 620/18/14, *Report of the committee of secrecy (commons, 1798)*, 134.
148. On 23 April, 1797, Higgins wrote that 'women are equally sworn with men', I.S.P.O. Reb. papers, 620/18/14.
149. Information of Bird, T.C.D. Sirr papers, Ms 869/9, ff 84–5.
150. E. Boyle to Cooke, 12 May, 1797, I.S.P.O. Reb. papers, 620/30/61, information of Spoule, 620/51/40. The Divisions corresponded to the 1786 police districts.
151. Camden to Pelham, 19 August, 1795, P.R.O.N.I. Pelham transcripts, T 755/2 f 157, Higgins, 30 September, 1796, I.S.P.O. Reb. papers, 620/18/14, Reynolds, *Life*, i, 187, 211.
152. E. Boyle to Cooke, 30 September, 1796, I.S.P.O. Reb. papers,

620/25/85, *Proceedings of the parliament of Ireland* (1793), 152, Whitelaw, 62–3.
153. 'List of meeting houses in and near Dublin,' I.S.P.O. Reb. papers, 620/31/183, 'Address to "The County Committee of Dublin City"', 1 February, 1798, 620/42/18. Reprinted in *State trials*, xxvii, 572–3.
154. Information of T. Boyle, April, 1797, I.S.P.O. Reb. papers, 620/18/3, *The Times*, 12 April, 1796.
155. Higgins, 9 April, 1797, I.S.P.O. Reb. papers, 620/18/14, *Morning Post*, 6 April, 1797.
156. *State trials*, xxvi, 1049, *F.D.J.*, 2 May, 1797.
157. Higgins, 30 April, 1797, I.S.P.O. Reb. papers, 620/18/14.
158. Gilbert, *Documents relating to Ireland*, 114, *State trials*, xxvi, 1063, Examination of William Walter, T.C.D. Sirr papers, Ms 869/5, ff 5–6, information of Sheehy, I.S.P.O. Reb. papers, 620/52/144.
159. Information of Boyle, undated, I.S.P.O. Reb. papers, 60/18/14. The Dubliners mistake was repeated elsewhere. A funeral in Wexford, 'attended by vast crowds, and put into marching order,' was organised by a young man 'who wished to imitate one he had seen in Dublin'. The consequences were similar. The magistrate, Hunter Gowan, was served notice 'that something extraordinary was going on in the county'. Miles Byrne, *Memoirs* (Paris, 1863, Shannon, 1972), i, 17.
160. The *Morning Post* referred to the depressed state of the building industry on 25 February, the *Dublin Evening Post* to heavy lay-offs on 7 & 30 March & 18 April. For the handbills, see Higgins, 31 March, I.S.P.O. Reb. papers, 620/18/14.
161 *D.E.P.*, 25 April, *The Times*, 29 May, 1797.
162. *Drennan letters*, 257, 'JW', 27 May, 1797, I.S.P.O. Reb. papers, 620/10/121/61.

CHAPTER 7:   THE POLITICS OF DISAFFECTION, 1795–9

1. Cooke to Pelham, 4 December, 1795, P.R.O.N.I. Pelham transcripts, T 755/5, Madden, *Lives of the United Irishmen*, 3rd ser. vol. i, 250–1, Information of Bird/Smith, 1796, I.S.P.O. Reb. papers, 620/27/1.
2. 'JW', I.S.P.O. Reb. papers, 620/10/121/137, Narrative of Bird/Smith, P.R.O.I. Frazer Ms, 1A 40 111a/18.
3. 'JW', 5 October, 1796, I.S.P.O. Reb. papers, 620/10/121/38.
4. Mugrave, 175, Camden to Portland, 6 October, 1797, P.R.O.N.I. Camden papers, T 2627/4/85.
5. Duggan, 'Carlow, 1791–1801', 83–4, G.Holdcroft to —— 6 October, 1797, I.S.P.O. S.O.C.P., 1016/39, Higgins, 27 June, 1797, Reb. papers, 620/18/14.
6. 'JW', 9 February, 1797, I.S.P.O. Reb. papers, 620/36/227, 620/29/1, *D.E.P.*, 5 October, 1797.
7. S. O'Loinsigh, 'The rebellion of 1798 in Meath', *Riocht na Midhe*,

vol. iv, no. 2 (1968), 38, G. Lambert to —— 2 June, 1797, I.S.P.O. S.O.C.P., 1016/36, 'JW', 1 February, 1798, Reb. papers, 620/36/226.

8. Byrne, *Memoirs*, 304, 325, Elliott, *Partners*, 304, O'Loinsigh, 'The rebellion in Meath', 37, G.Holdcroft to John Lees, 16 April, 1797, I.S.P.O. Reb. papers, 620/29/266, information of T. Boyle, undated, 620/18/3. Barren, 'A poitin affray near Ballybay in 1797', 186, 190–2.

9. *Report of the committee of secrecy . . . (commons, 1798)*, 153, I.S.P.O. Reb. papers, 620/53/9. Arthur O'Connor was an MP in the Longueville 'interest' (1790–95). After the Fitzwilliam episode he broke ranks by supporting catholic relief in a celebrated speech to parliament and resigning his seat. By 1797, along with his friend Lord Edward Fitzgerald, he had become a leading United Irishman: Frank McDermot, 'Arthur O'Connor', *I.H.S.*, xv, no. 52 (1966), 48–69.

10. Powell, 'Background to the rebellion in Wexford', 142–3, 'JW', I.S.P.O. Reb. papers, 620/10/121/44.

11. T. Knox to Cooke, 25 October, 1796, I.S.P.O. Reb. papers, 620/25/187, Rev. J. Cary to Cooke, 8 October, 1798, 620/40/140.

12. Lecky, iii, 479, Witherow, *Memorials of Presbyterianism*, 297, Young, *Ulster in '98'*, 59.

13. McCracken was a member of Belfast lodge 763, Kennedy of Belfast lodge, 763, Teeling of Lisburn lodge, 193: Members Register, Free-masons Hall. For McCabe (and Kennedy) see, Narrative of Bird/Smith, P.R.O.I. Frazer Ms, 1A 40 111a/19 & 40.

14. Pelham to Lake, 3 March, 1797, N.L.I. Lake correspondence, Ms 56, 31.

15. *Report of the committee of secrecy . . . (commons, 1797)*, 29, 40.

16. Madden, *Lives of the United Irishmen*, 3rd ser. vol. 1, 257, 312.

17. Narrative of Bird/Smith, P.R.O.I. Frazer Ms, 1A 40 111a/35, Major Meridith to Pelham, 21 February, 1798, I.S.P.O. Reb. papers, 620/35/148.

18. Madden, 314, R. Rochford to —— 6 March, 1796, I.S.P.O. Reb. papers, 620/24/43, Loftus to Pelham, 1 June, 1797, P.R.O.N.I. Pelham transcripts, T 755/5 f 120.

19. T. Judkin Fitzgerald to Castlereagh, 1 June, 1798, I.S.P.O. S.O.C.P., 1017/47, same to same, 24 June, Reb. papers, 620/38/247, information of Henry Rogers, 620/52/151, examination of Michael Donnoly, T.C.D. Sirr papers, Ms 869/5 f 13, *The Autobiography of William Farrell*, 35, Thomas Cloney, *Personal narrative* (1832), 6, *Auckland corr.*, iii, 413–17.

20. The figures were captured with Lord Edward Fitzgerald: Musgrave, 174.

21. Information of Nicholas Magin, P.R.O.N.I. Cleland Ms, D714/2/6.

22. Elliott, 'Origins of early Irish republicanism', 427.

23. I.S.P.O. Reb. papers, 620/29/262, information of Bird/Smith, T.C.D. Sirr papers, Ms 869/9. ff 84–5.

24. Sir Edward Newenham to Pelham, 31 May, 1797, I.S.P.O. Reb. papers, 620/30/257, Lord Ely to Camden, 29 May, 1797, 620/30/226, Maurice Tracy to Pelham, 26 May, 1797, 620/30/198.

25. Caesar Colclough to —— 22 April, 1797, I.S.P.O. Reb. papers, 620/29/299, see also 620/29/305, 620/30/3, Rev. Thomas Handcock to Pelham, 18 May, 620/30/103, T. Knox to Pelham, 5 June, 620/31/38 and 620/53/25.

26. 3 April, 1798, I.S.P.O. Reb. papers, 620/36/121.

27. Dr William Richardson to Abercorn, 14 & 22 February, 1797, P.R.O.N.I. Abercorn papers, T 2541/IB3/6/4–5.

28. Alexander Montgomery to Cooke, 17 & 20 February, 1798, I.S.P.O. Reb. papers, 620/35/144, 149.

29. Camden to Portland, 2 February, 1797, P.R.O.N.I. Pelham transcripts, T 755/4/1, f 106, Teeling, *Personal narrative*, 11, Musgrave, app. xvi, 78.

30. G. D. Zimmermann, *Irish political street ballads, 1708–1900* (Geneva, 1966), 37n. Copies of *Paddy's resource* are available in the Linen Hall library, Belfast. For reference to *The harp new strung*, see *Report of the secret committee . . . (lords, 1798)*.

31. The United Irishmen also, it bears repeating at this point, exhibited tragic misjudgement. By playing what would later be called the 'Orange card', they succeeded in swelling their own ranks only at the cost of fuelling sectarian hatreds.

32. Musgrave, 190.

33. McDowell, *Public opinion*, 209.

34. Richardson to Abercorn, 22 February, P.R.O.N.I. Abercorn papers, T 2541/IB3/6/5, Lake to Pelham, 16 April, Pelham transcripts, T 755/4/2, f 268. Inglis, *Freedom of the press*, 71.

35. George Gordon to Downshire, 26 October, 1796, P.R.O.N.I. Downshire papers, D207/D/257.

36. *N.S.*, 2–3 September, 21–25, 25–28 November, 1796. Musgrave states that the *Newsletter's* carriers were also intimidated (p. 171).

37. Camden to Portland, 30 May, 1797, P.R.O. H.O. 100/69/348. These remarks reveal as much about the Castle's cavalier attitude to the rule of law in the late 1790s, as they do about the influence of the *Northern Star*.

38. Justice Day to Pelham, 22 September, 1797, I.S.P.O. Reb. papers 620/32/136, Inglis, *Freedom of the press*, 88–89.

39. Inglis, *Freedom of th press*, 102–4, 'JW', 28 November, 1797, I.S.P.O. Reb. papers, 620/10/121/83.

40. 'Printed prospectus of *The Press*', P.R.O.I. Frazer Ms, 1A 40 111/19.

41. Knox, *Essays*, 51–2.

42. W. B. Kennedy, 'The Irish Jacobins', *Studia Hibernica*, xiv (1976), 119.

43. *N.S.*, 14–17 April, 1797, M. DeLatocnaye, *Rambles through Ireland; by a French emigrant, translated by an 'Irishman'* (London, 1799), ii,

106, Pollock to Downshire, 9 November, 1796, P.R.O.N.I. Downshire papers, D607/D/299, I.S.P.O. Reb. papers, 620/25/190, 620/42/18.

44. Jackson, *Ireland her own*, 132, Berrisford Ellis, *Irish working class*, 74, 79, Cronin *et al.*, *Freedom the Wolfe Tone way*, 55, 73, Yates, *Let the nation stand*, 55.

45. McDowell, *Public opinion*, 200–202, Elliott, *Tone*, 214, 220, 401, *Partners*, xvii, 27–8, 32, 369, 'The United Irishman as diplomat' in Corish, (ed.), *Radicals, rebels, establishments*, 70, 84, 'Origins of early Irish republicanism', 422, 426, 'The role of Ireland in French war strategy' in Dickson and Gough, eds, *Ireland and the French Revolution*, 202. Curtin, 'Transformation of . . . the United Irishmen', 465.

46. MacNevin, *Pieces of Irish history*, 177, 203, Elliott, 'Origins of early Irish republicanism', 422.

47. Moody, 'Political ideas of the United Irishmen', 23.

48. This kind of historians fallacy has been aptly described as 'negative bias': see Brendan Bradshaw, 'Nationalism and historical scholarship in modern Ireland', *I.H.S.*, xxvi, no. 104 (1989), 329–51, at 343.

49. 'Coigly's conception of liberty was wider than that of his fellow United Irishmen, and included the formation of a union of the underprivileged against their social superiors', Elliott, 'Irish republicanism in England, the first phase, 1797–9' in Bartlett and Hayton, eds, *Penal age*, 209. Note how Coigly is protrayed as a maverick.

50. McDowell, *Public opinion*, 202, Madden, *Lives of the United Irishmen*, 3rd ser, vol. ii, 155, 159.

51. Russell, *Letter to the people of Ireland*, 1–2, 14, 16, 18, 22. Russell was an anglican, McCracken a presbyterian.

52. Russell. *Letter to the people of Ireland*, 17.

53. G. Kates, 'From Liberalism to Radicalism: Tom Paine's Rights of Man', *Journal of the History of Ideas*, vol. 1, no. 4 (1989), 571.

54. Higgins, 15 August, I.S.P.O. Reb. papers, 620/18/14.

55. Thompson, *Making of the English working class*, 108.

56. Enclosure, R. Cornwall to —— 24 September, 1797, I.S.P.O. Reb. papers, 620/34/23. Administration convicted of high treason . . . (1798), 26.

57. Inglis, *Freedom of the press*, 88. See 'JW', 13 September, 1795, I.S.P.O. Reb. papers, 620/10/121/28, for the United Irish connections of this paper.

58. *Report of the committee of secrecy* (commons, 1797), 22, *Report of the committee of secrecy* (commons, 1798), 47.

59. *The union doctrine, or poor man's catechism* (c.1796), 3. A copy of this pamphlet is deposited in the Rebellion papers, I.S.P.O. 620/43/6.

60. *Catechism*, 3–4, 7.

61. *Catechism*, 7–8. The probability that this pamphlet was aimed at an essentially catholic audience is underlined by its subtitle, which may refer to an actual catholic catechism of the same name, which

was popular earlier in the century: Corish, *Catholic community*, 86–87, 109.

62. *Catechism*, 4–7.
63. T.C.D. Court martial papers, Ms 872/2.
64. Pakenham, *The year of liberty*, 286, Musgrave, *Memoirs of the different rebellions . . .* app. xxi. 9.
65. Miller, 'Presbyterianism and "modernization" in Ulster' in Philipin, (ed.), *Nationalism and popular protest*, 96–102.
66. Information of Bird/Smith, 1796, I.S.P.O. Reb. papers, 620/27/1. Gray, ' . . . Thomas Russell re-assessed', 8–9, J.Fruchtman jnr. 'The apocalyptic politics of Richard Price and Joseph Priestly: a study of late eighteenth-century millenialism', *Transactions of the American Philosophical Society*, vol. 73, pt. 4 (Philadelphia, 1983).
67. Thompson, *Making of the English working class*, 127–9. Extracts from Brothers' book were reprinted in the *Dublin Evening Post*, 9 April, 1795. See also, Patrick O'Farrell, 'Millenarianism, messianism and utopianism in Irish history', *Anglo-Irish Studies*, ii, (1976), 45–68.
68. Beresford to Auckland, 4 September, 1796, *Beresford corr.* ii, 128. Italics added.
69. I.S.P.O. Reb. papers, 620/27/2.
70. A.Cole Hamilton to ―― 2 March, 1796, I.S.P.O. Reb. papers, 620/29/8.
71. *N.S.*,17–20 August, 1795, *To the men of landed property in County Down*, I.S.P.O. Reb. papers, 620/33/139.
72. Tone described Clare as 'a man who expects no quarter and is therefore determined to give none': *Life*, ii, 468.
73. Lecky, iii, 540, McDowell, *Age*, 513.
74. Elliott, *Partners*,112, Dickson, *New foundations*, 187.
75. Clare to Auckland, 14 January, P.R.O.N.I. Sneyd papers, T 3229/1/12. Beresford remarked that 'no landing was made – providence prevented it; if there had, where was a stand to be made? It is clear that Cork was gone; who could answer afterwards for the loyalty of the country, then in possession of the French?' Cooke likewise speculated that 'had a complete landing being fully effected, I fear there would have been another tale': Beresford to Auckland, 28 January, 1797, *Auckland corr.*, iii, 375–7, Cooke to Auckland, 10 January, T 3229/2/19.
76. Byrne, *Memoir*, 8.
77. Clare to Auckland, 2 January, P.R.O.N.I. Sneyd papers, T 3229/1/11.
78. Cavan to Pelham, 27 June P.R.O.N.I. Pelham transcripts, T 755/5/206.
79. Knox to Abercorn, 12 March, 1797, P.R.O.N.I. Abercorn papers, T 2541/IB3/6/9.
80. Coote to Pelham, 17 April, Pelham to Coote, 29 April, 1797, P.R.O.N.I. Pelham transcipts, T 755/4/2/273–4, 321.
81. *The Press*, 23 November, 1797.
82. Pakenham, *The year of liberty*, 59–60. The enormous problems of

military organisation and discipline in these circumstances are discussed in P. C. Stoddart, 'Counter-Insurrgency and defence in Ireland, 1790–1808', unpublished D.Phil. (Oxford, 1973).

83. Knox to Lake, 11 March, 1797, P.R.O.N.I. Pelham transcripts, T 755/4/2/194, see also, Knox to Pelham, 28 May, T 755/5/101.
84. *The Press*, 2 November, 2 December, 1797, 2 January, 1798, *Autobiography of William Farrell*, 68.
85. *N.S.*, 4–9 July, 1796, *The Press*, 12 October, 1797, enclosure, 'An address to the Catholics', Downshire to Cooke, 6 October, 1796, I.S.P.O. Reb. papers, 620/25/150.
86. See note 102.
87. Lake to Pelham, 21 March, 1797, P.R.O.N.I. Pelham transcripts, T 755/4/2/196–7, Reynolds, *Life*, i, 216.
88. *Parl. reg.*, (1796–8), xvii, 131–40, Lecky, iv, 64.
89. Lecky, iv, 43–5, McDowell, *Age*, 597.
90. *D.E.P.*, 1 February, 1798, 'JW', 4 March, 26 July, 1798, I.S.P.O. Reb. papers, 620/10/121/93, 121
91. *Parl. reg.*, (1796–8), xvii, 133–6, Tone, *Life*, i, 108.
92. Cloney, *Narrative*, 192, T. Crofton Croker (ed.), *Memoirs of Joesph Holt* (London, 1838), i, 15–20.
93. MacNevin, *Pieces of Irish history*, 143, Cox, *Irish Magazine*, July, 1808, O'Connell quoted by Pakenham, *Year of liberty*, 398, Madden, *Lives of the United Irishmen*, 3rd ser. vol. i, xi, Dickson, *Wexford rising*, 36, 40, 182, 188.
94. MacNevin, *Pieces of Irish history*, 203n, *Irish Magazine*, December, 1809, 545. Castlereagh's remark was picked up by Karl Marx who also contended that the rebellion was fomented by the 'British ministry': K. Marx and F. Engels, *Ireland and the Irish question* (Moscow, 1978), 220–21.
95. Madden, *Lives of the United Irishmen*, 3rd ser, vol. i, 222.
96. See L. M. Cullen's path-breaking essay, 'The 1798 rebellion in Wexford: United Irishman organization, membership, leadership', in Kevin Whelan (ed.), *Wexford: history and society* (Dublin, 1987), 248–295.
97. *Irish Magazine*, July, 1808, 324, Roger Wells, *Insurrection, the British experience*, 134.
98. *D.E.P.*, 2 & 4 Feburary, 1797.
99. Castlereagh to Wickham, 3 November, 1798, *Castlereagh corr.*, i, 223–4.
100. Pakenham, *Year of liberty*, 45–7.
101. Lecky, vi, 84.
102. Pakenham, *Year of liberty*, 47–8, Inglis, *Freedom of the press*, 90, Higgin's 27 September, 1797, I.S.P.O. Reb. papers, 620/14/18, deposition of Rooney, T.C.D. Sirr papers Ms 869/5 f I, *The Press*, 14 December, 1797. Inglis argued that had Cox been a United Irishman then he would have been identified by a government informer. He was in fact identified by Thomas Boyle in November, 1797: I.S.P.O.

Reb. papers, 620/18/3. See also Cox's own account: *Irish Magazine*, October, 1810, 472.

103. 'JW' I.S.P.O. Reb. papers 620/10/121/51, 149.
104. William Sampson, *Memoirs* . . . (New York, 1807, London, 1832), 3–4, *F.D.J.*, 10 May, 1798.
105. Clare to Auckland, 21 May 1798, *Auckland corr.*, iii, 421–2.
106. Lake to Castlereagh, 15 June 1798, I.S.P.O. Reb. papers 620/38/153, Clare to Auckland, 5 June, 1798, *Auckland corr.*, iv, 2–3.
107. Musgrave, app. xxi. 12.
108. Musgrave, 214–15, Cox, *Irish Magazine*, July 1808, 231–4.
109. Musgrave, 213.
110. *Freemans Journal*, 26 May, 1798, Lake to Castlereagh, 15 June, 1798, I.S.P.O. Reb. papers 620/38/153.
111. Barrington, *The rise and fall of the Irish nation* (Dublin, 1833), 358.
112. Petition of Thomas Connor, Edward Neil and John Reilly, lamplighters, 7 July, 1798, I.S.P.O. S.S.P. carton 20, N.L.I. Ms 13, 837, *Freeman's Journal*, 29 & 31 May, 1798.
113. *Freemans Journal*, 29 May, 1798.
114. *Freemans Journal*, 26 May, *S.N.L.*, 4 June, 1798.
115. R. F. Foster, *Modern Ireland*, 280, Cullen, 'The 1798 rebellion in its eighteenth-century context' in Corish (ed.), *Radicals, rebels and establishments*, 91.
116. Dickson, *New foundations*, 193, Pakenham, *Year of liberty*, 17.
117. A powerful reinterpretation of the Wexford rebellion is now emerging from the detailed studies of L. M. Cullen and K. Whelan: Cullen, 'The 1798 rebellion in Wexford: United Irishman organization, membership, leadership', in Whelan (ed.), *Wexford: history and society*, 248–95, 'The 1798 rebellion in its eighteenth-century context', in Corish (ed.), *Radicals, rebels and establishments*, 91–113, *Emergence*, 210–33, Whelan, 'The religious factor in the 1798 rebellion in County Wexford', in P. O'Flanagan, P. Ferguson and K. Whelan, eds, *Rural Ireland, 1600–1900*, 62–85, and 'The role of the Catholic priest in the 1798 rebellion in County Wexford', *Wexford: history and society* 296–315, 'Politicisation in County Wexford and the origins of the 1798 rebellion' in Dickson and Gough, eds, *Ireland and the French Revolution*, 156–78. My discussion of the Wexford experience draws on this work.
118. Pakenham, *Year of liberty*, 155–6.
119. McDowell in Moody and Vaughan, eds, *New history of Ireland, iv*, 355.
120. *Hib. Jrnl.*, 7 September, 1792, Hay, *History of the insurrection in Wexford*, vi.
121. Whelan, 'Politicisation in County Wexford . . . ', 157–8, McDowell, 'Personnel . . . '.
122. Cullen, 'United Irishman organization, membership, leadership', 295.
123. Whelan, 'Religious factor in the 1798 rebellion', 75.
124. Pakenham, *Year of liberty*, 206, 285.

125. *Irish Magazine*, December, 1807, 24–5.
126. *Freemans Journal*, 4, 13 & 16 October, 1798.
127. Cornwallis to Portland, 14 February, Castlereagh to Portland, 3 June, 1799, *Castlereagh corr.*, 174–5, 325–7, Hudson to Charlemont, 22 March, 8 April, 1799, *Charl. Ms.* ii, 347–8, 366.
128. Elliott, *Wolfe Tone*, 393.

CONCLUSION

1. Elliott, 'The origins and transformation of early Irish republicanism', 405.
2. S. J. Connolly in Vaughan (ed.), *A new history of Ireland, v*, 19.
3. Elliott, *Partners*, 366, Beames, 'The Ribbon societies: lower-class nationalism in pre-famine Ireland', *Past and Present*, no. 97 (1982), 128–143, T. Garvin, 'Defenders, Ribbonmen and others: underground political networks in pre-famine Ireland', *Past and Present*, no. 96 (1982), 133–55, Beames's and Garvin's articles are reprinted in Philipin (ed.), *Nationalism and protest*.
4. *Life of Thomas Reynolds . . . i*, 169.
5. A. Cronin, *An Irish eye* (Kerry, 1985), 123–31.

Select Bibliography

BIBLIOGRAPHICAL GUIDES AND REFERENCE BOOKS

The best bibliography for both the 1790s and for the eighteenth century as a whole, is that compiled by David Dickson in T. W. Moody and W. E. Vaughan, eds, *A new history of Ireland, vi, eighteenth-century Ireland, 1690–1800* (Oxford, 1986). The essays by Sir Herbert Butterfield in T. W. Moody (ed.), *Irish historiography, 1936–1970* (Dublin, 1971), 55–71, and by J. I. McGuire in J. Lee (ed.), *Irish historiography, 1970–79* (Cork, 1981), 56–84, are also worth consulting.

Black, R. D. C. *A catalogue of pamphlets on economic subjects published between 1750 and 1900 and now housed in Irish libraries* (Belfast, 1969).

Hayes, R. J. (ed.), *Manuscript sources for the history of Irish civilization*, 11 vols (Boston, 1965), supplements, 3 vols (Boston, 1979).

Sayle, C. E. (ed.), *A catalogue of the Bradshaw collection of Irish books in the University of Cambridge* (Cambridge, 1916).

Webb, A. *A compendium of Irish biography* (Dublin, 1878).

Wilsons Dublin directory (1796).

PRIMARY SOURCES: MANUSCRIPTS

Belfast

Public Record Office, Nortern Ireland
D 272 McCance collection
D 607 Downshire papers
D 714 Cleland Ms.
D 1606/1.Gosford Ms.
T 755/2–5 Pelham transcripts (originals at British Museum, Add. Ms., 33101–33104, 1783–July, 1797)
T 2541 Abercorn papers
T 2627/4 Camden papers (photocopies from Kent Archives Office, ref. U840)
T 3019/3958–73 Wilmot papers (December, 1759, photocopies).
T 3048 McPeake papers
T 3229 Sneyd papers (typescript).

Dublin

Freemasons Hall
Grand Lodge, Freemasons of Ireland, members register, 1st series (microfilm).

Irish State Paper Office
Official papers
Rebellion papers, 620/1–67
State of the country papers, 1015/1–1017/66
State prisoners petitions, 1796–1799
Westmorland (Fane) correspondence.

National Library of Ireland
Ms 54, 54A Melville papers
Ms 56 Lake correspondence, 1796–1799
Ms 394 Townsend and Westmorland letters
Ms 886 Lord lieutenants correspondence, 1786–1798
Ms 13,837 (typescript) Letter, Dublin in 1798.

Public Record Office, Ireland
Frazer Ms.

Trinity College Dublin
Ms 868–9 Sirr papers
Ms 872 Court Martial papers, 1798
Ms 873 Madden papers
Ms 7253–6 Hope Ms.

London

Public Record Office
H.O. 100 Home Office papers.

PRIMARY SOURCES: PRINTED COLLECTIONS OF DOCUMENTS

Auckland correspondence, journal and correspondence of William, Lord Auckland (London, 1861–2), 4 vols.
Bartlett, Thomas. 'Select documents xxxviii: Defenders and Defenderism in 1795', *Irish Historical Studies*, xxiv, no. 95 (1985), 373–94.
Barren, Thomas, J. 'A poitin affray near Ballybay in 1797', *Clogher Record*, viii (1974), 182–93.

Beresford, Rt. Hon. William. (ed.), *The correspondence of the Rt. Hon. John Beresford* (London, 1854), 2 vols.

Chart, D.A. (ed.), *The Drennan letters . . . 1776–1819* (Belfast, 1931).

Edwards, R.D. (ed.), 'The minute book of the Catholic Committee, 1772–1792', *Archivium Hibernicum*, ix (1942), 1–172.

Gilbert, J.T. (ed.), *Documents relating to Ireland, 1795–1804* (Dublin, 1893, Shannon, 1970).

Howell, T.B. and T.J. eds., *A complete collection of State trials* (London, 1811–26), 34 vols.

Kelly, J. 'Select documents xliii: A secret return of the Volunteers of Ireland in 1784', *Irish Historical Studies*, xxvi, no. 103 (1989), 268–92.

Miller, D. W. *Peep O'Day Boys and Defenders, selected documents on the County Armagh disturbances, 1784–96* (Belfast P.R.O.N.I., 1990).

McDowell, R.B. 'Select documents ii, "United Irish plans of parliamentary reform in 1793"', *Irish Historical Studies*, iii, no. 9 (1942), 49–51.

——, 'The proceedings of the Dublin Society of United Irishmen', *Analecta Hibernia*, no. 17, (1949), 1–143.

O'Donovan, J. *The O'Connors of Connaught* (Dublin, 1891)

Russell, Lord John. (ed.), *Correspondence of John, fourth duke of Bedford* (London, 1842–1846).

Correspondence between the Rt. Hon. William Pitt and Charles, duke of Rutland, 1781–1787 (Edinburgh, 1890).

Robert Steward, 2nd marquess of Londonderry [Vicount Castlereagh], memoirs and correspondence (London, 1848–1849), vols 1–4.

PUBLICATIONS OF THE HISTORICAL MANUSCRIPTS COMMISSION

The manuscripts and correspondence of James, first earl of Charlemont, 13th report, app. part 8, vol. ii (London, 1894).

The manuscripts of J. B. Fortescue esq, preserved at Dropmore, 13th report, app. part 3 and 14th report, app. part 5 (London, 1892–4).

Rutland manuscripts, iii, 14th report, app. part 1 (London, 1894).

Mrs Stopford-Sackville manuscripts (London, 1904).

PARLIAMENTARY PROCEEDINGS AND REPORTS

The Parliamentary register: or history of the proceedings and debates of the house of commons of Ireland, vi (1786), xii–xvii (1792–98)

Proceedings of the parliament of Ireland, 1793, 3 vols.

Journals of the house of commons of the kingdom of Ireland, x, part 1, (1779–1782), xv–xvii (1792–1798) (Dublin, 1796–1800).

Report from the committee of secrecy of the house of commons (London,

1798). This pamphlet includes the reports from the lords secret committee (1793) and the reports from the commons and lords secret committees (1797). These reports are also reproduced in the *Journal of the house of commons* (1798).
Report of the committee of secrecy of the house of lords of Ireland (London, 1798).

NEWSPAPERS

Belfast Newsletter
Cork Gazette
Dublin Evening Post
Faulkners Dublin Journal
Hiberian Journal
Irish Magazine and monthly asylum for neglected biography, 1807–15.
Morning Post
National Evening Star
Northern Star
The Press
Saunders Evening Newsletter
The Times.

CONTEMPORARY ACCOUNTS, PAMPHLETS, MEMOIRS

Administration convicted of high treason against king and people . . . in a letter to the marquess of Landsdowne from an Irish farmer (1798).
Advise to the patriots of the Coomb, the Liberties, and the suburbs of Dublin, lately assembled in parliament, of whatever trade, sex or denomination, by a faithful Irishman (Dublin, 1759).
An advice to the rich by an independent country gentleman, pointing out the road to security and peace (Dublin, 1796).
Barrington, Sir Jonah. *Personal sketches* (London, 1827–1832).
——, *The rise and fall of the Irish nation* (Dublin, 1833).
Bell, Robert. *A description of the condition . . . character, education etc. of the peasantry of Ireland . . . between 1780 and 1790 . . .* (London, 1804).
Byrne, John. *An impartial account of the late disturbances in the county of Armagh . . . since the year 1784, down to the year 1791* (Dublin, 1792).
Byrne, Miles. *Memoirs . . .* (Paris, 1863, Shannon, 1972) 2 vols.
A candid and impartial account of the disturbances in the county of Meath in the years 1792, 1793, 1794, by a County Meath freeholder (Dublin, 1794).

Cary, William Paulet. *An appeal to the people of Ireland* (Dublin, 1794).

Clifford, Robert. *Application of Barruel's memoirs of Jacobinism to the secret societies of Ireland and Great Britain* (London, 1798).

Cloney, Thomas. *Personal narrative* (1832).

The clothier's letter to the inhabitants of the Liberties (Dublin, 1759).

The life of the Rev. James Coigly . . . as written by himself (London, 1798).

Cosgrave, J. *A genuine history of the lives and actions of the most notorious Irish highwaymen, Tories and Rapparees* (Dublin, 12th edition, c.1760).

Croker, T. Crofton, *Researches in the south of Ireland* (Dublin, 1824).

Dermot, Laurence. *Ahimam Rezon: or, a help to a Brother . . .* (Belfast, 1783).

DeLatocnaye. M. *Rambles through Ireland; by a French emigrant, translated by an 'Irishman'* (London, 1799) 2 vols.

A dialogue between a protestant and a papist; concerning some late strange reports about an union, and the seditious consequences of them (Dublin c.1759).

A narrative of the confinement and exile of William Steele Dickson . . . (Dublin, 1812).

Downes, Charles. *Downes list of Irish Masonic lodges in 1804* (Comber, 1908).

Drummond, W. H. (ed.), *Autobiography of A. Hamilton Rowan* (Dublin, 1840, Shannon, 1972).

An enquiry into the causes of popular discontents in Ireland, by an Irish country gentleman (London, 1805).

Gorden, Rev. James. *History of the rebellion in Ireland in the year 1798 etc. containing an account of the proceedings of the Irish revolutionists, from the year 1782 till the supression of the rebellion* (Dublin, 1801).

Grattan, jnr. Henry. *Memoirs of the life and times of the Rt. Hon. Henry Grattan* (London, 1839–46) 5 vols.

Hay, Edward. *History of the insurrection of the county of Wexford, A.D. 1798* (Dublin, 1803).

Holt, Joseph. *Memoirs . . .* (T. Crofton Croker, ed.) (London, 1838) 2 vols.

Knox, Alexander. *Essays on the political circumstances of Ireland, written during the administration of Earl Camden . . . by a gentleman of the north of Ireland* ((Dublin, 1798).

LaTouche, James Digges. *A short but true history of the rise, progress, and happy supression, of several late insurrections commonly called rebellions in Ireland* (Dublin, 1760).

Lawless, John. *The Belfast politics enlarged; being a compendium of the political history of Ireland for the last forty years* (Belfast, 1818).

A letter to the inhabitants of Dublin and the Liberty by T. B. Journeyman Weaver (Dublin, 1759).

Roger McHugh (ed.), *Carlow in '98. The autobiography of William Farrell of Carlow,* (Dublin, 1948).

MacNevin, William James. *Pieces of Irish history* (New York, 1807).

Musgrave, Sir Richard. *Memoirs of the different rebellions in Ireland . . .*

(Dublin, 1801).

Newell, Edward John. *The apostacy of Newell* (London, 1798).

Paddy's resource: being a select collection of original and modern patriotic songs for the use of the people of Ireland nos. 1 and 2 (Belfast, 1795, 1796).

Paine, Thomas. (Isaac Kramnick, ed,) *Common Sense* (Harmonsworth, 1982).

Paine, Thomas. (H. Collins, ed,) *The Rights of Man* (Harmondsworth, 1976).

Plowden, Francis. *A historical review of the state of Ireland, from the invasion of that country under Henry II to its union with Great Britain* (London, 1803) 2 vols.

——, *An historical disquisition concerning the rise, progress, nature and effects of the Orange societies in Ireland* (Dublin, 1810).

Reynolds, jnr. Thomas. *Life of Thomas Reynolds* (London, 1839) 2 vols.

Russell, Thomas. *A letter to the people of Ireland on the present situation of the country* (Belfast, 1796).

Memoirs of William Sampson (New York, 1807).

Society of United Irishmen of Dublin (1794).

Teeling, Charles Hamilton. *Observations on the history and consequences of the battle of the Diamond* (Belfast, 1838).

——, *History of the Irish rebellion of 1798: a personal narrative and sequel to the history of the Irish rebellion of 1798* (Glasgow, 1876, Shannon, 1972).

Tone, William T. W. (ed.), *Life of Wolfe Tone . . .* (Washington, 1826) 2 vols.

Tracts on Catholic affairs (Dublin, 1792).

The union doctrine, or poor mans catechism (c1796?). There is a copy of this pamphlet in the Rebellion papers, 620/43/6, it also reprinted as 'The Catechism of the United Irishmen' in Musgrave, who claims it was 'published and circulated' soon after the rebellion: *Memoirs of the different rebellions . . .* app. xxi. 9.

A view of the present state of Ireland, with an account of the origin and progress of the disturbances in that country; and a narrative of facts, addressed to the people of England, by an observer (London, 1797).

Wakefield, Edward. *An account of Ireland, statistical and political* (London, 1812) 2 vols.

Whitelaw, Rev. James. *An essay on the population of Dublin, 1798* (Dublin, 1805).

Young, Arthur. *A tour in Ireland, 1776–1779,* (4th edn London, 1892, Shannon, 1970) 2 vols.

SECONDARY SOURCES

Adams, J. R. R. 'Reading societies in Ulster', *Ulster Folklife,* xxvi, no. 26

(1980), 55–64.

——, *The printed word and the common man, popular culture in Ulster, 1700–1900* (Belfast, 1987).

Aspinall, Arthur. *Politics and the press, 1780–1850* (Brighton, 1973).

Bartlett, Thomas. 'An end to moral economy: the Irish militia disturbances of 1793', *Past and Present*, no. 99 (1983), 41–64.*

——, 'A new history of Ireland', *Past and Present*, no. 116 (1987), 206–17.

Bartlett, Thomas and Hayton, David. eds., *Penal age and golden era* (Belfast, 1979).

Beames, Michael R. 'Peasant movements, Ireland, 1785–1795', *Journal of Peasant Studies*, vol. 2, no. 4 (1975), 502–6.

——, 'The Ribbon societies: lower-class nationalism in pre-famine Ireland', *Past and Present*, no. 97 (1982), 128–143.*

——, *Peasants and power, the Whiteboy movements and their control in pre-famine Ireland* (Brighton, 1983).

Boyd, A. *The rise of the Irish trade unions, 1729–1970* (Tralee, 1972).

Boyle, K. 'Police in Ireland before the union', *Irish Jurist*, vii–viii (1972–3).

Brady, J. 'Lawrence O'Conner – a Meath schoolmaster', *Irish Ecclesiastical Record*, 5th ser. xlix (1937), 281–7.

Bric, Maurice J. 'Priests, parsons and politics: the Rightboy protest in County Cork, 1785–1788', *Past and Present*, no. 100 (1983), 100–23.*

——, 'The tithe system in eighteenth-century Ireland', *Proceedings of the Royal Irish Academy*, vol. 86, c. (1986), 271–88.

Brooke, Peter. *Ulster Presbyterianism, the historical perspective, 1610–1970* (Dublin, 1987).

Burke, Peter. *Popular culture in early modern Europe* (London, 1978).

Christianson, G. E. 'Secret societies and agrarian violence in Ireland, 1790–1840', *Agricultural History*, no. 46 (1972), 469–84.

Clark, J. C. D. *English society, 1688–1832* (Cambridge, 1986).

Clark, Samuel and Donnelly, J. S. eds, *Irish peasants, violence and political unrest, 1780–1914* (Wisconsin, 1983).

Connell, K. H. *Irish peasant society* (Oxford, 1968).

Connolly, Sean J. *Priests and people in pre-famine Ireland, 1780–1845* (Dublin, 1982).

——, 'Religion and history', in *Irish Economic and Social History*, x (1985), 66–80.

Corish, Patrick J. *The Catholic community in the seventeenth and eighteenth centuries* (Dublin, 1981).

—— (ed.), *Radicals, rebels and establishments* (Belfast, 1985).

Corkery, Daniel. *The hidden Ireland, a study of Gaelic Munster in the eighteenth century* (Dublin, 1925).

Cosgrove, Art. *Dublin through the ages* (Dublin, 1988).

Coughlan, R. J. *Napper Tandy* (1976).

Cox, L. 'Westmeath in the 1798 period', *Irish Sword*, ix (1969–70), 1–15.

Cronin, Sean. *Irish nationalism, a history of its roots and ideology* (Dublin, 1980).

Crossle, P. *Irish Masonic records* (Dublin, 1973).

Crossle and Lepper, J. H. *A history of the Grand Lodge of free and accepted Masons of Ireland* (Dublin, 1925).

Cullen, L. M. 'The hidden Ireland: re-assessment of a concept', *Studia Hibernica*, no. 9 (1969), 7–47.

——, *An economic history of Ireland since 1660* (London, 1976).

——, 'The cultural bias of modern Irish nationalism', in Mitchison, R. (ed.), *The roots of nationalism, studies in northern Europe* (Edinburgh, 1980), 91–106.

——, *The emergence of modern Ireland, 1600–1900* (London, 1981).

——, 'Catholics under the penal laws', *Eighteenth-Century Ireland*, i (1986), 23–36.

Curtin, Nancy J. 'The transformation of the society of United Irishmen into a mass-based organisation, 1794–6', *Irish Historical Studies*, xxiv, no. 96 (1985), 463–492.

Davitt, Michael *The fall of feudalism in Ireland* (London and New York, 1904, Shannon, 1970).

Devine, T. M. 'Unrest and stability in rural Ireland and Scotland, 1780–1840', in Mitchison R. and Roebuck, P. eds, *Economy and society in Scotland and Ireland* (Edinburgh, 1988), 126–39.

Dickinson, H. T. *Liberty and property, political ideology in eighteenth-century Britain* (London, 1977).

——, *British radicalism and the French revolution, 1789–1815* (Oxford, 1985).

——, (ed.), *Britain and the French revolution* (London, 1989).

Dickson, Charles. *The Wexford rising in 1798, its causes and course* (Tralee, 1955).

——, *Revolt in the North: Antrim and Down in 1798* (Dublin, 1960).

Dickson, David. 'The place of Dublin in the eighteenth-century Irish economy', in Dickson and Devine, T. M., eds, *Ireland and Scotland; 1600–1850* (Edinburgh, 1983), 177–92.

——, *New foundations: Ireland 1660–1800* (Dublin, 1987).

——, Dickson and Gough, Hugh. eds., *Ireland and the French revolution* (Dublin, 1990).

Dobson, C. R. *Masters and journeymen, a prehistory of industrial relations, 1717–1800* (London, 1980).

Donnelly, James S. 'The Whiteboy movement, 1761–5', *Irish Historical Studies*, xxi, no. 81 (1978), 20–54.

——, 'The Rightboy movement', *Studia Hibernica*, nos 17 and 18 (1977–8), 120–202.

——, 'Hearts of Oak, Hearts of Steel', *Studia Hibernica*, no. 21 (1981), 7–73.

——, 'Propagating the cause of the United Irishmen', *Studies*, lxix, 273 (1981), 5–23.

——, 'Irish agrarian rebellions: the Whiteboys of 1769–76', *Proceedings of the Royal Irish Academy*, 83, c. no. 12 (1983), 293–332.

Dowling, P. J. *The hedge schools of Ireland* (Dublin, 1935).

Doyle, D. N. *Ireland, Irishmen and revolutionary America, 1760–1820* (Dublin and Cork, 1981).

Dunne, Tom. *Wolfe Tone, colonial outsider* (Cork, 1982).

Ehrman, John. *The younger Pitt, ii, the reluctant transition* (London, 1983).

Elliott, Marrianne. 'The "Despard Conspiracy" reconsidered', *Past and Present*, no. 75 (1977), 46–61.

——, 'The origins and transformation of early Irish republicanism', *International Review of Social History*, xxii, pt. 3 (1978), 405–28.

——, *Partners in revolution, the United Irishmen and France* (New Haven, 1982).

——, *Watchmen in Sion: the Protestant idea of liberty* (*Field Day* pamphlet, 1985).

——, *Wolfe Tone, prophet of Irish independence* (New Haven and London, 1989).

Falkiner, C. L. *Studies in Irish history and biography* (London, 1902).

Ferguson, P., O'Flanagan, P. and Whelan, K. eds, *Rural Ireland: modernisation and change, 1600–1900* (Cork, 1987).

Fitzhenry, Edna C. *Henry Joy McCracken* (Dublin, 1936).

Fitzpatrick, W. J. *The secret service under Pitt* (London, 1892).

Foster, R. F. *Modern Ireland 1600–1972* (Harmonsworth, 1988).

Froude, James Anthony. *The English in Ireland in the eighteenth century* (London, 1882) 3 vols.

Fruchtman, jnr. J. 'The apocalytic politics of Richard Price and Joseph Priestly: a study in late eighteenth-century millenialism', *Transactions of the American Philosophical Society*, (Philadelphia, 1983).

Garvin, Thomas. 'Defenders, Ribbonmen and others: underground political networks in pre-famine Ireland', *Past and Present*, no. 96 (1982), 133–55.*

Geoghegan, William. *The history and antiquities of the first Volunteer lodge of Ireland* (Dublin, 1921).

Gibbon, Peter. 'The origins of the Orange Order and the United Irishmen', *Economy and Society*, i (1972), 135–63.

Gill, Conrad. *The rise of the Irish linen industry* (Oxford, 1925).

Goodwin, Albert. *The friends of liberty: the English democratic movement in the age of the French revolution* (London, 1979).

Gray, John. 'Millennial vision . . . Thomas Russell re-assessed', *The Linen Hall Review*, vol. 6, no. 1 (1989), 5–9.

Haire, J. L. M. (ed.), *Challenge and conflict, essays in Irish Presbyterian history and doctrines* (Antrim, 1981).

Hayes, R. 'Priests in the independence movement of '98', *Irish Ecclesiastical Record* (1945), 258–70.

Hayton, David. 'Anglo-Irish attitudes: changing perceptions of national identity among the Protestant Ascendancy in Ireland, ca. 1690–1750', *Studies in Eighteenth-Century Culture*, vol. 17 (1987), 145–57.

Hill, Jacqueline. 'The meaning and significance of Protestant Ascendancy,

1787–1840' in *Ireland after the Union* (Oxford, 1989), 1–22.

Hobsbawn, E. J. *Primitive rebels* (Manchester, 1959).

——, *Bandits* (London, 1969).

Hobsbawn and Scott, J. W. 'Political shoemakers', *Past and Present*, no. 89 (1980), 86–114.

Houstan, R. A. *Scottish literacy and the Scottish identity, illiteracy and society in Scotland and northern England, 1600–1800* (Cambridge, 1985).

Inglis, Brian. *The freedom of the press in Ireland, 1784–1841* (London, 1954).

Jacob, Rosamond. *The rise of the United Irishmen* (London, 1937).

James, F. G. *Ireland in the empire, 1688–1770* (Cambridge, Mass. 1973).

Johnson, J. H. 'The two "Irelands" at the beginning of the nineteenth century', in Stephens, N. and Glassock, R. E. eds, *Irish Geographical Studies* (Belfast, 1970), 224–43.

Johnston, E. M. *Great Britain and Ireland 1760–1800, a study in political administration* (Edinburgh, 1963).

——, *Ireland in the eighteenth century* (Dublin, 1974).

Kates, G. 'From liberalism to radicalism: Tom Paine's *Rights of Man*', *Journal of the History of Ideas*, vol. 1, no. 4 (1989), 569– 87.

Kee, Robert. *The green flag, a history of Irish nationalism* (London, 1972).

Kelly, James 'The origins of the act of union: an examination of unionist opinion, 1650–1800', *Irish Historical Studies*, xxv, no. 99 (1987), 236–63.

——, 'The parliamentary reform movement of the 1780s and the catholic question', *Archivium Hibernicum* xliii (1988), 95–117.

Kelly, Rev. L. 'Defenderism in Leitrim during the 1790s', *Breifne*, vol. vi, no. 24 (1986), 341–54.

Kennedy, W. B. 'The Irish Jacobins', *Studia Hibernica*, xiv (1976), 109–21.

Latimer, William T. *Ulster biographies, relating chiefly to the rebellion of 1798* (1897).

Lecky, W. E. H. *A history of Ireland in the eighteenth century* (London, 1892) 5 vols.

Lewis, George Cornewall. *On local disturbances in Ireland and on the Irish Church question* (London, 1836).

Logue, K. J. *Popular disturbances in Scotland, 1780–1815* (Edinburgh, 1979).

Lynd, Staughton. *Intellectual origins of American radicalism* (Harvard, 1982).

Madden, R. R. *Lives of the United Irishmen* (Dublin, 1842–6) 7 vols.

——, *The history of Irish periodical literature* (London, 1867) 2 vols.

MacDonagh, Oliver *'The hereditary bondsman', Daniel O'Connell, 1775–1829* (London, 1988).

Maguire, W. A. 'Lord Donegall and the Hearts of Steel', *Irish Historical Studies*, xxi, no. 84, (1981), 351–76.

Mahoney, T. H. D. *Edmund Burke and Ireland* (London, 1960).

Malcomson, A. P. W. *John Foster, the politics of the Anglo-Irish Ascendancy* (Oxford, 1978).

——, 'A lost natural leader: John James Hamilton, first marquess of Abercorn (1756–1818)', *Proceedings of the Royal Irish Academy*, vol. 88, c, no. 4 (1988), 61–86.

Miller, David. W. 'Presbyterianism and "modernization" in Ulster', *Past and Present*, no. 80 (1978), 66–90.*

——, *Queen's rebels, Ulster loyalism in historical perspective* (Dublin, 1978).

Moody, T. W. 'The political ideas of the United Irishmen', *Ireland Today*, iii, no. 1 (1938), 15–25.

Moody and Vaughan, W. E. eds, *A new history of Ireland, iv, eighteenth-century Ireland, 1690–1800* (Oxford, 1986).

'JM' (James Morgan), 'Sketch of the life of Thomas Russell', in *Ulster Magazine* (1830) (copy in NLI.)

Murphy, Sean. 'Charles Lucas and the Dublin election of 1748–1749', *Parliamentary History*, no. 2 (1983), 93–111.

McAnally, H. *The Irish militia, 1793–1816* (Dublin and London, 1949).

McClelland, A. 'Orangism in Co. Monagahan', *Clogher Record*, ix (1978).

McCormick, W. J. *Ascendancy and tradition in Anglo-Irish literary history from 1789 to 1939* (Oxford, 1981).

MacDermott, Frank. *Theobald Wolfe Tone: a biographical study* (Tralee, 1969).

——, 'Arthur O'Connor', *Irish Historical Studies*, xv, no. 57 (1966), 48–69.

McDowell, R. B. 'The Irish government and the provincial press', *Hermathena*, liii (1939), 138–47.

——, 'The personnel of the Dublin Society of United Irishmen, 1791–4', *Irish Historical Studies*, ii (1940–1), 12–53.

——, *Irish public opinion, 1750–1800* (London, 1944).

——, 'The Fitzwilliam episode', *Irish Historical Studies*, xvi, no. 58 (1966), 115–30.

——, *Ireland in the age of imperialism and revolution* (Oxford, 1979).

McEvoy, Rev. B. 'The United Irishmen in Co. Tyrone', *Seanchas Ardmhacha*, iii (1959), 283–305, iv (1960–1), 1–32, v (1969), 37–65.

——, 'Father James Quigley', *Seanchas Ardmhacha*, v (1970), 247–59.

——, 'The Peep of Day Boys and Defenders in the County Armagh', *Seanchas Ardmhacha* (1986), 123–163 (1987), 60–127.

McNeill, Mary. *The life and times of Mary Ann McCracken, 1770–1866, a Belfast panorama* (Dublin, 1960).

McSkimmin, Samuel. *Annals of Ulster, 1790–1798* (1849, E. J. Crum, ed., Belfast, 1906).

O'Brien, Gerard. (ed.), *Parliament, politics and people, essays in eighteenth-century Irish history* (Dublin, 1989).

O'Coindealbain S. O. 'The United Irishmen in Cork County', *Cork Archeological and Historical Society Journal*, 2nd ser. liii, liv (1948–53).

O'Connell, M. R. *Irish politics and social conflict in the age of the American revolution* (Philadelphia, 1965).

——, 'Class conflict in a pre-industrial society: Dublin in 1780', *Irish Ecclesiastical Record*, ciii (1965), 93–106.

O'Farrell, Patrick. 'Millenarianism, messianism and utopianism in Irish history', *Anglo-Irish Studies*, ii (1976), 45–68.

O'Flaherty, Eamon. 'The Catholic Convention and Anglo-Irish politics, 1791–93', *Archivium Hibernicum* xl (1985), 14–34.

O'Loinsigh, Seamus. 'The rebellion of 1798 in Meath', *Riocht na Midhe* iii–iv (1966–71).

Pakenham, Thomas. *The year of liberty, the story of the great rebellion of 1798* (London, 1982).

Palmer, R. R. *The age of the democratic revolution: a political history of Europe and America, 1760–1800* (Princeton, 1959, 1964), 2 vols.

Palmer, S. H. *Police and protest in England and Ireland, 1780–1850* (Cambridge, 1988).

Parssinen, T. M. 'Association, convention and anti-parliament in British radical politics, 1771–1848', *English Historical Review*, lxxxviii, no. 348 (1973), 504–33.

Paterson, T. G. F. 'The County Armagh Volunteers of 1778–1793', *Ulster Journal of Archeology*, 3rd ser. iv–vii (1941–4).

Philpin, C. H. E. (ed.), *Nationalism and popular protest in Ireland* (Cambridge, 1987).

Pollard, M. 'John Chambers, printer and United Irishman', *The Irish Book*, iii (1964), 1–22.

Power, T. P., and Whelan, K. (eds), *Endurance and emergence, catholics in Ireland in the eighteenth century* (Dublin, 1990).

Robbins, Caroline. '"When is it that colonies may turn independent": an analysis of the environment of Francis Hutcheson (1694–1746)', *William and Mary Quarterly* 3rd. ser xi (1954), 214–51.

——, *The eighteenth-century commonwealthman* (Cambridge, Mass. 1959).

Roberts, J. M. *The mythology of the secret societies* (London, 1972).

Robinson, Philip. 'Hanging ropes and buried secrets', *Ulster Folklife*, no. 32 (1986), 4–15.

Rogers, Patrick. *The Irish Volunteers and catholic emancipation, 1778–1793* (London, 1934).

Rule, John. *The experience of labour in eighteenth-century industry* (London, 1981).

Rudé, George *The crowd in history* (New York, 1974).

—— *Paris and London in the eighteenth century, studies in popular protest* (London, 1974).

——, *Ideology and popular protest* (London, 1980).

Senior, Hereward. *Orangism in Ireland and Britain, 1795–1836* (London, 1966).

Simms, J. G. *Colonial nationalism, 1698–1776* (Cork, 1976).

——, (Patrick H. Kelly, (ed.),) *William Molyneux of Dublin* (Dublin, 1984).

Simms, Samuel. *Rev. James O'Coigly, United Irishman* (Belfast, 1937).

Smith, Olivia. *The politics of language* (Oxford, 1984).

Stewart, A. T. Q. '"A Stable Unseen Power". Dr William Drennan and the origins of the United Irishmen', in John Bossy and Peter Jupp eds., *Essays presented to Michael Roberts* (Belfast, 1976), 80–92.

——, *The narrow ground, aspects of Ulster, 1609–1969* (London, 1977).

——, '"The Harp New-Strung": nationalism, culture and the United Irishmen', in MacDonagh, O. and Mandle, W.F. eds., *Ireland and Irish Australia, studies in cultural history* (London, 1986), 258–69.

Stone, Lawrence. 'Literacy and education in England, 1640–1900', *Past and Present*, no. 42 (1969), 69–139.

Thompson, E. P. 'The moral economy of the English crowd in the eighteenth century', *Past and Present*, no. 50 (1971), 76–136.

——, *The making of the English working class* (1963, Harmondsworth, 1979).

Tohall, P. 'The Diamond fight of 1795 and the resultant expulsions', *Seanchas Ardmhacha*, no. 3 (1958–9), 17–50.

Vaughan, W. E. (ed.), *A new history of Ireland, v, Ireland under the union, I, 1801–1870* (Oxford, 1989).

Vance, Norman. 'Celts, Carthaginians and constitutions: Anglo-Irish literary relations, 1780–1820', *Irish Historical Studies*, xxii, no. 87 (1981), 216–36.

Wall, Maureen. 'The United Irish movement', *Historical Studies*, v (1965), 122–40.

——, (O'Brien, G. ed.), *Catholic Ireland in the eighteenth century: collected essays of Maureen Wall* (Dublin, 1989).

Wells, Roger. *Insurrection: the British experience, 1795–1803* (Gloucester, 1983).

Whelan, Kevin. (ed.), *Wexford: history and society* (Dublin, 1987).

Williams, T. D. (ed.), *Secret societies in Ireland* (Dublin, 1973).

Witherow, Thomas. *Historical and literary memorials of Presbyterianism in Ireland* (London, 1889–90) 2 vols.

Woods, C. J. 'The secret mission to Ireland of Captain Bernard MacSheehy, an Irishman in French service', *Cork Archeological and Historical Society Journal*, lxxviii (1973), 93–108.

Young, R. M. *Ulster in '98, episodes and anecdotes* (Belfast, 1893).

Zimmermann, G. D. *Irish political street ballads, 1780–1900* (Geneva, 1966).

Those articles which first appeared in *Past and Present*, and here marked with an astrix (*), are reprinted in Philipin (ed.), *Nationalism and popular protest in Ireland* (Cambridge, 1987).

UNPUBLISHED DISSERTATIONS

Duggan, Mary L. 'County Carlow, 1791–1801, a study in an era of revolution', MA, N.U.I. (1969).

Fitzpatrick, A. J. 'Economic effects of the French revolution and Napoleonic wars on Ireland', Ph.D, Manchester (1973).

Kerrane, J. G. O. 'The background to the 1798 rebellion in County Meath', MA, N.U.I. (1971).

O'Flaherty, Eamon. 'The Catholic question in Ireland, 1774–1793', MA, N.U.I. (1981).

Powell, T. 'The background to the 1798 rebellion in County Wexford', MA, N.U.I. (1972).

Price, J. S. 'Dublin, 1750 to 1850: spacial distribution and organisation of economic activity', Msc, T.C.D. (1981).

Stoddart, P. C. 'Counter-insurgency and defence in Ireland, 1790–1805', D. Phil. Oxford (1973).

Index